Time

Other New Titles from
HACKETT
READINGS IN
PHILOSOPHY

Time

Edited and Introduced by

Jonathan Westphal and Carl Levenson

Hackett Publishing Company, Inc.
Indianapolis/Cambridge
1993

The editors wish to thank Bill King for his advice and assistance in preparation of this volume.

99 98 97 96 95 94 93   1 2 3 4 5 6 7

Text design by Dan Kirklin

For further information, please address
  Hackett Publishing Company, Inc.
  P.O. Box 44937
  Indianapolis, Indiana 46244-0937

Library of Congress Cataloging-in-Publication Data

Time/edited and introduced by Jonathan Westphal & Carl Levenson.
        p.   cm. (Readings in philosophy)
     ISBN 0-87220-207-0 (cloth: alk. paper)   ISBN 0-87220-206-2
  (paper: alk. paper)
     1. Time. I. Westphal, Jonathan, 1951–   . II. Levenson, Carl
  Avren, 1949–   . III. Series.
     BD638.T54   1993
  115—dc20   93-14608
                                                              CIP

The paper used in this publication meets the minimum requirements of American National Standard for Information. Sciences—Permanence of Paper for Printed Library Materials, ANSI Z39.48-1984.
                                    ∞

Contents

Introduction

1. Proust's great novel *Remembrance of Things Past* (*A la Recherche du Temps Perdu*) is often thought to be a novel about time. Marcel, the main character, is afraid of losing the things he values most. As soon as he falls in love, the possibility of losing his loved one contaminates the relationship. Even when he is with her, he is nervous that he will not be able to find in her the qualities that originally attracted him. This is not because he is neurotic, but because of the transitoriness of the present, of which he is acutely aware.

One day Marcel discovers that time can be overcome, through the apparently trivial experience of eating a piece of cake, a "petite madeleine," dipped in a cup of tea. He suddenly remembers his early childhood, when he often ate these cakes. He feels something enormous and wonderful but nameless; then he is able to recognize it. He does not have a memory of childhood in the sense of a mental picture of it, but it is more as if

> all the flowers in our garden . . . and the good folk of the village and their little dwellings and the parish church and the whole of Combray and of its surroundings, taking their proper shapes and growing solid, sprang into being, town and gardens alike, from my cup of tea.

In the novel this overcoming of time not only brings Marcel ordinary happiness, but he ceases to feel insignificant and accidental, and he is raised above his usual state to a "new sensation"—a sensation which has had "the effect which love has of filling me with a precious essence."

2. St. Augustine too is bothered by transience and the loss of the past. In the first nine books of the *Confessions*, his autobiography, time is a central theme, as in Proust's novel. Time can take away what we love best. But St. Augustine also writes about how thrilling it is to desire things we do not have in the present (joy, love, honor, etc.), to let longing arouse our vital powers.

By Book XI of the *Confessions*, from which our selection has been taken, these autobiographical themes have given way to a more purely theoretical interest in the problem of time. "I know well enough what time is, provided nobody asks me to explain. But if I am asked what it is and try to explain, I am baffled." When St. Augustine looks for time, he cannot find it. He looks for the past, but it has already gone. He looks for the future, but it has not yet arrived. As for the present, he finds that a century cannot be present, because it splits up into the years which have passed, and those which are yet to come. A year cannot be present, because it splits up into the months which have passed, and those which are yet to come. . . . So no unit of time can be present, and the present also does not exist. By this repeated mental exercise, St. Augustine arrives to his horror at the conclusion that time only exists to the extent that it doesn't. "Time is insofar as it tends not to be." The essence of time is to absent itself.

Still, St. Augustine knows that time is something, because it is long or short. If it were nothing, how could it be measured? His answer is that time has being, after all, but only in the mind. The past passes away, but the mind keeps it in memory. The future is not yet present, but the mind anticipates it. Within the mind it is not true that the present has no duration. We give it a duration through memory and expectations. These reflections are all part of St. Augustine's attempt to understand the relation between time and eternity, in particular how God, who is outside time, could create something within time.

3. Two different kinds of twentieth-century responses to St. Augustine's problem about the existence of time are represented by Wittgenstein and Husserl. Wittgenstein says in our excerpt from the *Blue Book* that "Philosophy . . . is a fight against the fascination which forms of expression exert on us." Words like "chair" have a factual definition. Obsession with these expressions makes us expect a similar definition for time. When we don't find one, we think that time must be very mysterious, perhaps something which lacks an essence or a definition. "Augustine, we might say, thinks of the process of measuring a *length;* say the distance between two marks on a travelling band which passes us. . . ." How could one measure a piece of string when one end refused to appear at all, the other was permanently lost, and the middle bit so short as not to be measurable at all? The trouble, according to Wittgenstein, is the bewitchment of our thought about time by spatial and physical concepts of length, motion, and substance, our desire to think of time as being like a piece of string.

4. For Husserl, philosophy is description rather than argument. What it describes is the way in which the world manifests itself to us. So

when Husserl writes about time, he intends to describe it as a phenomenon. Rather than criticizing Augustine's meditation on time, Husserl continues it. In our selection from *The Phenomenology of Internal Time Consciousness,* Husserl describes what Augustine calls memory as *retention.* Suppose I am listening to a sound. The precise point of sound I am listening to *now* does not vanish in the next instant, but is to some extent "retained." It fades away gradually, blending in with other sounds.

> The further we withdraw from the now, the greater the blending and drawing together. If in reflection we immerse ourselves in the unity of a structured process, we observe that an articulated part of the process "draws together" as it sinks into the past—a kind of temporal perspective ... analogous to spatial perspective.

Husserl thinks that such "running-off phenomena" (the German is the rather fearsome *Ablaufsphänomene*) can be precisely diagrammed. His style is difficult, but we can judge for ourselves the accuracy of his description by snapping our fingers, and seeing whether his words correspond to the perceived phenomena.

5. Isaac Newton, the great seventeenth-century mathematician and physicist, also wants to give a theoretical description of time. Unlike Husserl, Newton wants to sever it from a relation to "sensible objects" or phenomena. He distinguishes between "absolute and relative, true and apparent, mathematical and common" time.

> Absolute, true and mathematical time, of itself, and from its own nature, flows equably without relation to anything external, and by another name is called duration.

The other kind of time, "relative, apparent and common," is merely a measure of duration by motion, "which is commonly used instead of true time: such as an hour, a day, a month, a year." Newton's absolute time is almost like a kind of eternity. "The duration or perseverance of the existence of things remains the same, whether the motions are swift or slow, or none at all."

6. The idea of absolute time was sharply criticized by Leibniz, a philosopher and mathematician who independently invented the calcu-

lus at the same time as Newton. *The Leibniz-Clarke Correspondence* is a debate between Leibniz and Newton's representative, Samuel Clarke. Leibniz argues that a completely uniform time would consist of a series of instants which were indistinguishable. But this offends against his principle of the identity of indiscernibles, which states that here are no two things "exactly alike." Newton's conception of real time also conflicts with the principle of sufficient reason, which says that there is a good reason why anything happens. There would be no good reason for God to create the universe at one instant in the infinite and absolute time rather than another. Indeed, the placings of the universe in time would be indiscernible and therefore according to Leibniz identical. Leibniz's Fifth Paper ends with a thoroughly Augustinian argument. "How could a thing exist, no part of which ever exists?" He concludes that time is "an ideal thing," a measure, not a real one.

7. Plato's view of time is the first and still the most essential account of the relation between time and eternity. Reality, Plato writes, is all present in eternity at once, for

> days and nights and months and years . . . are all parts of time . . . which we unconsciously but wrongly transfer to eternal being, for we say that it "was," or "is," or "will be," but the truth is that "is" alone is properly attributed to it. . . .

As for time, it is "the moving image of eternity." What this means is that time differs from eternity in virtue of its movement with the heavenly bodies circling through the sky, but time also resembles eternity because its movement is lawful and unending. The sun, the stars always move in the same patterns.

Plato's treatment of time in the *Parmenides* is less abstract and poetic but it is also extremely difficult. Readers should be alerted that the One in the *Parmenides* is related to eternity in the *Timaeus*, but it is also in some way the unity or "oneness" of anything, such as a chair. They will also want to know that "the others" Plato talks about are anything other than the One, anything dispersed or dissected. In Plato's text the time-transcending One is drawn into time through its relation to "the others." This entrance of eternity into time could be viewed as a remote cosmic event, but it could also be taken as a description of time and eternity in present experience.

8. The discussion of time in Book IV of Aristotle's *Physics* is an attempt to explain the queerer logical features of time, by inquiring what time is. Aristotle gives an earlier formulation of St. Augustine's puzzle about time's tendency not to be.

> It either does not exist at all or barely, in an obscure way. One part of it has been and is not, while the other is going to be and is not yet. Yet time—both infinite time and any time you like to take—is made up of these. One would naturally suppose that what is made up of things which do not exist could have no share in reality.

Aristotle also asks how time can both be always different, in the sense that it is always a different time, and remain the same, unaltered in the sense that one minute is identical, in quantity of time, to any other. His answer is that time is the measure of change, so that in one way it is always the same, as a unit of measurement (a time) is always the same, but in another not, as the time measured is always a different one. The perspective of eternity is absent in Aristotle's careful unpicking of these logical problems.

9. Plotinus, in the third of his six *Enneads* ("Groups of Nine"), gives the most full-blooded description of eternity in our anthology. It is not a static changelessness, it is a superabundance of being and life, which is limitless in the sense that it is "all the life there is." It has the compendious richness of memories of early life and dreams and hopes of the future. According to Plotinus the soul was suffocated by this richness. It wanted the thrill of desire. It was "set on governing itself and realizing itself and it chose to aim at something more than its present." So it "produced an image of Eternity, produced Time."

10. Plotinus is clearly what could be called a "friend of eternity." In our anthology, the other firm friends of eternity are Plato, Plotinus, St. Augustine, and Eliade. It may not be immediately obvious to readers in what way McTaggart also belongs to this group. He has a destructive proof of the impossibility or unreality of time, which depends on the idea that a particular event cannot belong to the past, present, and future, since these are contradictory. (McTaggart has a profound answer to the obvious objection that an event belongs to these categories successively, not simultaneously.) But this means that we cannot even say that one event is earlier or later than another. This leaves him with

an eternal or nontemporal ordering of events, in what he calls the C-series, held together by a mysterious quality that remains undefined in his essay.

11–12. Our two commentaries on McTaggart's proof criticize it at two different places. Michael Dummett argues that what McTaggart has really shown is that time and reality are incompatible and that if there is such a thing as a complete description of reality, then time cannot exist. Or, if we are to say that time exists, then we must give up the idea of a complete description of reality. This is because the reality of time requires that the present should be distinguished from all other moments—in reality. Paul Horwich suggests in our excerpt from his recent book on *Asymmetries in Time* that McTaggart's error is to suppose that time requires the real changes which are involved in the passage from past to present and future.

13. A very famous attack on the idea, not of time itself, but of the notion of the *passage* of time, of the moving present, is D. C. Williams's "The Myth of Passage." If time moves, Williams asks, what does it move *in*, and at what rate? It cannot move in time, because then there would have to be a stationary time which it moves in. Williams offers instead what he calls the "pure theory of the manifold," in which instead of saying that "Time flows or flies or marches, years roll, hours pass," we simply say that there is a succession of events, that "rivers flow and winds blow, that things burn and burst, that men strive and guess and die. All this is the concrete stuff of the manifold. . . ."

14. The attempt to get rid of time and replace it with an eternally ordered series is even more determined in our passage from Quine. Quine argues that we should understand time like space. He proposes a method for translating all temporal statements into a canonical atemporal idiom. In this way he arrives at a time as merely a slice of something called space-time, events considered as arranged in a huge block of space and time. One advantage of this is that it fits in with modern physical theory. It produces a sort of eternity, but one which is a frozen order of prearranged events, which would certainly not satisfy the friends of eternity.

15. O. K. Bouwsma's hilarious rendition of thoughts derived from Wittgenstein, to the effect that a man who understands only linoleum—

a spatial concept—will have some difficulty understanding time, is actually just as serious an attempt as Quine's to exorcise the by now familiar perplexities originally described by Aristotle and St. Augustine. Bouwsma's essay makes the mystery of time into a confusion, but his best powers are devoted to describing the mystery, and one suspects him of getting a positive pleasure out of the misrepresentations necessary to state the problem.

16. Just as Bouwsma elaborates Wittgenstein's view, so Merleau-Ponty elaborates Husserl's. Merleau-Ponty continues the attempt to describe the phenomena of time. The present moment, for him, is "sheer being" or fullness. It plays the role of the eternal in Plato, Plotinus, and Augustine. Consciousness, like Plotinus' desire, opens up in this fullness an empty space for the future and the past to occupy. Merleau-Ponty knows that he is approaching a classical notion of eternity, which he is uneasy about. "But if we are in fact destined to make contact with a sort of eternity, it will be at the core of our experience of time, and not in some nontemporal subject."

17. James F. Sheridan, an American phenomenologist with a special interest in science, describes how time may have first appeared to human consciousness in the experience of a caveman. In his entertaining piece, Sheridan offers a phenomenological solution to several traditional questions about time, such as the relation of time to measurement. He speaks of a sense of "lostness" which he thinks probably dominated the earliest experience of time. He also makes the intriguing suggestion that "like myself, totality is lost."

18. The experience of time among archaic people is Mircea Eliade's special theme. Eliade was a Roumanian historian of religion working at the University of Chicago. He says that archaic people are aware of two kinds of time, profane time, which is linear, and sacred time, in which the very same event, such as a season or a festival, is repeated. Sacred time is the time of gods and myths, full of meaning and life. This kind of time approaches eternity in the classical sense. Eliade's archaic people evoke sacred time by means of symbol, ritual, dance, and festival. Through these they feel themselves able to reenact the moment of creation when the world emerges from chaos, and time from eternity.

19. Our selection from Thomas Mann's *The Magic Mountain* is a meditation on the passage of time in the life of a young man, Hans Castorp, who is confined to a sanitorium high in the Swiss Alps. The theme of the meditation is that the richest times of our life, though they pass very quickly, "expand" as we view them in retrospect. This will be a familiar experience to many readers.

20. Our final selection is Simone's Weil's "The Renunciation of Time," a brief chapter from her *Gravity and Grace*. Just as for Proust there is a marvelous quality in the recollected past, which the past could not have had when it was merely present, so for Weil there is a marvelousness in anticipation, which the future loses when it becomes present—even if it satisfies all our expectations.

> When we are disappointed by a pleasure which we have been expecting and which comes, the disappointment is because we were expecting the future, and as soon as it is there, it is present. We want the future to be there without ceasing to be future. This is an absurdity of which eternity alone is the cure.

Marcel Proust,
"Combray," from *Rembrance of Things Past*

Marcel Proust (1871–1922) was a French novelist with philosophical interests. His views on love, art, time, jealousy, and many other topics may be found in his book Remembrance of Things Past, *one of the greatest (and longest) novels to be written in the twentieth century. In the following selection, Proust's hero and narrator, Marcel, succeeds, for a moment, in recapturing a part of his childhood, his summers in the village of Combray.*

And so it was that, for a long time afterwards, when I lay awake at night and revived old memories of Combray, I saw no more of it than this sort of luminous panel, sharply defined against a vague and shadowy background, like the panels which a Bengal fire or some electric sign will illuminate and dissect from the front of a building the other parts of which remain plunged in darkness: broad enough at its base, the little parlour, the dining-room, the alluring shadows of the path along which would come M. Swann, the unconscious author of my sufferings, the hall through which I would journey to the first step of that staircase, so hard to climb, which constituted, all by itself, the tapering 'elevation' of an irregular pyramid; and, at the summit, my bedroom, with the little passage through whose glazed door Mamma would enter; in a word, seen always at the same evening hour, isolated from all its possible surroundings, detached and solitary against its shadowy background, the bare minimum of scenery necessary (like the setting one sees printed at the head of an old play, for its performance in the provinces) to the drama of my undressing, as though all Combray had consisted of but two floors joined by a slender staircase, and as though there had been no time there but seven o'clock at night. I must own that I could have assured any questioner that Combray did include other scenes and did exist at other hours than these. But since the facts which I should then have recalled would have been prompted only by an exercise of the will, by my intellectual memory, and since the pictures which that kind of memory shews us of the past preserve nothing of the past itself, I should never have had any wish to ponder over this residue of Combray. To me it was in reality all dead.

Permanently dead? Very possibly.

There is a large element of hazard in these matters, and a second hazard, that of our own death, often prevents us from awaiting for any length of time the favours of the first.

I feel that there is much to be said for the Celtic belief that the souls of those whom we have lost are held captive in some inferior being, in an animal, in a plant, in some inanimate object, and so effectively lost to us until the day (which to many never comes) when we happen to pass by the tree or to obtain possession of the object which forms their prison. Then they start and tremble, they call us by our name, and as soon as we have recognized their voice the spell is broken. We have delivered them: they have overcome death and return to share our life.

And so it is with our own past. It is a labour in vain to attempt to recapture it: all the efforts of our intellect must prove futile. The past is hidden somewhere outside the realm, beyond the reach of intellect, in some material object (in the sensation which that material object will give us) which we do not suspect. And as for that object, it depends on chance whether we come upon it or not before we ourselves must die.

Many years had elapsed during which nothing of Combray, save what was comprised in the theatre and the drama of my going to bed there, had any existence for me, when one day in winter, as I came home, my mother, seeing that I was cold, offered me some tea, a thing I did not ordinarily take. I declined at first, and then, for no particular reason, changed my mind. She sent out for one of those short, plump little cakes called 'petites madeleines,' which look as though they had been moulded in the fluted scallop of a pilgrim's shell. And soon, mechanically, weary after a dull day with the prospect of a depressing morrow, I raised to my lips a spoonful of the tea in which I had soaked a morsel of the cake. No sooner had the warm liquid, and the crumbs with it, touched my palate than a shudder ran through my whole body, and I stopped, intent upon the extraordinary changes that were taking place. An exquisite pleasure had invaded my senses, but individual, detached, with no suggestion of its origin. And at once the vicissitudes of life had become indifferent to me, its disasters innocuous, its brevity illusory—this new sensation having had on me the effect which love has of filling me with a precious essence; or rather this essence was not in me, it was myself. I had ceased now to feel mediocre, accidental, mortal. Whence could it have come to me, this all-powerful joy? I was conscious that it was connected with the taste of tea and cake, but that it infinitely transcended those savours, could not, indeed, be of the same nature as theirs. Whence did it come? What did it signify? How could I seize upon and define it?

I drink a second mouthful, in which I find nothing more than in the first, a third, which gives me rather less than the second. It is time to stop; the potion is losing its magic. It is plain that the object of my quest, the truth, lies not in the cup but in myself. The tea has called up in me, but does not itself understand, and can only repeat indefinitely with a gradual loss of strength, the same testimony; which I, too, cannot interpret, though I hope at least to be able to call upon the tea for it again and to find it there presently, intact and at my disposal, for my final enlightenment. I put down my cup and examine my own mind. It is for it to discover the truth. But how? What an abyss of uncertainty whenever the mind feels that some part of it has strayed beyond its own borders; when it, the seeker, is at once the dark region through which it must go seeking, where all its equipment will avail it nothing. Seek? More than that: create. It is face to face with something which does not so far exist, to which it alone can give reality and substance, which it alone can bring into the light of day.

And I begin again to ask myself what it could have been, this unremembered state which brought with it no logical proof of its existence, but only the sense that it was a happy, that it was a real state in whose presence other states of consciousness melted and vanished. I decide to attempt to make it reappear. I retrace my thoughts to the moment at which I drank the first spoonful of tea. I find again the same state, illuminated by no fresh light. I compel my mind to make one further effort, to follow and recapture once again the fleeting sensation. And that nothing may interrupt it in its course I shut out every obstacle, every extraneous idea, I stop my ears and inhibit all attention to the sounds which come from the next room. And then, feeling that my mind is growing fatigued without having any success to report, I compel it for a change to enjoy that distraction which I have just denied it, to think of other things, to rest and refresh itself before the supreme attempt. And then for the second time I clear an empty space in front of it. I place in position before my mind's eye the still recent taste of that first mouthful, and I feel something start within me, something that leaves its resting-place and attempts to rise, something that has been embedded like an anchor at a great depth; I do not know yet what it is, but I can feel it mounting slowly; I can measure the resistance, I can hear the echo of great spaces traversed.

Undoubtedly what is thus palpitating in the depths of my being must be the image, the visual memory which, being linked to that taste, has tried to follow it into my conscious mind. But its struggles are too far off, too much confused; scarcely can I perceive the colourless reflection in which are blended the uncapturable whirling medley of radiant hues, and I cannot distinguish its form, cannot invite it, as the one possible interpreter, to translate to me the evidence of its contemporary, its inseparable paramour, the taste of cake soaked in tea; cannot ask it to inform me what special circumstance is in question, of what period in my past life.

Will it ultimately reach the clear surface of my consciousness, this memory, this old, dead moment which the magnetism of an identical moment has travelled so far to importune, to disturb, to raise up out of the very depths of my being? I cannot tell. Now that I feel nothing, it has stopped, has perhaps gone down again into its darkness, from which who can say whether it will ever rise? Ten times over I must essay the task, must lean down over the abyss. And each time the natural laziness which deters us from every difficult enterprise, every work of importance, has urged me to leave the thing alone, to drink my tea and to think merely of the worries of to-day and of my hopes for to-morrow, which let themselves be pondered over without effort or distress of mind.

And suddenly the memory returns. The taste was that of the little crumb of madeleine which on Sunday mornings at Combray (because on those mornings I did not go out before church-time), when I went to say good day to her in her bedroom, my aunt Léonie used to give me, dipping it first in her own cup of real or of lime-flower tea. The sight of the little madeleine had recalled nothing to my mind before I tasted it; perhaps because I had so often seen such things in the interval, without tasting them, on the trays in pastry-cooks' windows, that their image had dissociated itself from those Combray days to take its place among others more recent; perhaps because of those memories, so long abandoned and put out of mind, nothing now survived, everything was scattered; the forms of things, including that of the little scallop-shell of pastry, so richly sensual under its severe, religious folds, were either obliterated or had been so long dormant as to have lost the power of expansion which would have allowed them to resume their place in my consciousness. But when from a long-distant past nothing subsists, after the people are dead, after the things are broken and scattered, still, alone, more fragile, but with more vitality, more unsubstantial, more persistent, more faithful, the smell and taste of things remain poised a long time, like souls, ready to remind us, waiting and hoping for their moment, amid the ruins of all the rest; and bear unfaltering, in the tiny and almost impalpable drop of their essence, the vast structure of recollection.

And once I had recognized the taste of the crumb of madeleine soaked in her decoction of lime-flowers which my aunt used to give me (although I did not yet know and must long postpone the discovery of why this memory made me so happy) immediately the old grey house upon the street, where her room was, rose up like the scenery of a theatre to attach itself to the little pavilion, opening on to the garden, which had been built out behind it for my parents (the isolated panel which until that moment had been all that I could see); and with the house the town, from morning to night and in all weathers, the Square where I was sent before luncheon, the streets along which I used to run errands, the country roads we took when it was fine. And just as the Japanese amuse themselves by filling a porcelain bowl with water and steeping in it little crumbs of paper which until then are without character or form, but, the moment they become wet, stretch themselves and bend, take on colour and distinctive shape, become flowers or houses or people, permanent and recognisable, so in that moment all the flowers in our garden and in M. Swann's park, and the water-lilies on the Vivonne and the good folk of the village and their little dwellings and the parish church and the whole of Combray and of its surroundings, taking their proper shapes and growing solid, sprang into being, towns and gardens alike, from my cup of tea.

2

St. Augustine
"Time Tends Not to Be,"
from the *Confessions*

St. Augustine (354–430), Bishop of Hippo in North Africa, was the last of the great thinkers in the tradition of classical philosophy. At the same time he was the most important of the Church Fathers and his work is the foundation of medieval theology and Protestant thought alike. The eleventh chapter of St. Augustine's Confessions, *presented here in its entirety, is focused on the question of time and blends prayers and mystical poetry with philosophical discussion.*

I

But, Lord, since You are in eternity, are You unaware of what I am saying to You? Or do you see in time what takes place in time? But if You *do* see, why am I giving You an account of all these things? Not, obviously, that You should learn them from me; but I excite my own love for You and the love of those who read what I write, that we all may say: *The Lord is great, and exceedingly to be praised.* I have said before and I will say again: "It is for love of Your love that I do it." We pray [for what we want], yet Truth Himself has said: *Your Father knows what is needful for you before you ask Him.* Thus we are laying bare our love for You in confessing to You our wretchedness and Your mercies toward us: that You may free us wholly as You have already freed us in part, so that we may cease to be miserable in ourselves and come to happiness in You. For You have called us to be poor in spirit, to be meek, to mourn, to hunger and thirst after justice, to be merciful and clean of heart and peacemakers.

From St. Augustine, *Confessions*, Book Eleven, translated by Frank Sheed, 1993, Hackett Publishing Company, Inc., Indianapolis, Ind., and Cambridge, Mass.

Thus I have told You many things, with such power and will as I had, because You, O Lord my God, had first willed that I should confess to You: *for Thou art good and Thy mercy endureth forever.*

II

But when will the voice of my pen have power to tell all Your exhortations and all Your terrors, Your consolations and the guidance by which You have brought me to be to Your people a preacher of Your word and a dispenser of Your Sacrament? Even had I the power to set down all these things duly, the drops of my time are too precious.

For a long time now I burn with the desire to meditate upon Your law, and to confess to You both my knowledge of it and my ignorance of it—the first beginnings of Your light and what remains of my own darkness—until my weakness shall be swallowed up in Your strength. And I do not want to see scattered and wasted upon other things such time as I find free from necessary care of the body, intellectual labour, and the service which either I owe men or do not owe but render all the same.

O Lord my God, be attentive to my prayer. Let Thy mercy grant my desire, since it does not burn for myself alone, but longs to serve the charity I have for my brethren: and in my heart Thous seest that it is so. Let me offer in sacrifice to Thee the service of my mind and my tongue, and do Thou give me what I may offer Thee. For I am needy and poor, *Thou art rich unto all who call upon Thee.* Thou art free from care for Thyself and full of care for us. Circumcise the lips of my mouth and the lips of my mind of all rash speech and lying. May Thy Scriptures be for my chaste delight; let me not deceive others about them nor be myself deceived. O Lord, hearken and have mercy, O Lord my God, Light of the blind and Strength of the strong; hearken to my soul, hear it crying from the depths. Unless Thine ears are attentive to us in the abyss, whither shall we go? To whom shall we cry?

Thine is the day, and Thine is the night: at Thy will the moments flow and pass. Grant me, then, space for my meditations upon the hidden things of Thy law, nor close Thy law against me as I knock. Not for nothing hast Thou willed that the deep secrets of all those pages should be written, not for nothing have those woods their *stags*, which retire to them and are restored, walk in them and are fed, lie down in them and ruminate. Complete Thy work in me, O Lord, and open those pages to me. Thy voice is my joy, abounding above all joys. Grant me what I love, for I do love it. And this too is of Thy gift. Do not abandon what Thou hast given, nor scorn Thy grass that is athirst for Thee. Let me confess to Thee whatsoever I shall find in Thy books, and *let me hear the voice of Thy praise,* and drink of Thee and *consider the wondrous things of Thy law* from the first beginning, when Thou didst make heaven and earth, until our everlasting reign with Thee in Thy holy city.

O Lord have mercy on me and grant what I desire. For, as I think, my desire is not of the earth, not of gold and silver and gems or fine raiment or power and glory or lusts of the flesh or the necessities of my body and of this our earthly pilgrimage: *all these things shall be added unto us who seek the Kingdom of God and Thy justice.*

See, O my God, whence comes my desire. *The wicked have told me fables but not as Thy law.* That is the source of my desire. See, Father: gaze and see and approve: and may it be pleasing in the sight of Thy mercy that I should find grace before Thee, that the inner secret of Thy words may be laid open at my knock. I beseech it by our Lord Jesus Christ Thy Son, *the Man of Thy right hand, the Son of Man, whom Thou hast confirmed for Thyself* as Mediator between Thyself and us: by whom Thou didst seek us when we sought not Thee, didst seek us indeed that we might seek Thee: Thy Word, by which Thou hast made all things and me among them: Thy Only One, by whom Thou hast called the people of the faithful, and me among them, unto adoption. I beseech it by Him who sits at Thy right hand and makes intercession for us, *in whom are hidden all the treasures of wisdom and knowledge.* These treasures are what I seek in Thy books. Moses wrote of Him: this He says, who is Truth.

III

Grant me to hear and understand what is meant by *In the beginning You made heaven and earth.* For so Moses wrote, wrote and went his way: passed from this world to You and is no longer here before me. Were he here, I should lay hold of him, and ask him, and in Your name beg him, to explain the sense of those words to me; I should lend my bodily ear to the sounds that should issue from his mouth. If he spoke in Hebrew, his voice would beat upon my ear to no purpose, nothing of what it said would reach my mind: if he spoke in Latin, I should know what he said. But how should I know that what he said was true? And if I did know it, would it be from him that I knew it? No: but within me, in the inner retreat of my mind, the Truth, which is neither Hebrew nor Greek, nor Latin, nor Barbarian, would tell me, without lips or tongue or sounded syllables: "He speaks truth:" and I (at once assured) would say to Your servant in all confidence: "You speak truth." Since, then, I cannot question him, I ask Thee, the Truth, filled with whom Moses spoke truth: I ask Thee, my God: pardon my sins, and as Thou didst grant to Thy servant to speak those words, grant me to understand them.

IV

We look upon the heavens and the earth, and they cry aloud that they were made. For they change and vary. (If anything was not made and yet exists, there is nothing in it that was not there before: and it is the essence of change and variation that something should be made that was not there before.) They cry aloud, too, that they did not make themselves. "We exist, because we were made; but we did not exist before we existed to be able to give ourselves existence!" And their visible presence is itself the voice with which they speak.

It was You, Lord, who made them: for You are beautiful, and they are beautiful: You are good, and they are good: You are, and they are. But they neither are beautiful nor are good nor simply are at You their Creator: compared with You they are not beautiful and are not good and are not. These truths, thanks to You, we know; and our knowledge compared with Your knowledge is ignorance.

V

But *how* did You make heaven and earth? What instrument did You use for a work so mighty? You are not like an artist; for he forms one body from another as his mind chooses; his mind has the power to give external existence to the form it perceives within itself by its inner eye—and whence should it have that power unless You made it? It impresses that form upon a material already existent and having the capacity to be thus formed, such as clay or stone or wood or gold or such like. And how should these things have come to be unless You made them to be? It was You who made the workman his body, and the mind that directs his limbs, the matter of which he makes what he makes, the intelligence by which me masters his art and sees inwardly what he is to produce exteriorly, the bodily sense by which he translates what he does from his mind to his material, and then informs the mind of the result of his workmanship, so that the mind may judge by that truth which presides within it whether the work is well done.

All these things praise You, the Creator of them all. But how do You create them? How, O God, did You create heaven and earth? Obviously it was not *in* heaven or on earth that You made heaven and earth; nor in the air nor in the waters, since these belong to heaven and earth; nor did You make the universe in the universe, because there was no place for it to be made in until it was made. Nor had You any material in Your hand when You were making heaven and earth: for where should You have got what You had not yet made to use as material? What exists, save because You exist? You spoke and heaven and earth were created; in Your word You created them.

VI

But *how* did You speak? Was it perhaps as when that voice sounded from the cloud saying: *This is my beloved Son?* That voice sounded and ceased to sound, had a beginning and an end. The syllables sounded and died away, the second after the first, the third after the second, and so in order, until the last after the rest, and silence after the last. From this it is clear beyond question that that voice was sounded by the movement of something created by You, a movement in time but serving Your eternal will.

These words were uttered in time and the bodily ear conveyed them to the understanding mind, whose spiritual ear is attuned to Your eternal World. And the mind compared these words sounding in time with Your eternal Word and its silence: and it said: "It is other, far other. These words are far less than I, indeed they are not at all, for they pass away and are no more: but the Word of God is above me and endures for ever."

Thus, had it been by words sounding and passing away that You said "Let heaven and earth be made," and so created heaven and earth, there would have had to be some bodily creature before heaven and earth, by the movement of which in time that voice came and went in time.

But there was no bodily thing before heaven and earth: or if there were then certainly You did not use some still earlier utterance in time to produce it, that by it You might utter in time the decree that heaven and earth should be made. Whatever it may have been that produced such a voice, it must have been made by You, otherwise it would not have existed at all. But to produce the bodily thing capable of uttering those words, what word did You utter?

VII

Clearly You are calling us to the realization of that Word—God with You, God as You are God—which is uttered eternally and by which all things are uttered eternally.

For this is not an utterance in which what is said passes away that the next thing may be said and so finally the whole utterance be complete: but all in one act, yet abiding eternally: otherwise it would be but time and change and no true eternity, no true immortality.

I know it, O my God, and I give You thanks. I know it, Lord, I confess it to You: and every man knows it as I do and praises You as I do who is not ungrateful for Your sure truth. We know, Lord, we know, that in the degree that anything is no longer what it was, and is now what it once was not, it is in the process of dying and beginning anew. But of Your Word nothing passes or comes into being, for it is truly immortal and eternal. Thus it is by a Word co-eternal with Yourself that in one eternal act You say all that You say, and all things are made that You say are to be made. You create solely by thus saying. Yet all things You create by saying are not brought into being in one act and from eternity.

VIII

Tell me, O Lord my God, how this can be? In a kind of way I see, but how to express it I do not know: save that whatever comes into being and ceases to be, begins at the moment and ends at the moment when the eternal reason—which has in itself no beginning or ending— knows that it should begin or end. That eternal reason is Your Word, *the Beginning who also speaks unto us.* This He tells us in the Gospel to our bodily ear, this He uttered exteriorly in the ears of men: that we might believe in Him, and seek Him within us and find Him in the eternal Truth, where the one good Master teaches all His disciples.

There it is that I hear Your voice, Lord, telling me that only one who teaches us is speaking to us, and that whoever does not teach us may be speaking, but not to us. Yet who teaches us save Truth unchanging? When from changing creatures we learn anything, we are led to Truth that does not change: and there we truly learn, as we stand and hear Him and rejoice with joy for the voice of the bridegroom, returning to the Source of our being. Thus it is that He is the Beginning: unless He remained when we wandered away, there should be no abiding place for our return. But when we return from error, we return by realizing the Truth; that we may realize it, He instructs us for He is the *Beginning who also speaks unto us.*

IX

This then, O God, was the Beginning in which You created Heaven and Earth: marvellously speaking and marvellously creating in Your Word, Who is Your Son and Your Strength and Your Wisdom and Your Truth. Who shall understand this? Who shall relate it? What is that light which shines upon me but not continuously, and strikes upon my heart with no wounding? I draw back in terror: I am on fire with longing: terror in so far as I am different from it, longing in the degree of my likeness to it. It is Wisdom, Wisdom Itself, which in those moments shines upon me, cleaving through my cloud. And the cloud returns to wrap me round once more as my strength is beaten down under its darkness and the weight of my sins: *for my strength is weakened through poverty*, so that I can no longer support my good, until Thou, Lord who art merciful to my iniquities, shalt likewise heal my weakness: redeeming my life from corruption and crowning me with pity and compassion, and filling my desire with good things: *my youth shall be renewed like the eagle's. For we are saved by hope and we wait with patience for Thy promises.*

Let him who can hear Thy voice speaking within him; I, relying upon Thy inspired word, shall cry aloud: *How great are Thy works, O Lord! Thou hast made all things in wisdom.* Wisdom is "the Beginning": and it is in that Beginning that You made heaven and earth.

X

Surely those are still in their ancient error who say to us: "What was God doing before He made heaven and earth?" If, they say, He was at rest and doing nothing, why did He not continue to do nothing for ever after as for ever before? If it was a new movement and a new will in God to create something He had never created before, how could that be a true eternity in which a will should arise which did not exist before? For the will of God is not a creature: it is prior to every creature, since nothing would be created unless the will of the Creator first so willed. The will of God belongs to the very substance of God. Now if something arose in the substance of God which was not there before, that substance could not rightly be called eternal; but if God's will that creatures should be is from eternity, why are creatures not from eternity?

XI

Those who speak thus do not yet understand You, O Wisdom of God, Light of minds: they do not yet understand how the things are made that are made by You and in You. They strive for the savour of eternity, but their mind is still tossing about in the past and future movements of things, and is still in vain.

Who shall lay hold upon their mind and hold it still, that it may stand a little while, and a little while glimpse the splendor of eternity which stands for ever: and compare it with time whose moments never stand, and see that it is not comparable. Then indeed it would see that a long time is long only from the multitude of movements that pass away in succession, because they cannot co-exist: that in eternity nothing passes but all is present, whereas time cannot be present all at once. It would see that all the past is thrust out by the future, and all the future follows upon the past, and past and future alike are wholly created and upheld in their passage by that which is always present? Who shall lay hold upon the mind of man, that it may stand and see that time with its past and future must be determined by eternity, which stands and does not pass, which has in itself no past or future. Could my hand have the strength [so to lay hold upon the mind of man] or could my mouth by its speaking accomplish so great a thing?

XII

I come now to answer the man who says: "What was God doing before He made Heaven and earth?" I do not give the jesting answer—said to have been given by one who sought to evade the force of the question—"He was getting Hell ready for people who pry to deep." To poke fun at a questioner is not to see the answer. My reply will be different. I would much rather say "I don't know," when I don't, than hold one up to ridicule who had asked a profound question and win applause for a worthless answer.

But, O my God, I say that You are the Creator of all creation, and if by the phrase heaven and earth we mean all creation, then I make bold to reply: Before God made heaven and earth, He did not make anything. For if He had made something, what would it have been but a creature? And I wish I knew all that it would be profitable for me to know, as well as I know that no creature was made before any creature was made.

XIII

But a lighter mind, adrift among images of time and its passing, might wonder that You, O God almighty and all-creating and all-conserving, Maker of heaven and earth, should have abstained from so vast a work for the countless ages that passed before You actually wrought it. Such a mind should awaken and realize how ill-grounded is his wonder.

How could countless ages pass when You, the Author and Creator of all ages, had not yet made them? What time could there be that You had not created? or how could ages pass, if they never were?

Thus, since You are the Maker of all times, if there actually was any time before You made heaven and earth, how can it be said that You were not at work? If there was time, You made it, for time could not pass before You made time. On the other hand, if before heaven and earth were made there was not time, then what is meant by the question "What were You doing *then?*" If there was not any time, there was not any "then."

It is not in time that You are before all time: otherwise You would not be before all time. You are before all the past by the eminence of Your ever-present eternity: and You dominate all the future in as much as it is still to be: and once it has come it will be past: but *Thou art always the self-same, and Thy years shall not fail.* Your years neither go not come: but our years come and go, that all may come. Your years abide all in one act of abiding: for they abide and the years that go are not thrust out by those that come, for none pass: whereas our years shall not all be, till all are no more. Your years are as a single day; and Your day comes not daily but is today, a today which does not yield place to any tomorrow or follow upon any yesterday. In You today is eternity: thus it is that You begot one co-eternal with Yourself to whom you said: *Today have I begotten Thee.* You are the Maker of all time, and before all time You are, nor was there ever a time when there was no time!

XIV

At no time then had You not made anything, for time itself You made. And no time is co-eternal with You, for You stand changeless; whereas if time stood changeless, it would not be time. What then is time? Is there any short and easy answer to that? Who can put the answer into words or even see it in his mind? Yet what commoner or more familiar word do we use in speech than time? Obviously when we use it, we know what we mean, just as when we hear another use it, we know what he means.

What this *is* time? If no one asks me, I know; if I want to explain it to a questioner, I do not know. But at any rate this much I dare affirm I know: that if nothing passed there would be no past time; if nothing were approaching, there would be no future time; if nothing were, there would be no present time.

But the two times, past and future, how can they *be*, since the past is no more and the future is not yet? On the other hand, if the present were always present and never flowed away into the past, it would not be time at all, but eternity. But if the present is only time, because it flows away into the past, how can we say that it *is*? For it is, only because it will cease to be. Thus we can affirm that time *is* only in that it tend towards not-being.

XV

Yet we speak of a long time or a short time, applying these phrases only to past or future. Thus for example we call a hundred years ago a long time past, and a hundred years hence a long time ahead, and ten days ago a short time past, ten days hence a short time ahead. But in what sense can that which does not exist be long or short? The past no longer is, the future is not yet. Does this mean that we must not say: "It is long," but of the past "It was long," of the future "It will be long?"

O, my Lord, my Light, here too man is surely mocked by Your truth! If we say the past was long, was it long when it was already past or while it was still present? It could be long only while it was in existence to *be* long. But the past no longer exists; it cannot be long, because it is not at all.

Thus we must not say that the past was long: for we shall find nothing in it capable of being long, since, precisely because it is past, it is not at all. Let us say then that a particular time was long while it was present, because in so far as it was present, it was long. For is had not yet passed away and so become non-existent; therefore it still was something and therefore capable of being long: though once it passed away, it ceased to be long by ceasing to be.

Let us consider, then, O human soul, whether present time can be long: for it has been given you to feel and measure time's spaces. What will you answer me?

Are the present hundred years a long time? But first see whether a hundred years *can* be present. If it is the first year of the hundred, then that year is present, but the other ninety-nine are still in the future, and so as yet are not: if we are in the second year, then one year is past, one year is present, the rest future. Thus whichever year of our hundred-year period we choose as present, those before it have passed away, those after it are still to come. Thus a hundred years cannot be present.

But now let us see if the chosen year is itself present. If we are in the first month, the others are still to come, if in the second, the first has passed away and the rest are not yet. Thus a year is not wholly present, then the year is not present. For a year is twelve months, and the month that happens to be running its course is the only one present, the others either are no longer or as yet are not. Even the current month is not present, but only one day of it: if that day is the first, the rest are still to come; if the last, the rest are passed away; if somewhere between, it has days past on one side and days still to come on the other.

Thus the present, which we have found to be the only time capable of being long, is cut down to the space of scarcely one day. But if we examine this one day, even it is not wholly present. A day is composed of twenty-four hours—day-hours, night-hours: the first hour finds the rest still to come, the last hour finds the rest passed away, any hour between has hours passed before it, hours to come after it. And that one hour is made of fleeing moments: so much of the hour as has fled away is past, what still remains is future. If we conceive of some point of time which cannot be divided into even the minutest parts of moments, that is the only point that can be called present: and that point flees at such lightening speed from being future to being past, that it has no extent of duration at all. For if it were so extended, it would be divisible into past and future: the present has no length.

Where, then, is there a time that can be called long? Is it the future? But we cannot say of the future "It is long" We say "It will be long." But when will it be long? While it is still in the future, it will not be long, because it does not yet exist and so cannot be long. Suppose we say, then, that it is to be long only when, coming out of the future [which is not yet], it begins to be and is now present—and thus something, and thus capable of being long. But the present cries aloud, as we have just heard, that it cannot have length.

XVI

Yet, Lord, we are aware of periods of time; we compare one period with another and say that some are longer, some shorter. We measure how much one is longer than another and say that it is double, or triple, or single, or simply that one is as long as the other. But it is time actually passing that we measure by our awareness; who can measure times past which are now no more or times to come which are not yet, unless you are prepared to say that that which does not exist can be measured? Thus while time is passing, it can be perceived and measured; but when it has passed it cannot, for it *is* not.

XVII

I am seeking, Father, not saying, O, my God aid me and direct me.

Perhaps it might be said that there are not three times, past, present and future, as we learnt in boyhood and have taught boys: but only present, because the other two do not exist. Or perhaps that these two do exist, but that time comes forth from some secret place when from future it becomes present, and departs into some secret place when from present it becomes past. For where have those who prophesied the future seen the future, if it does not yet exist? What does not exist cannot be seen. And those who describe the past could not describe it truly if they did not mentally see it: and if the past were totally without existence it would be totally impossible to see it. Hence both past and future must exist.

XVIII

Suffer me, Lord, to push my inquiry further; O my Hope, let not my purpose go awry.

If the future and the past exist, I want to know where they are. And if I cannot yet know this, at least I do know that wherever they are, they are there not as future or past, but present. If wherever they are they are future, then in that place they are not yet; if past, then they are there no more. Thus wherever they are and whatever they are, they *are* only as present. When we relate the past truly, it is not the things themselves that are brought forth from our memory—for these have passed away: but words conceived from the images of the things: for the things stamped their prints upon the mind as they passed through it by way of the senses. Thus for example my boyhood, which no longer exists, is in time past, which no longer exists; but the likeness of my boyhood, when I recall it and talk of it, I look upon in time present, because it is still present in my memory.

Whether the case is similar with prophecies of things to come—namely that images of things which are not yet are seen in advance as now existent—I confess, O my God, that I do not know. But this I do know, that we ordinarily consider our future actions in advance, and that this consideration is present, but the action we are thinking of does not yet exist, because it is future; when we have actually set about it and have begun to do what we planned, then that action will exist, because then it will not be future but present.

Whatever may be the mode of this mysterious foreseeing of things to come, unless the thing is it cannot be seen. But what now is, is not future but present. Therefore when we speak of seeing the future, obviously what is seen is not the things which are not yet because they are still to come, but their causes and signs do exist here and now. Thus to those who see them now, they are not future but present, and from them things to come are conceived by the mind and foretold. These concepts already exist, and those who foretell are gazing upon them, present within themselves.

Let me take one example from a vast number of such things.

I am looking at the horizon at dawn: I foretell that the sun is about to rise. What I am looking at is present, what I foretell is future—not the sun, of course, for it now is, but its rising which is not yet. But unless I could imagine the actual rising in my mind, as now when I speak of it, I could not possibly foretell it. But the dawn which I see in the sky is not the sunrise, although it precedes the sunrise; nor is the dawn the image of the sunrise that is in my mind. But both—the dawn and the image of the sunrise—are present and seen by me, so that the sunrise which is future can be told in advance. Thus the future is not yet; and if it is not yet, it is not; and if it is not, then it is totally impossible to see it. But it can be foretold from things present which now exist and are seen.

XIX

But You, O Ruler of Your creation, how is it that you can show souls things that are to come? For such things You have told Your prophets. In what manner do You show the future to man, for whom nothing future is yet is? Or do You show only present signs of things to come? For what does not exist obviously cannot be shown. The means You use is altogether beyond my gaze; my eyes have not the strength; of myself I shall never be able to see so deep, but in You I shall be able, when you grant it, O lovely Light of the eyes of my spirit.

XX

At any rate it is now quite clear that neither future nor past actually exists. Nor is it right to say there are three times, past, present and future. Perhaps it would be more correct to say: there are three times, a present of things past, a present of things present, a present of things future. For these three exist in the mind, and I find them nowhere else: the present of things past is memory, the present of things present it sight, the present of things future is expectation. If we are allowed to speak thus, I see and admit that there are three times, that three times truly are.

By all means continue to say that there are three times, past, present and future; for, though it is incorrect, custom allows it. By all means say it. I do not mind, I neither argue nor object: provided that you understand what you are saying and do not think future or past now exists. There are few things that we phrase properly; most things we phrase badly: but what we are trying to say is understood.

XXI

I said a little while ago that we measure time in its passing, so that we are able to say that this period of time is to that as two to one, or that this is of the same duration as that, and can measure and describe any other proportions of time's parts.

Thus, as I said, we measure time *in its passing*. If you ask me how I know this, my answer is that I know it because we measure time, and we cannot measure what does not exist, and past and future do not exist. But how do we measure time present, since it has no extent? It is measured while it is passing; once it has passed, it cannot be measured, for then nothing exists to measure.

But where does time come from, and by what way does it pass, and where does it go, while we are measuring it? Where is it from?— obviously from the future. By what way does it pass?—by the present. Where does it go?—into the past. In other words it passes from that which does not yet exist, by way of that which lacks extension, into what which is no longer.

But how are we measuring time unless in terms of some kind of duration? We cannot say single or double or triple or equal or proportioned in any other way, save of the duration of periods of time. But in what duration do we measure time while it is actually passing? In the future, from which it comes? But what does not yet exist cannot be measured. In the present, then, by which it passes? But that which has no space cannot be measured. In the past, to which it passes? But what no longer exists cannot be measured.

XXII

My mind burns to solve this complicated enigma. O Lord my God, O good Father, for Christ's sake I beseech Thee, do not shut off these obscure familiar problems from my longing, do not shut them off and leave them impenetrable but let them shine clear for me in the light of Thy mercy, O Lord. Yet whom shall I question about them? And to whom more fruitfully than to Thee shall I confess my ignorance: for Thou art not displeased at the zeal with which I am on fire for Thy Scriptures. Grant me what I love: for it is by Your gift that I love. Grant me this gift, Father, *who dost know how to give good gifts to Thy children.* Grant is because I have *studied that I might know and it is a labour in my sight* until Thou shalt open it to me. For Christ's sake I beseech Thee, in the name of Him who is the Holy of Holies, that no one prevent me. *I have believed, therefore have I spoken.* This is my hope; for this do I live, *that I may see the delight of the Lord. Behold Thou hast made my days old,* and they pass away: but how I know not.

We are forever talking of time and of times. "How long did he speak," "How long did it take him to do that," "For how long a time did I fail to see this," "This syllable is double the length of that." So we speak and so we hear others speak, and others understand us, and we them. They are the plainest and commonest of words, yet again they are profoundly obscure and their meaning still to be discovered.

XXIII

I once heard a learned man say that time is simply the movement of the sun and moon and stars. I did not agree. For why should not time rather by the movement of all bodies? Supposing the light of heaven were to cease and the potter's wheel we could measure its rotations and say that these were at equal intervals, or some slower, some quicker, some taking longer, some shorter? And if we spoke thus, should we not ourselves be speaking in time: would there not be in our words some syllables long, some short—because some would sound for a longer time, some for a shorter?

O God, grant unto men to see by some small example the elements in common between small things and great. There are stars and the lights of heaven *to be for signs and for seasons and for days and years.* This is evident; but just as I would not affirm that one turn of that little wooden wheel is a day, neither should my philosopher say that it is no time at all.

What I am trying to come at is the force and nature of time, by which we measure the movement of bodies and say for example that this movement is twice as long as that. A day means not only the length of time that the sun is above the earth—so that we distinguish day from night—but the time of the sun's whole circuit from east to east— as we say that so many days have passed, so many days being used to include their nights, for the nights are not reckoned separately. Thus, since a day is constituted by the movement of the sun and its completed circle from east to east, I wish to know whether a day is that movement itself, or simply the time the movement takes, or both.

If the movement of the sun through one complete circuit were the day, then it would be a day even if the sun sped through its course in a space of time equal to an hour. If the time the sun now takes to complete its circuit is the day, then it would not be a day if between one sunrise and the next there were only the space of an hour: the sun would have to go round twenty-four times to make one day. But if to constitute a day there is needed both the movement of the sun through one circuit and the time the sun now takes, then you would not have a day if the sun completed its whole circuit in an hour, nor again if the sun stood still and as much time passed as the sun normally takes to complete its journey from one morning to the next.

But I shall not at the moment pursue the question of what it is that we call a day. I shall continue to seek what time is, by which we measure the sun's journey: so that we should say that it had gone round in half its accustomed time, if it went round in a space of time equivalent to twelve hours. And comparing its normal time with this twelve-hour time, we should say that the latter was single, the former double; yet the sun would in the one case have made its journey from east to east in the shorter time, in the other in the longer [so that time is something independent of the sun's movement].

Let no one tell me that the movement of the heavenly bodies is time: when at the prayer of a man the sun stood still that he might complete his victory in battle, the sun stood still but time moved on. The battle was continued for the necessary length of time and was finished.

Therefore I see time as in some way extended. But do I see it? Or do I only seem to see it? Thou wilt show me, O Light, O Truth.

XXIV

Would You have me agree with one who said that time is the movement of a body? You would not: for I learn that no body moves save in time: You have said it. But I do not learn that the movement of the body is time: You have not said it. For when a body is in motion, it is by time that I measure how long it is in motion from the beginning of its movement till it ceases to move. And if I did not see when the movement began, and if it moved on without my seeing when it ceased, I should be able to measure only from the moment I began to look until the moment I stopped looking. If I look for a long time, all I can say is that the time is long, but not how long it is, because when we say how long a time, we say it by comparison: as for example: this is as long as that, or this is twice that, and such like. But if we could note the point of space from which a body in motion comes or the point to which it goes, or could distinguish its parts if it is moving on its axis, we should be able to say how much time has elapsed for the movement of the body, or its part, from one place to another.

Thus since the movement of a body is not the same as our measurement of how long the movement takes, who can fail to see which of these is more deserving of the name of time? A body moves at different speeds, and sometimes stands still; but time enables us to measure not only its motion but its rest as well; and we say "It was at rest for the same length of time as it was in motion," or "It was at rest twice or thrice as long as it was in motion" or any other proportion, whether precisely measured or roughly estimated.

Therefore time is not the movement of a body.

XXV

I confess to You, Lord, that I still do not know what time is. And again I confess to You, Lord, that I know that I am uttering these things in time: I have been talking of time for a long time, and this long time would not be a long time unless time had passed. But how do I know this, since I do not know how to express what I know. Alas for me, I do not even know what I do not know! See me, O my God, I stand before You and I do not lie: as my speech is, so is my heart. *For Thou lightest my lamp, O Lord; O my God, enlighten my darkness.*

XXVI

Does not my soul speak truly to You when I say that I can measure time? For so it is, O Lord my God, I measure it and I do not know what it is that I am measuring. I measure the movement of a body, using time to measure it by. Do I not then measure time itself? Could I measure the movement of a body—its duration and how long it takes to move from place to place—if I could not measure the time in which it moves?

But if so, what do I use to measure time with? Do we measure a longer time by a shorter one, as we measure a beam in terms of cubits? Thus we say that the duration of a long syllable is measured by the space of a short syllable and is said to be double. Thus we measure the length of poems by the lengths of the lines, and the lengths of the lines by the lengths of the feet, and the lengths of the feet by the syllables, and the lengths of long syllables by the lengths of short. We do not measure poems by pages, for that would be to measure space not time; we measure by the way the voice moves in uttering the poem, and we say: "It is a long poem, for it consists of so many lines; the lines are long for they are composed of so many feet; the feet are long for they include so many syllables; this syllable is long for it is the double of a short syllable."

But not by all this do we arrive at an exact measure of time. It may well happen that a shorter line may take longer if it is recited slowly than a longer line hurried through. And the same is true of a poem or a foot or a syllable.

Thus it seems to me that time is certainly extendedness—but I do not know what it is extendedness of: probably of the mind itself. Tell me, O my God, what am I measuring, when I say either, with no aim at precision, that one period is longer than the other, or, precisely, that one is double the other? That I measure time, I know. But I do not measure the future, for it is not yet; nor the present, for it is not extended in space; nor the past, which no longer exists. So what do I measure? Is it time in passage but not past? So I have already said.

XXVII

Persevere, O my soul, fix all the power of your gaze. *God is our helper. He made us, and not we ourselves.* Fix your gaze where truth is whitening toward the dawn.

Consider the example of a bodily voice. It begins to sound, it sound and goes on sounding, then it ceases: and now there is silence, the sound has passed, the sound no longer is. It was future before it began to sound, and so could not be measured, for as yet it did not exist; and now it cannot be measured because now it exists no longer. Only while sounding could it be measured for then it was, and so was measurable. But even then it was not standing still; it was moving, and moving out of existence. Did this make it more measurable? Only in the sense that by its passing it was spread over a certain space of time which made it measurable: for the present occupies no space.

At any rate, let us grant that it could be measured. And now again imagine a voice. It begins to sound and goes on sounding continuously without anything to break its even flow. Let us measure it, while it is sounding. For when it has ceased to sound, it will be past and will no longer be measurable. Let us measure it then and say how long it is. But it is still sounding and can be measured only from its beginning when it begins to sound to its end, when it ceased. For what we measure in the interval between some starting point and some conclusion. This means that a sound which is not yet over cannot be measured so that we may say how long or short it is, nor can it be said either to be equal to some other sound or single or double or any other proportion in relation to it. But when it *is* over, it will no longer be. Then how will it be possible to measure it? Yet we do measure time—not that which is not yet, nor that which is no longer, nor that which has no duration, nor that which lacks beginning and end. Thus is seems that we measure neither time future nor time past nor time present nor time passing: and yet we measure time.

Deus creator omnium: This line is composed of eight syllables, short and long alternately: the four short syllables, the first, third, fifth, seventh are single in relation to the four long syllables, the second, fourth, sixth, eighth. Each long syllable has double the time of each short syllable. I pronounce them and I say that it is so, and so it is, as it quite obvious to the ear. As my ear distinguishes I measure a long syllable by a short and I perceive that it contains it twice. But since I hear a syllable only when the one before it has ceased—the one before being short and the one following long—how am I to keep hold of the short syllable, and how shall I set it again the long one to measure it and find that the long one is twice its length—given that the long syllable does not begin to sound until the short one has ceased? And again can I measure the long one while it is present, since I cannot measure it until it is completed? And its completion is its passing our of existence.

What then is it that I measure? Where is the short syllable by which I measure? Where is the long syllable which I measure? Both have sounded, have fled away, have gone into the past, are now no more: yet I do measure, and I affirm with confidence, in so far as a practiced sense can be trusted, that one is single, the other double, in the length of time it occupies. And I could not do this unless they had both passed away and ended. Thus it is not the syllables themselves that I measure, for they are now no more, but something which remains engraved in my memory.

It is in you, O my mind, that I measure time. Do not bring against me, do not bring against yourself the disorderly throng of your impressions. In you, I say, I measure time. What I measure is the impress produced in you by things as they pass and abiding in you when they have passed: and it is present. I do not measure the things themselves whose passage produced the impress; it is the impress that I measure when I measure time. Thus either that is what time is, or I am not measuring time at all.

But when we measure silences, and say that some particular silence lasted as long as some particular phrase, do we not stretch our mind to measure the phrase as though it were actually sounded, so as to be able to form a judgment of the relation between the space of the silence and that space of time? For without voice or lips we can go through poems and verses and speeches in our minds, and we can allow for the time it takes for their movement, one part in relation to another, exactly as if we were reciting them aloud. If a man decides to utter a longish sound and settles in his mind how long the sound is to be, he goes through that space of time in silence, entrusts it to his memory, then begins to utter the sound, and it sounds until it reaches the length he had fixed for it. Or rather I should say [not that it sounds but] that it has sounded and will sound: for as much of it as has been uttered at a given moment has obviously sounded, and what remains will sound: and so he completes the sound: at every moment his attention, which is present, causes the future to make its way into the past, the future diminishing and the past growing, until the future is exhausted and everything is past.

XXVIII

But how is the future diminished or exhausted, since the future does not yet exist: or how does the past grow, since it no longer is? Only because, in the mind which does all this, there are three acts. For the mind expects, attends and remembers: what it expects passes, by way of what it attends to, into what it remembers. Would anyone deny that the future is as yet not existent? But in the mind there is already an expectation of the future. Would anyone deny that the past no longer exists? Yet still there is in the mind a memory of the past. Would anyone deny that the present time lacks extension, since it is but a point that passes on? Yet the attention endures, and by it that which is to be passes on its way to being no more. Thus it is not the future that is long, for the future does not exist: a long future is merely a long expectation of the future; nor is the past long since the past does not exist: a long past is merely a long memory of the past.

Suppose that I am about to recite a psalm that I know. Before I begin, my expectation is directed to the whole of it; but when I have begun, so much of it as I pluck off and drop away into the past becomes matter for my memory; and whole energy of the action is divided between my memory, in regard to what I have said, and my expectation, in regard to what I am still to say. But there is a present act of attention, by which what was future passes on its way to becoming past. The further I go in my recitation, the more my expectation is diminished and my memory lengthened, until the whole of my expectation is used up when the action is completed and has passed wholly into my memory. And what is true of the whole psalm, is true for each part of the whole, and for each syllable: and likewise for any longer action, of which the canticle may be only a part: indeed it is the same for the whole life of man, of which all a man's actions are parts: and likewise for the whole history of the human race, of which all the lives of all men are parts.

XXIX

But *Thy mercy is better than lives,* and behold my life is but a scattering. *Thy right hand has held me up* in my Lord, the Son of Man who is the Mediator in many things and in divers manners—that *I may apprehend by Him in whom I am apprehended* and may be set free from what I once was, following your Oneness: *forgetting the things that are behind* and not poured out upon things to come and things transient, but *stretching forth to those that are before* (not by dispersal but by concentration of energy) *I press towards the prize of the supernal vocation,* where *I may hear the voice of Thy praise* and contemplate Thy delight which neither comes nor passes away.

But now my years are wasted in sighs, and Thou, O Lord, my eternal Father, art my only solace; but I am divided up in time, whose order I do not know, and my thoughts and the deepest places of my soul are torn with every kind of tumult until the day when I shall be purified and melted in the fire of Thy love and wholly joined to Thee.

XXX

And I shall stand and be established in You, in my own true form, in Your truth. I shall no longer suffer the questions of men who, by a disease they have merited for their punishment, ever thirst more than they can drink. Thus they ask: "What was God making before He made Heaven and earth?" "Or how did the idea of creating something come into His mind whereas He had never created anything before?"

Grant them, Lord, to think well what they are saying, and to realize that one cannot use the word "never" made anything, obviously this means that He did not make anything "at any time." Let them see than that there can be no time apart from creation, and let them cease to talk such nonsense. *Let them stretch forth to the things that are before*, and let them realize that before all times You are the Eternal Creator of all times, and that no times are co- eternal with You, nor in any creature, even if there were a creature above time.

XXXI

O Lord, My God, how deep is the abyss of Thy secret, and how far from it have the consequences of my sins held me? Cleanse my eyes and let me rejoice in Thy Light. Assuredly if there were a mind of such vast knowledge and fore-knowledge that all the past and all the future were as clearly known to it as some familiar canticle is known to me, such a mind would be marvelous beyond measure, would strike us silent with awe. For to such a mind nothing would be hidden of ages past or ages still to come, any more than when I am singing my canticle anything is unknown to me of what I have sung from the beginning, of what remains to me to sing to the end. Yet far from me be it to think that You, O Creator of the Universe, Creator of souls and bodies, had only such knowledge as that of the future and the past. Far more marvellously, far more mysteriously, do You hold Your knowledge. For when a man is singing a song he knows, or hearing a song he knows, his impressions vary and his senses are divided between the expectation of sounds to come and the memory of sounds already uttered. No such thing happens to You, the immutable and eternal, the eternal Creator of minds. In the beginning You knew heaven and earth without any element of change in your knowledge; and similarly in the beginning You created heaven and earth without any element of change in Your action. Let him who understands praise You, and let him who does not understand praise You likewise. You are the highest, and the humble of heart are Your dwelling place. For You *lift up them that are cast down,* and those do not fall who have You for their high place.

3

Ludwig Wittgenstein, "St. Augustine's Puzzle about Time," from *The Blue Book*

Ludwig Wittgenstein (1889–1951), the author of the Tractatus Logico-Philosophicus *and the* Philosophical Investigations, *is thought by some to be the greatest philosopher of the twentieth century. In this passage from* The Blue Book *he is discussing our tendency to believe that language must be an abstract system which proceeds according to exact rules.*

Consider as an example the question "What is time?" as Saint Augustine and others have asked it. At first sight what this question asks for is a definition, but then immediately the question arises: "What should we gain by a definition, as it can only lead us to other undefined terms?" And why should one be puzzled just by the lack of a definition of time, and not by the lack of a definition of "chair"? Why shouldn't we be puzzled in all cases where we haven't got a definition? Now a definition often clears up the *grammar* of a word. And in fact it is the grammar of the word "time" which puzzles us. We are only expressing this puzzlement by asking a slightly misleading question, the question: "What is . . . ?" This question is an utterance of unclarity, of mental discomfort, and it is comparable with the question "Why?" as children so often ask it. This too is an expression of a mental discomfort, and doesn't necessarily ask for either a cause or a reason. (Hertz, *Principles of Mechanics.*) Now the puzzlement about the grammar of the word "time" arises from what one might call apparent contradictions in that grammar.

It was such a "contradiction" which puzzled Saint Augustine when he argued: How is it possible that one should measure time? For the past can't be measured, as it is gone by; and the future can't be measured

From *The Blue Book* by Ludwig Wittgenstein, Oxford, 1958, reprinted by permission of Basil Blackwell Publishers and the Wittgenstein Trustees.

because it has not yet come. And the present can't be measured for it has no extension.

The contradiction which here seems to arise could be called a conflict between two different usages of a word, in this case the word "measure". Augustine, we might say, thinks of the process of measuring a *length*: say, the distance between two marks on a travelling band which passes us, and of which we can only see a tiny bit (the present) in front of us. Solving this puzzle will consist in comparing what we mean by "measurement" (the grammar of the word "measurement") when applied to a distance on a travelling band with the grammar of that word when applied to time. The problem may seem simple, but its extreme difficulty is due to the fascination which the analogy between two similar structures in our language can exert on us. (It is helpful here to remember that it is sometimes almost impossible for a child to believe that one word can have two meanings.)

Now it is clear that this problem about the concept of time asks for an answer given in the form of strict rules. The puzzle is about rules.— Take another example: Socrates' question "What is knowledge?" Here the case is even clearer, as the discussion begins with the pupil giving an example of an exact definition, and then analogous to this a definition of the word "knowledge" is asked for. As the problem is put, it seems that there is something wrong with the ordinary use of the word "knowledge". It appears we don't know what it means, and that therefore, perhaps, we have no right to use it. We should reply: "There is no one exact usage of the word 'knowledge'; but we can make up several such usages, which will more or less agree with the ways the word is actually used".

The man who is philosophically puzzled sees a law in the way a word is used, and, trying to apply this law consistently, comes up against cases where it leads to paradoxical results. Very often the way the discussion of such a puzzle runs is this: First the question is asked "What is time?" This question makes it appear that what we want is a definition. We mistakenly think that a definition is what will remove the trouble (as in certain states of indigestion we feel a kind of hunger which cannot be removed by eating). The question is then answered by a wrong definition; say: "Time is the motion of the celestial bodies". The next step is to see that this definition is unsatisfactory. But this only means that we don't use the word "time" synonymously with "motion of the celestial bodies". However in saying that the first definition is wrong, we are now tempted to think that we must replace it by a different one, the correct one.

Compare with this the case of the definition of number. Here the explanation that a number is the same thing as a numeral satisfies that first craving for a definition. And it is very difficult not to ask: "Well, if it isn't the numeral, *what is it?*"

Philosophy, as we use the word, is a fight against the fascination which forms of expression exert upon us.

I want you to remember that words have those meanings which we have given them; and we give them meanings by explanations. I may have given a definition of a word and used the word accordingly, or those who taught me the use of the word may have given me the explanation. Or else we might, by the explanation of a word, mean the explanation which, on being asked, we are ready to give. That is, if we *are* ready to give any explanation; in most cases we aren't. Many words in this sense then don't have a strict meaning. But this is not a defect. To think it is would be like saying that the light of my reading lamp is no real light at all because it has no sharp boundary.

Philosophers very often talk about investigating, analysing, the meaning of words. But let's not forget that a word hasn't got a meaning given to it, as it were, by a power independent of us, so that there could be a kind of scientific investigation into what the word *really* means. A word has the meaning someone has given to it.

There are words with several clearly defined meanings. It is easy to tabulate these meanings. And there are words of which one might say: They are used in a thousand different ways which gradually merge into one another. No wonder that we can't tabulate strict rules for their use.

It is wrong to say that in philosophy we consider an ideal language as opposed to our ordinary one. For this makes it appear as though we thought we could improve on ordinary language. But ordinary language is all right. Whenever we make up 'ideal languages' it is not in order to replace our ordinary language by them; but just to remove some trouble caused in someone's mind by thinking that he has got hold of the exact use of a common word. That is also why our method is not merely to enumerate actual usages of words, but rather deliberately to invent new ones, some of them because of their absurd appearance. . . .

4

Edmund Husserl,
"The Constitution of Temporal Objects,"
from *The Phenomenology of the Internal Time-Consciousness*

The phenomenological method of Edmund Husserl (1859–1938), which brackets (sets aside) the question of external reality and carefully describes phenomena or appearances, is one of the most fruitful approaches to philosophy in the twentieth century. In the following pages from The Phenomenology of *Internal Time-Consciousness,* Husserl *applies his method to the problem of time, describing how temporal objects (e.g. a sound) are "constituted" within consciousness.*

The Consciousness of the Appearances of
Immanent Objects [*Objekte*]

On closer inspection, we are able to distinguish still other lines of thought with reference to the description: (1) We can make self-evident assertions concerning the immanent Object in itself, e.g., that it now endures, that a certain part of the duration has elapsed, that the duration of the sound apprehended in the now (naturally, with the content of the sound) constantly sinks back into the past and an ever new point of duration enters into the now or is now, that the expired duration recedes from the actual now-point (which is continually filled up in some way or other) and moves back into an ever more "distant" past, and so on. (2) We can also speak of the way in which we are "conscious of" all differences in the "appearing" of immanent sounds and their content of duration. We speak here with reference to the perception of the duration of the sound which extends into the actual now, and

Excerpts from Edmund Husserl, *The Phenomenology of Internal Time-Consciousness,* edited by Martin Heidegger, translated by James S. Churchill, 1973, Indiana University Press.

say that the sound, which endures, is perceived, and that of the interval of duration of the sound only the point of duration characterized as now is veritably perceived. Of the interval that has expired we say that we are conscious of it in retentions, specifically, that we are conscious of those parts or phases of the duration, not sharply to be differentiated, which lie closest to the actual now-point with diminishing clarity, while those parts lying further back in the past are wholly unclear; we are conscious of them only as empty [*leer*]. The same thing is true with regard to the running-off of the entire duration. Depending on its distance from the actual now, that part of the duration which lies closest still has perhaps a little clarity; the whole disappears in obscurity, in a void retentional consciousness, and finally disappears completely (if one may say so) as soon as retention ceases.[1]

In the clear sphere we find, therefore, a greater distinction and dispersion (in fact, the more so, the closer the sphere to the actual now). The further we withdraw from the now, however, the greater the blending and drawing together. If in reflection we immerse ourselves in the unity of a structured process, we observe that an articulated part of the process "draws together" as it sinks into the past—a kind of temporal perspective (within the originary temporal appearance) analogous to spatial perspective. As the temporal Object moves into the past, it is drawn together on itself and thereby also becomes obscure.

We must now examine more closely what we find here and can describe as the phenomena of temporally constitutive consciousness, that consciousness in which temporal objects with their temporal determinations are constituted. We distinguish the enduring, immanent Object in its modal setting [*das Objekt im Wie*], the way in which we are conscious of it as actually present or as past. Every temporal being "appears" in one or another continually changing mode of running-off, and the "Object in the mode of running-off" is in this change always something other, even though we still say that the Object and every point of its time and this time itself are one and the same. The "Object in the mode of running-off" we cannot term a form of consciousness (any more than we can call a spatial phenomenon, a

---

1. It is tempting to draw a parallel between these modes of the consciousness and appearance of temporal Objects and the modes in which a spatial thing appears and is known with changing orientation, to pursue further the "temporal orientations" in which spatial things (which are also temporal Objects) appear. Yet, for the time being, we shall remain in the immanent sphere.

body in its appearance from one side or the other, from far or near, a form of consciousness). "Consciousness," "lived experience," refers to an Object by means of an appearance in which "the Object in its modal setting" subsists. Obviously, we must recognize talk of "intentionality" as ambiguous, depending on whether we have in mind the relation of the appearance to what appears or the relation of consciousness on the one hand to "what appears in its modal setting" and on the other to what merely appears.

The Continua of Running-off Phenomena— The Diagram of Time

We should prefer to avoid talk of "appearance" when referring to phenomena which constitute temporal Objects, for these phenomena are themselves immanent Objects and are appearances in a wholly different sense. We speak here of "running-off phenomena" [*Ablaufsphänomene*], or better yet of "modes of temporal orientation," and with reference to the immanent Objects themselves of their "running-off characters" (e.g., now, past). With regard to the running-off phenomenon, we know that it is a continuity of constant transformations which form an inseparable unit, not severable into parts which could be by themselves nor divisible into phases, points of the continuity, which could be by themselves. The parts which by a process of abstraction we can throw into relief can be only in the entire running-off. This is also true of the phases and points of the continuity of running-off. It is evident that we can also say of this continuity that in certain ways it is unalterable as to form. It is unthinkable that the continuity of phases would be such that it contained the same phase-mode twice or indeed contained it extended over an entire part-interval. Just as every temporal point (and every temporal interval) is, so to speak, different from every other "individual" point and cannot occur twice, so also no mode of running-off can occur twice. However, we shall carry our analysis still further here and hence must make our distinctions clear.

To begin with, we emphasize that modes of running-off of an immanent temporal Object have a beginning, that is to say, a source-point. This is the mode of running-off with which the immanent Object begins to be. It is characterized as now. In the continuous line of advance, we find something remarkable, namely, that every subsequent phase of running-off is itself a continuity, and one constantly expanding, a continuity of pasts. The continuity of the modes of running-off of the duration of the Object we contrast to the continuity of the modes of running-off of each point of the duration which obviously is enclosed in the continuity of those first modes of running-off; therefore, the continuity of running-off of an enduring Object is a continuum whose phases are the continua of the modes of running-off of the different temporal points of the duration of the Object. If we go along the concrete continuity, we advance in continuous modifications, and in this process the mode of running-off is constantly modified, i.e., along the continuity of running-off of the temporal points concerned. Since a new now is always presenting itself, each now is changed into a past, and thus the entire continuity of the running-off of the pasts of the preceding points moves uniformly "downward" into the depths of the past. In our figure the solid horizontal line illustrates the modes of

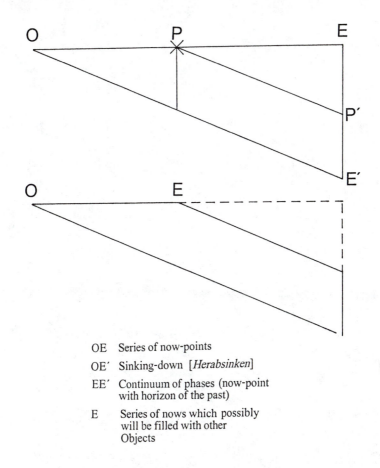

OE   Series of now-points

OE′ Sinking-down [*Herabsinken*]

EE′ Continuum of phases (now-point
      with horizon of the past)

E   Series of nows which possibly
     will be filled with other
     Objects

running-off of the enduring Object. These modes extend from a point O on for a definite interval which has the last now as an end-point. Then the series of modes of running-off begins which no longer contains a now (of this duration). The duration is no longer actual but past and constantly sinks deeper into the past. The figure thus provides a complete picture of the double continuity of modes of running-off.

5

Sir Isaac Newton,
"Scholium on Absolute Space and Time,"
from the *Principia*

The work of the great Sir Isaac Newton (1642–1727), including the Principia *and the* Opticks, *completely changed the understanding of the physical world. He was also a mathematician of genius, discovering the calculus at the same time as Leibniz.*

Hitherto I have laid down the definitions of such works as are less known, and explained the sense in which I would have them to be understood in the following discourse. I do not define time, space, place, and motion, as being well known to all. Only I must observe, that the common people conceive those quantities under no other notions but from the relation they bear to sensible objects. And thence arise certain prejudices, for the removing of which it will be convenient to distinguish them into absolute and relative, true and apparent, mathematical and common.

I. Absolute, true, and mathematical time, of itself, and from its own nature, flows equably without relation to anything external, and by another name is called duration: relative, apparent, and common time, is some sensible and external (whether accurate or unequable) measure of duration by the means of motion, which is commonly used instead of true time; such as an hour, a day, a month, a year.

II. Absolute space, in its own nature, without relation to anything external, remains always similar and immovable. Relative space is some movable dimension or measure of the absolute spaces; which our senses determine by its position to bodies; and which is commonly taken for immovable space; such is the dimension of a subterraneous, an aerial,

From Isaac Newton, *Mathematical Principles of Natural Philosophy and His System of the World*, translated by Florian Cajori, edited by Andrew Motte, © 1934, renewed 1962, Regents of the University of California, with permission of the University of California Press.

or celestial space, determined by its position in respect of the earth. Absolute and relative space are the same in figure and magnitude; but they do not remain always numerically the same. For if the earth, for instance, moves, a space of our air, which relatively and in respect of the earth remains always the same, will at one time be one part of the absolute space into which the air passes; at another time it will be another part of the same, and so, absolutely understood, it will be continually changed.

III. Place is a part of space which a body takes up, and is according to the space, either absolute or relative. I say, a part of space; not the situation, nor the external surface of the body. For the places of equal solids are always equal; but their surfaces, by reason of their dissimilar figures, are often unequal. Positions properly have no quantity, nor are they so much the places themselves, as the properties of places. The motion of the whole is the same with the sum of the motions of the parts; that is, the translation of the whole, out of its place, is the same thing with the sum of the translations of the parts out of their places; and therefore the place of the whole is the same as the sum of the places of the parts, and for that reason, it is internal, and in the whole body.

IV. Absolute motion is the translation of a body from one absolute place into another; and relative motion, the translation from one relative place into another. Thus in a ship under sail, the relative place of a body is that part of the ship which the body possesses; or that part of the cavity which the body fills, and which therefore moves together with the ship: and relative rest is the continuance of the body in the same part of the ship, or of its cavity. But real, absolute rest, is the continuance of the body in the same part of that immovable space, in which the ship itself, its cavity, and all that it contains, is moved. Wherefore, if the earth is really at rest, the body, which relatively rests in the ship, will really and absolutely move with the same velocity which the ship has on the earth. But if the earth also moves, the true and absolute motion of the body will arise, partly from the true motion of the earth, in immovable space, partly from the relative motion of the ship on the earth; and if the body moves also relatively in the ship, its true motion will arise, partly from the true motion of the earth, in immovable space, and partly from the relative motions as well of the ship on the earth, as of the body in the ship; and from these relative motions will arise the relative motion of the body on the earth. As if that part of the earth, where the ship is, was truly moved towards the east, with a velocity of 10010 parts; while the ship itself, with a fresh gale, and full sails, is carried towards the west, with a velocity expressed by 10 of those parts; but a sailor walks in the ship towards the east, with 1 part of the said velocity; then the sailor will be moved truly in immovable space towards the east, with a velocity of 10001 parts, and relatively on the earth towards the west, with a velocity of 9 of those parts.

Absolute time, in astronomy, is distinguished from relative, by the equation or correction of the apparent time. For the natural days are truly unequal, though they are commonly considered as equal, and used for a measure of time; astronomers correct this inequality that they may measure the celestial motions by a more accurate time. It may be, that there is no such thing as an equable motion, whereby time may be accurately measured. All motions may be accelerated and retarded, but the flowing of absolute time is not liable to any change. The duration or perseverance of the existence of things remains the same, whether the motions are swift or slow, or none at all: and therefore this duration ought to be distinguished from what are only sensible measures thereof; and from which we deduce it, by means of the astronomical equation. The necessity of this equation, for determining the times of a phenomenon, is evinced as well from the experiments of the pendulum clock, as by eclipses of the satellites of Jupiter.

As the order of the parts of time is immutable, so also is the order of the parts of space. Suppose those parts to be moved out of their places, and they will be moved (if the expression may be allowed) out of themselves. For times and spaces are, as it were, the places as well of themselves as of all other things. All things are placed in time as to order of succession; and in space as to order of situation. It is from their essence or nature that they are places; and that the primary places of things should be movable, is absurd. These are therefore the absolute places; and translations out of those places, are the only absolute motions.

But because the parts of space cannot be seen, or distinguished from one another by our senses, therefore in their stead we use sensible measures of them. For from the positions and distances of things from any body considered as immovable, we define all places; and then with respect to such places, we estimate all motions, considering bodies as transferred from some of those places into others. And so, instead of absolute places and motions, we use relative ones; and that without any inconvenience in common affairs; but in philosophical disquisitions, we ought to abstract from our senses, and consider things themselves, distinct from what are only sensible measures of them. For it may be that there is no body really at rest, to which the places and motions of others may be referred.

But we may distinguish rest and motion, absolute and relative, one from the other by their properties, causes, and effects. It is a property of rest, that bodies really at rest do rest in respect to one another. And therefore as it is possible, that in the remote regions of the fixed stars, or perhaps far beyond them, there may be some body absolutely at rest; but impossible to know, from the position of bodies to one another in our regions, whether any of these do keep the same position to that remote body, it follows that absolute rest cannot be determined from the position of bodies in our regions.

It is a property of motion, that the parts, which retain given positions to their wholes, do partake of the motions of those wholes. For all the parts of revolving bodies endeavor to recede from the axis of motion; and the impetus of bodies moving forwards arises from the joint impetus of all the parts. Therefore, if surrounding bodies are moved, those that are relatively at rest within them will partake of their motion. Upon which account, the true and absolute motion of a body cannot be determined by the translation of it from those which only seem to rest; for the external bodies ought not only to appear at rest, but to be really at rest. For otherwise, all included bodies, besides their translation from near the surrounding ones, partake likewise of their true motions; and though that translation were not made, they would not be really at rest, but only seem to be so. For the surrounding bodies stand in the like relation to the surrounded as the exterior part of a whole does to the interior, or as the shell does to the kernel; but if the shell moves, the kernel will also move, as being part of the whole, without any removal from near the shell.

A property, near akin to the preceding, is this, that if a place is moved, whatever is placed therein moves along with it; and therefore a body, which is moved from a place in motion, partakes also of the motion of its place. Upon which account, all motions, from places in motion, are no other than parts of entire and absolute motions; and every entire motion is composed of the motion of the body out of its first place, and the motion of this place out of its place; and so on, until we come to some immovable place, as in the before-mentioned example of the sailor. Wherefore, entire and absolute motions can be no otherwise determined than by immovable places; and for that reason

I did before refer those absolute motions to immovable places, but relative ones to movable places. Now no other places are immovable but those that, from infinity to infinity, do all retain the same given position one to another; and upon this account must ever remain unmoved; and do thereby constitute immovable space.

The causes by which true and relative motions are distinguished, one from the other, are the forces impressed upon bodies to generate motion. True motion is neither generated nor altered, but by some force impressed upon the body moved; but relative motion may be generated or altered without any force impressed upon the body. For it is sufficient only to impress some force on other bodies with which the former is compared, that by their giving way, that relation may be changed, in which the relative rest or motion of this other body did consist. Again, true motion suffers always some change from any force impressed upon the moving body; but relative motion does not necessarily undergo any change by such forces. For if the same forces are likewise impressed on those other bodies, with which the comparison is made, that the relative position may be preserved, then that condition will be preserved in which the relative motion consists. And therefore any relative motion may be changed when the true motion remains unaltered, and the relative may be preserved when the true suffers some change. Thus, true motion by no means consists in such relations.

The effects which distinguish absolute from relative motion are, the forces of receding from the axis of circular motion. For there are no such forces in a circular motion purely relative, but in a true and absolute circular motion, they are greater or less, according to the quantity of the motion. If a vessel, hung by a long cord, is so often turned about that the cord is strongly twisted, then filled with water, and held at rest together with the water; thereupon, by the sudden action of another force, it is whirled about the contrary way, and while the cord is untwisting itself, the vessel continues for some time in this motion; the surface of the water will at first be plain, as before the vessel began to move; but after that, the vessel, by gradually communicating its motion to the water, will make it begin sensibly to revolve, and recede by little and little from the middle, and ascend to the sides of the vessel, forming itself into a concave figure (as I have experienced), and the swifter the motion becomes, the higher will the water rise, till at last, performing its revolutions in the same times with the vessel, it becomes relatively at rest in it. This ascent of the water shows its endeavor to recede from the axis of its motion; and the true and absolute circular motion of the water, which is here directly contrary to the relative, becomes known, and may be measured by this endeavor. At first, when the relative motion of the water in the vessel was greatest, it produced no endeavor to recede from the axis; the water showed no tendency to the circumference, nor any ascent towards the sides of the vessel, but remained of a plain surface, and therefore its true circular motion had not yet begun. But afterwards, when the relative motion of the water had decreased, the ascent thereof towards the sides of the vessel proved its endeavor to recede from the axis; and this endeavor showed the real circular motion of the water continually increasing, till it had acquired its greatest quantity, when the water rested relatively in the vessel. And therefore this endeavor does not depend upon any translation of the water in respect of the ambient bodies, nor can true circular motion be defined by such translation. There is only one real circular motion of any one revolving body, corresponding to only one power of endeavoring to recede from its axis of motion, as its proper and adequate effect; but relative motions, in one and the same body, are innumerable, according to the various relations it bears to external bodies, and, like other relations, are alto-gether destitute of any real effect, any otherwise than they may perhaps partake of that one only true motion. And therefore in their system who suppose that our heavens, revolving below the sphere of the fixed stars, carry the planets along with them; the several parts of those heavens, and the planets, which are indeed relatively at rest in their heavens, do yet really move. For they change their position one to another (which never happens to bodies truly at rest), and being carried together with their heavens, partake of their motions, and as parts of revolving wholes, endeavor to recede from the axis of their motions.

Wherefore relative quantities are not the quantities themselves, whose names they bear, but those sensible measure of them (either accurate or inaccurate), which are commonly used instead of the mea-sured quantities themselves. And if the meaning of words is to be determined by their use, then by the names time, space, place, and motion, their [sensible] measures are properly to be understood; and the expression will be unusual, and purely mathematical if the measured quantities themselves are meant. On this account, those violate the accuracy of language, which ought to be kept precise, who interpret these words for the measured quantities. Nor do those less defile the purity of mathematical and philosophical truths, who confound real quantities with their relations and sensible measures.

It is indeed a matter of great difficulty to discover, and effectually to distinguish, the true motions of particular bodies from the apparent; because the parts of that immovable space, in which those motions are performed, do by no means come under the observation of our senses. Yet the thing is not altogether desperate; for we have some arguments to guide us, partly from the apparent motions, which are the differences of the true motions; partly from the forces, which are the causes and effects of the true motions. For instance, if two globes, kept at a given distance one from the other by means of a cord that connects them, were revolved about their common centre of gravity, we might, from the tension of the cord, discover the endeavor of the globes to recede from the axis of their motion, and from thence we might compute the quantity of their circular motions. And then if any equal forces should be impressed at once on the alternate faces of the globes to augment or diminish their circular motions, from the increase or decrease of the tension of the cord, we might infer the increment or decrement of their motions; and thence would be found on what faces those forces ought to be impressed, that the motions of the globes might be most augmented; that is, we might discover their hindmost faces, or those which, in the circular motion, do follow. But the faces which follow being known, and consequently the opposite ones that precede, we should likewise know the determination of their motions. And thus we might find both the quantity and the determination of this circular motion, even in an immense vacuum, where there was nothing external or sensible with which the globes could be compared. But now, if in that space some remote bodies were placed that kept always a given position one to another, as the fixed stars do in our regions, we could not indeed determine from the relative translation of the globes among those bodies, whether the motion did belong to the globes or to the bodies. But if we observed the cord, and found that its tension was that very tension which the motion of the globes required, we might conclude the motion to be in the globes and the bodies to be at rest; and then, lastly, from the translation of the globes among the bodies, we should find the determination of their motions. But how we are to obtain the true motions from their causes, effects, and apparent differences, and the converse, shall be explained more at large in the following treatise. For to this end it was that I composed it.

6

G. W. Leibniz,
"Time Is a Relation,"
from *The Leibniz-Clarke Correspondence*

The philosopher Leibniz (1646–1716) was in Bertrand Russell's words "one of the supreme intellects of all time." He argued for a philosophy of spiritual atoms or "monads," each mirroring the whole universe in its own way. The only book he published during his lifetime was the Theodicy, *essays on the goodness of God, human freedom, and the origin of evil. His notation for calculus, still used today, is superior to Newton's. He also discovered binary arithmetic. In the* Leibniz-Clarke Correspondence *he is attacking the claim made by Newton's representative Samuel Clarke that space is absolute and exists independently of the things which occupy it.*

Leibniz's Third Paper

1. According to the usual way of speaking, *mathematical principles* concern only pure mathematics, namely, numbers, figures, arithmetic, geometry. But *metaphysical principles* concern more general notions, such as cause and effect.

2. The author grants me this important principle, that nothing happens without a sufficient reason why it should be so rather than otherwise. But he grants it only in words and in reality denies it. This shows that he does not fully perceive the strength of it. And therefore, he makes use of an instance, which exactly falls in with one of my demonstrations against real absolute space, the idol of some modern Englishmen. I call it an idol, not in a theological sense, but in a philosophical one, as Chancellor Bacon says that there are idols of the tribe and idols of the cave.[1]

From G. W. Leibniz, *Philosophical Essays*, translated by Roger Ariew & Daniel Garber, 1989, Hackett Publishing Company, Inc., Indianapolis, Ind., and Cambridge, Mass.

1. See Bacon, *New Organon*, book I, aphorisms 41–42.

3. These gentlemen maintain, therefore, that space is a real absolute being. But this involves them in great difficulties, for it appears that such a being must be eternal and infinite. Hence some have believed it to be God himself, or one of his attributes, his immensity. But since space consists of parts, it is not a thing which can belong to God.

4. As for my own opinion, I have said more than once that I hold space to be something merely relative, as time is, that I hold it to be an order of coexistences, as time is an order of successions. For space denotes, in terms of possibility, an order of things which exist at the same time, considered as existing together, without entering into their particular manners of existing. And when many things are seen together, one perceives this order of things among themselves.

5. I have many demonstrations to confute the fancy of those who take space to be a substance, or, at least, an absolute being. But I shall only use, at present, one demonstration, which the author here gives me occasion to insist upon. I say, then, that if space were an absolute being, something would happen for which it would be impossible that there should be a sufficient reason—which is against my axiom. And I can prove it thus. Space is something absolutely uniform, and without the things placed in it, one point of space absolutely does not differ in anything from another point of space. Now, from hence it follows (supposing space to be something in itself, besides the order of bodies among themselves) that is impossible there should be a reason why God, preserving the same situations of bodies among themselves, should have placed them in space after one certain particular manner and not otherwise—why everything was not placed the quite contrary way, for instance, by changing east into west. But if space is nothing else but this order or relation, and is nothing at all without bodies but the possibility of placing them, then those two states, the one such as it is now, the other supposed to be the quite contrary way, would not at all differ from one another. Their difference therefore is only to be found in our chimerical supposition of the reality of space in itself. But in truth, the one would exactly be the same thing as the other, they being absolutely indiscernible, and consequently there is no room to inquire after a reason for the preference of the one to the other.

6. The case is the same with respect to time. Supposing anyone should ask why God did not create everything a year sooner, and the same person should infer from this that God has done something concerning which it is not possible that there should be a reason why he did it so and not otherwise; the answer is that his inference would

be right if time was anything distinct from things existing in time. For it would be impossible that there should be any reason why things should be applied to such particular instants rather than to others, their succession continuing the same. But then the same argument proves that instants, considered without the things, are nothing at all and that they consist only in the successive order of things; this order remaining the same, one of the two states, namely, that of a supposed anticipation, would not at all differ, nor could be discerned from the other which now is.

7. It appears from what I have said that my axiom has not been well understood and that the author denies it, though he seems to grant it. It is true, says he, that there is nothing without a sufficient reason why it is, and why it is thus rather than otherwise, but he adds that this sufficient reason is often the simple or mere will of God—as when it is asked why matter was not placed otherwise in space, the same situations of bodies among themselves being preserved. But this is plainly to maintain that God wills something without any sufficient reason for his will, against the axiom or the general rule of whatever happens. This is falling back into the loose indifference which I have amply refuted and showed to be absolutely chimerical, even in creatures, and contrary to the wisdom of God, as if he could operate without acting by reason.

8. The author objects against me that, if we don't admit this simple and mere will, we take away from God the power of choosing and bring in a fatality. But quite the contrary is true. I maintain that God has the power of choosing, since I ground that power upon the reason of a choice agreeable to his wisdom. And it is not this fatality (which is only the wisest order of providence) but a blind fatality or necessity void of all wisdom and choice which we ought to avoid. . . .

. . .

17. Theologians will not grant the author's position against me, namely, that there is no difference, with respect to God, between natural and supernatural; and it will be still less approved by most philosophers. There is an infinite difference between these two things, but it plainly appears that it has not been duly considered. The supernatural exceeds all the powers of creatures. I shall give an instance which I have often made use of with good success. If God wanted to cause a body to move free in the aether round about a certain fixed center, without any other creature acting upon it, I say it could not be done without a miracle, since it cannot be explained by the nature of bodies. For a free body naturally recedes from a curve in the tangent.

And therefore, I maintain that the attraction of bodies, properly so called, is a miraculous thing, since it cannot be explained by the nature of bodies.

Leibniz's Fourth Letter

1. In things absolutely indifferent there is no foundation for choice,[2] and consequently no election or will, since choice must be founded on some reason or principle.

2. A mere will without any motive is a fiction, not only contrary to God's perfection, but also chimerical and contradictory, inconsistent with the definition of the will, and sufficiently confuted in my *Theodicy*.

3. It is an indifferent thing to place three bodies, equal and perfectly alike, in any order whatsoever, and consequently they will never be placed in any order by him who does nothing without wisdom. But then, he being the author of things, no such things will be produced by him at all, and consequently, there are no such things in nature.

4. There is no such thing as two individuals indiscernible from each other. An ingenious gentleman of my acquaintance, discoursing with me in the presence of Her Electoral Highness, the Princess Sophia, in the garden of Herrenhausen, thought he could find two leaves perfectly alike. The princess defied him to do it, and he ran all over the garden a long time to look for some; but it was to no purpose. Two drops of water or milk, viewed with a microscope, will appear distinguishable from each other. This is an argument against atoms, which are confuted, as well as the void, by the principles of true metaphysics.

5. Those great principles of sufficient reason and of the identity of indiscernibles change the state of metaphysics. That science becomes real and demonstrative by means of these principles, whereas before it did generally consist in empty words.

6. To suppose two things indiscernible is to suppose the same thing under two names. And therefore the hypothesis that the universe could have had at first another position of time and place than that which it actually had, and yet that all the parts of the universe should have had the same situation among themselves as that which they actually had—such a supposition, I say, is an impossible fiction.

7. The same reason which shows that extramundane space is imagi-

2. In Leibniz's original, the claim is that "there is no choice at all."

nary proves that all empty space is an imaginary thing, for they differ only as greater and less.

8. If space is a property or attribute, it must be the property of some substance. But of what substance will that bounded empty space be an affect or property, which the persons I am arguing with suppose to be between two bodies?

9. If infinite space is immensity, finite space will be the opposite to immensity, that is, it will be mensurability, or limited extension. Now extension must be the affect of something extended. But if that space is empty, it will be an attribute without a subject, an extension without anything extended. Wherefore, by making space a property, the author falls in with my opinion, which makes it an order of things and not anything absolute.

10. If space is an absolute reality, far from being a property or an accident opposed to substance, it will have a greater reality than substances themselves. God cannot destroy it, nor even change it in any respect. It will be not only immense in the whole but also immutable and eternal in every part. There will be an infinite number of eternal things besides God.

11. To say that infinite space has no parts is to say that it is not composed of finite spaces, and that infinite space might subsist though all finite space should be reduced to nothing. It would be as if one should say, in accordance with the Cartesian supposition of a material extended unlimited world, that such a world might subsist, though all the bodies of which it consists should be reduced to nothing.

· · ·

13. To say that God can cause the whole universe to move forward in a right line or in any other line, without otherwise making any alteration in it, is another chimerical supposition. For two states indiscernible from each other are the same state, and consequently, it is a change without any change. Besides, there is neither rhyme nor reason in it. But God does nothing without reason, and it is impossible that there should be any here. Besides, it would be *agendo nihil agere*, as I have just now said, because of the indiscernibility.

14. These are idols of the tribe, mere chimeras, and superficial imaginations. All this is only grounded upon the supposition that imaginary space is real.[3]

3. See Bacon, *New Organon*, book I, aphorism 41.

15. It is a like fiction (that is), an impossible one, to suppose that God might have created the world some millions of years sooner. They who run into such kind of fictions can give no answer to those who would argue for the eternity of the world. For since God does nothing without reason, and no reason can be given why he did not create the world sooner, it will follow either that he has created nothing at all, or that he created the world before any assignable time, which is to say that the world is eternal. But when once it has been shown that the beginning, whenever it was, is always the same thing, the question why it was not otherwise becomes needless and insignificant.

16. If space and time were anything absolute, that is, if they were anything else besides certain orders of things, then indeed my assertion would be a contradiction. But since it is not so, the hypothesis (that space and time are anything absolute)[4] is contradictory, that is, it is an impossible fiction.

17. And the case is the same as in geometry, where by the very supposition that a figure is greater than it really is, we sometimes prove that it is not greater. This indeed is a contradiction, but it lies in the hypothesis, which appears to be false for that very reason.[5]

18. Space being uniform, there can neither be any external nor internal reason by which to distinguish its parts and to make any choice among them. For any external reason to discern between them can only be grounded upon some internal one. Otherwise we should discern what is indiscernible or choose without discerning. A will without reason would be the chance of the Epicureans. A God who should act by such a will would be a God only in name. The cause of these errors proceeds from want of care to avoid what derogates from the divine perfections.

19. When two incompatible things are equally good, and neither in themselves, nor by their combination with other things, has the one any advantage over the other, God will produce neither of them.

20. God is never determined by external things but always by what is in himself, that is, by his knowledge, before anything exists outside himself.

---

4. The parenthetical remark is Clarke's addition.
5. Leibniz's text reads: ". . . which is found to be false for that reason."

Leibniz's Fifth Paper

. . .

23. I said that in sensible things two that are indiscernible can never be found, that, for instance, two leaves in a garden or two drops of water perfectly alike are not to be found. The author acknowledges it as to leaves and perhaps as to drops of water. But he might have admitted it without any hesitation, without a 'perhaps' (an Italian would say *senza forse*), as to drops of water likewise.

24. I believe that these general observations in things sensible also hold in proportion in things insensible, and that one may say in this respect what Harlequin says in the *Emperor of the Moon:* it is there just as it is here. And it is a great objection against indiscernibles that no instance of them is to be found. But the author opposes this consequence, because (says he) sensible bodies are composed, whereas he maintains there are insensible bodies which are simple. I answer again that I don't admit simple bodies. There is nothing simple, in my opinion, but true monads, which have neither parts nor extension. Simple bodies, and even perfectly similar ones, are a consequence of the false hypothesis of the void and of atoms, or of lazy philosophy, which does not sufficiently carry on the analysis of things and fancies it can attain to the first material elements of nature, because our imagination would be therewith satisfied.

25. When I deny that there are two drops of water perfectly alike, or any two other bodies indiscernible from each other, I don't say it is absolutely impossible to suppose them, but that it is a thing contrary to the divine wisdom, and which consequently does not exist.

26. I own that if two things perfectly indiscernible from each other did exist they would be two; but that supposition is false and contrary to the grand principle of reason. The vulgar philosophers were mistaken when they believed that there are two things different in number alone, or only because they are two, and from this error have arisen their perplexities about what they called the *principle of individuation.* Metaphysics has generally been handled like a science of mere words, like a philosophical dictionary, without entering into the discussion of things. *Superficial philosophy*, such as is that of the atomists and vacuists, forges things which superior reasons do not admit. I hope my demonstrations will change the face of philosophy, notwithstanding such weak objections as the author raises here against me.

27. The parts of time and place, considered in themselves, are ideal things, and therefore they perfectly resemble one another like two abstract units. But it is not so with two concrete ones, or with two real times, or two spaces filled up, that is, truly actual.

28. I don't say that two points of space are one and the same point, nor that two instants of time are one and the same instant, as the author seems to impute to me. But a man may fancy, for want of knowledge, that there are two different instants where there is but one; in like manner, as I observed in the seventeenth paragraph of the foregoing answer, that frequently in geometry we suppose two, in order to represent the error of a gainsayer, and only find one. If any man should suppose that a right line cuts another in two points, it will be found, after all, that these two pretended points must coincide and make but one point.

29. I have demonstrated that space is nothing else but an order of the existence of things observed as existing together, and therefore the fiction of a material finite universe moving forward in an infinite empty space cannot be admitted. It is altogether unreasonable and impracticable. For besides the fact that there is no real space out of the material universe, such an action would be without any design in it; it would be working without doing anything, in acting nothing would be done by the action. There would happen no change which could be observed by any person whatsover. These are the imaginations of philosophers who have incomplete notions, who make space an absolute reality. Mere mathematicians who are only taken up with the conceits of imagination are apt to forge such notions, but they are destroyed by superior reason.

. . .

49. It cannot be said that a certain duration is eternal but that things, which continue always, are eternal, gaining always new duration. Whatever exists of time and of duration, being successive, perishes continually, and how can a thing exist eternally which (to speak exactly) does not exist at all? For how can a thing exist of which no part does ever exist? Nothing of time does ever exist but instants, and an instant is not even itself a part of time. Whoever considers these observations will easily apprehend that time can only be an ideal thing. And the analogy between time and space will easily make it appear that the one is as merely ideal as the other. (But if in saying that the duration of a thing is eternal, it only meant that the thing endures eternally, I have nothing to say against it.) . . .

7

Plato,
"The Moving Image of Eternity,"
from the *Timaeus*, and
"Time and the One,"
from the *Parmenides*

Plato (428–347 B.C.), a student of Socrates, founded the Academy at Athens and is the first philosopher of whose work we possess more than fragments. He has also been regarded as the greatest philosopher. His difficult but important notion of the emergence of time from eternity is set out in the Myth of the Creator or Demiurge.

Now when the Creator had framed the soul according to his will, he formed within her the corporeal universe, and brought the two together, and united them centre to centre. The soul, interfused everywhere from the centre to the circumference of heaven, of which also she is the external envelopment, herself turning in herself, began a divine beginning of never-ceasing and rational life enduring throughout all time. The body of heaven is visible, but the soul is invisible, and partakes of reason and harmony, and being made by the best of intellectual and everlasting natures, is the best of things created. And because she is composed of the same and of the other and of the essence, these three, and is divided and united in due proportion, and in her revolutions returns upon herself, the soul, when touching anything which has essence, whether dispersed in parts or undivided, is stirred through all her powers, to declare the sameness or difference of that thing and some other; and to what individuals are related, and by what affected, and in what way and how and when, both in the world of generation and in the world of immutable being. And when reason, which works with equal truth, whether she be in the circle of the diverse or of the

Jowett translation.

same—in voiceless silence holding her onward course in the sphere of the self-moved—when reason, I say, is hovering around the sensible world and when the circle of the diverse also moving truly imparts the intimations of sense to the whole soul, then arise opinions and beliefs sure and certain. But when reason is concerned with the rational, and the circle of the same moving smoothly declares it, then intelligence and knowledge are necessarily perfected. And if any one affirms that in which these two are found to be other than the soul, he will say the very opposite of the truth.

When the father and creator saw the creature which he had made moving and living, the created image of the eternal gods, he rejoiced, and in his joy determined to make the copy still more like the original; and as this was eternal, he sought to make the universe eternal, so far as might be. Now the nature of the ideal being was everlasting, but to bestow this attribute in its fullness upon a creature was impossible. Wherefore he resolved to have a moving image of eternity, and when he set in order the heaven, he made this image eternal but moving according to number, while eternity itself rests in unity; and this image we call time. For there were no days and nights and months and years before the heaven was created, but when he constructed the heaven he created them also. They are all parts of time, and the past and future are created species of time, which we unconsciously but wrongly transfer to the eternal essence; for we say that he 'was,' he 'is,' he 'will be,' but the truth is that 'is' alone is properly attributed to him, and that 'was' and 'will be' are only to be spoken of becoming in time, for they are motions, but that which is immovably the same cannot become older or younger by time, nor ever did or has become, or hereafter will be, older or younger, nor is subject at all to any of those states which affect moving and sensible things and of which generation is the cause. These are the forms of time, which imitates eternity and revolves according to a law of number. Moreover, when we say that what has become *is* become and what becomes *is* becoming, and that what will become *is* about to become and that the non-existent *is* non-existent,—all these are inaccurate modes of expression. But perhaps this whole subject will be more suitably discussed on some other occasion.

Time, then, and the heaven came into being at the same instant in order that, having been created together, if ever there was to be a dissolution of them, they might be dissolved together. It was framed after the pattern of the eternal nature, that it might resemble this as far as was possible; for the pattern exists from eternity, and the created heaven has been, and is, and will be, in all time. Such was the mind and thought of God in the creation of time. . . .

Conceptually more elaborate and entertaining than our selection from the Timaeus *is this dialogue about time from the* Parmenides. *"The One" mentioned in the dialogue is a pure time-transcending unity; "the Others" represent the spatio-temporal order into which "the One" has somehow entered.*

Does the one also partake of time? And is it and does it become older and younger than itself and others, and again, neither younger nor older than itself and others, by virtue of participation in time?

How do you mean?

If one is, being must be predicated of it?

Yes.

But to be (εἶναι) is only participation of being in present time, and to have been is the participation of being at a past time, and to be about to be is the participation of being at a future time?

Very true.

Then the one, since it partakes of being, partakes of time?

Certainly.

And is not time always moving forward?

Yes.

Then the one is always becoming older than itself, since it moves forward in time?

Certainly.

And do you remember that the older becomes older than that which becomes younger?

I remember.

Then since the one becomes older than itself, it becomes younger at the same time?

Certainly.

Thus, then, the one becomes older as well as younger than itself?

Yes.

And it is older (is it not?) when in becoming, it gets to the point of time between 'was' and 'will be,' which is 'now': for surely in going from the past to the future, it cannot skip the present?

No.

And when it arrives at the present it stops from becoming older, and no longer becomes, but is older, for if it went on it would never be reached by the present, for it is the nature of that which goes on, to touch both the present and the future, letting go the present and seizing the future, while in process of becoming between them.

True.

But that which is becoming cannot skip the present; when it reaches the present it ceases to become, and is then whatever it may happen to be becoming.

Clearly.

And so the one, when in becoming older it reaches the present, ceases to become, and is then older.

Certainly.

And it is older than that than which it was becoming older, and it was becoming older than itself.

Yes.

And that which is older is older than that which is younger?

True.

Then the one is younger than itself, when in becoming older it reaches the present?

Certainly.

But the present is always present with the one during all its being; for whenever it is it is always now.

Certainly.

Then the one always both is and becomes older and younger than itself?

Truly.

And is it or does it become a longer time than itself or an equal time with itself?

An equal time.

But if it becomes or is for an equal time with itself, it is of the same age with itself?

Of course.

And that which is of the same age, is neither older nor younger?

No.

The one, then, becoming and being the same time with itself, neither is nor becomes older or younger than itself?

I should say not.

And what are its relations to other things? Is it or does it become older or younger than they?

I cannot tell you.

You can at least tell me that others than the one are more than the

one—other would have been one, but the others have multitude, and
are more than one?

They will have multitude.

And a multitude implies a number larger than one?

Of course.

And shall we say that the lesser or the greater is the first to come
or to have come into existence?

The lesser.

Then the least is the first? And that is the one?

Yes.

Then the one of all things that have number is the first to come
into being; but all other things have also number, being plural and not
singular.

They have.

And since it came into being first it must be supposed to have come
into being prior to the others, and the others later; and the things
which came into being later, are younger than that which preceded
them? And so the other things will be younger than the one, and the
one older than other things?

True.

What would you say of another question? Can the one have come
into being contrary to its own nature, or is that impossible?

Impossible.

And yet, surely, the one was shown to have parts; and if parts, then
a beginning, middle and end?

Yes.

And a beginning, both of the one itself and of all other things, comes
into being first of all; and after the beginning, the others follow, until
you reach the end?

Certainly.

And all these others we shall affirm to be parts of the whole and of
the one, which, as soon as the end is reached, has become whole and
one?

Yes; that is what we shall say.

But the end comes last, and the one is of such a nature as to come
into being with the last; and, since the one cannot come into being
except in accordance with its own nature, its nature will require that
it should come into being after the others, simultaneously with the
end.

Clearly.

Then the one is younger than the others and the others older than the one.

That also is clear in my judgment.

Well, and must not a beginning or any other part of the one or of anything, if it be a part and not parts, being a part, be also of necessity one?

Certainly.

And will not the one come into being together with each part—together with the first part when that comes into being, and together with the second part and with all the rest, and will not be wanting to any part, which is added to any other part until it has reached the last and become one whole; it will be wanting neither to the middle, nor to the first, nor to the last, nor to any of them, while the process of becoming is going on?

True.

Then the one is of the same age with all the others, so that if the one itself does not contradict its own nature, it will be neither prior nor posterior to the others, but simultaneous; and according to this argument the one will be neither older nor younger than the others, nor the others than the one, but according to the previous argument the one will be older and younger than the others and the others than the one.

Certainly.

After this manner then the one is and has become. But as to its becoming older and younger than the others, and the others than the one, and neither older nor younger, what shall we say? Shall we say as of being so also of becoming, or otherwise?

I cannot answer.

But I can venture to say, that even if one thing were older or younger than another, it could not become older or younger in a greater degree than it was at first; for equals added to unequals, whether to periods of time or to anything else, leave the difference between them the same as at first.

Of course.

Then that which is, cannot become older or younger than that which is, since the difference of age is always the same; the one is and has become older and the other younger; but they are no longer becoming so.

True.

And the one which is does not therefore become either older or younger than the others which are.

No.

But consider whether they may not become older and younger in another way.

In what way?

Just as the one was proven to be older than the others and the others than the one.

And what of that?

If the one is older than the others, it has come into being a longer time than the others.

Yes.

But consider again; if we add equal time to a greater and a less time, will the greater differ from the less time by an equal or by a smaller portion than before?

By a smaller portion.

Then the difference between the age of the one and the age of the others will not be afterwards so great as at first, but if an equal time be added to both of them they will differ less and less in age?

Yes.

And that which differs in age from some other less than formerly, from being older will become younger in relation to that other than which it was older?

Yes, younger.

And if the one becomes younger the others aforesaid will become older than they were before, in relation to the one.

Certainly.

Then that which had become younger becomes older relatively to that which previously had become and was older; it never really is older, but is always becoming, for the one is always growing on the side of youth and the other on the side of age. And in like manner the older is always in process of becoming younger than the younger; for as they are always going in opposite directions they become in ways the opposite to one another, the younger older than the older, and the older younger than the younger. They cannot, however, have become; for if they had already become they would be and not merely become. But that is impossible; for they are always becoming both older and younger than one another: the one becomes younger than the others because it was seen to be older and prior, and the others become older than the one because they came into being later; and in the same way the others are in the same relation to the one, because they were seen to be older and prior to the one.

That is clear.

Inasmuch then, as the one thing does not become older or younger than another, in that they always differ from each other by an equal number, the one cannot become older or younger than the others, nor the others than the one; but inasmuch as that which came into being earlier and that which came into being later must continually differ from each other by a different portion—in this point of view the others must become older and younger than the one, and the one than the others.

Certainly.

For all these reasons, then, the one is and becomes older and younger than itself and the others, and neither is nor becomes older or younger than itself or the others.

Certainly.

But since the one partakes of time, and partakes of becoming older and younger, must it not also partake of the past, the present, and the future?

Of course it must.

Then the one was and is and will be, and was becoming and is becoming and will become?

Certainly.

And there is and was and will be something which is in relation to it and belongs to it?

True.

And since we have at this moment opinion and knowledge and perception of the one, there is opinion and knowledge and perception of it?

Quite right.

Then there is name and expression for it, and it is named and expressed, and everything of this kind which appertains to other things appertains to the one.

Certainly, that is true.

8

Aristotle,
"Time,"
from the *Physics*

Aristotle (384–322 B.C.), was a more empirically minded philosopher than his teacher Plato. He has been regarded as the "greatest mind" of antiquity and, until the scientific revolution, the greatest intellectual authority in philosophy and the sciences. In the following passage he is working out a theory of how time exists.

I

Next for discussion after the subjects mentioned is time. The best plan will be to begin by working out the difficulties connected with it, making use of the current arguments. First, does it belong to the class of things that exist or to that of things that do not exist? Then secondly, what is its nature? To start, then: the following considerations would make one suspect that it either does not exist at all or barely, and in the obscure way. One part of it has been and is not, while the other is going to be and is not yet. Yet time—both infinite time and any time you like to take—is made up of these. One would naturally suppose that what is made up of things which do not exist could have no share in reality.

Further, if a divisible thing is to exist, it is necessary that, when it exists, all or some of its parts must exist. But of time some parts have been, while others are going to be, and no part of it *is*, though it is divisible. For the 'now' is not a part: a part is a measure of the whole, which must be made up of parts. Time, on the other hand, is not held to be made up of 'nows'.

Again, the 'now' which seems to bound the past and the future—does it always remain one and the same or is it always other and other? It is hard to say.

If it is always different and different, and if none of the *parts* in time which are other and other are simultaneous (unless the one contains and the other is contained, as the shorter time is by the longer), and if the 'now' which is not, but formerly was, must have ceased to be at some time, the '*nows*' too cannot be simultaneous with one another, but the prior 'now' must always have ceased to be. But the prior 'now' cannot have ceased to be in itself (since it then existed); yet it cannot have ceased to be in another 'now'. For we may lay it down that one 'now' cannot be next to another, anymore than a point to a point. If then it did not cease to be in the next 'now' but in another, it would exist simultaneously with the innumerable 'nows' between the two—which is impossible.

Yes, but neither is it possible for the 'now' to remain always the same. No determinate divisible thing has a single termination, whether is it continuously extended in one or in more than one dimension; but the 'now' is a termination, and it is possible to cut off a determinate time. Further, if coincidence in time (i.e. being neither prior nor posterior) means to be in one and the same 'now', then, if both what is before and what is after are in this same 'now', things which happened ten thousand years ago would be simultaneous with what has happened to-day, and nothing would be before or after anything else.

This may serve as a statement of the difficulties about the attributes of time.

As to what time is or what is its nature, the traditional accounts give us as little light as the preliminary problems which we have worked through.

Some assert that it is the movement of the whole, others that it is the sphere itself.

Yet part, too, of the revolution is a time, but it certainly is not a revolution; for what is taken is part of a revolution, not a revolution. Besides, if there were more heavens than one, the movement of any of them equally would be time, so that there would be many times at the same time.

Those who said that time is the sphere of the whole thought so, no doubt, on the ground that all things are in time and all things are in the sphere of the whole. The view is too naive for it to be worth while to consider the impossibilities implied in it.

But as time is most usually supposed to be motion and a kind of change, we must consider this view.

Now the change or movement of each thing is only *in* the thing which changes or *where* the thing itself which moves or change may chance to be. But time is present equally everywhere and with all things.

Again, change is always faster or slower, whereas time is not; for fast and slow are defined by time—fast is what moves much in a short time, slow what moves little in a long time; but time is not defined by time, by being either a certain amount or a certain kind of it.

Clearly then it is not movement. (We need not distinguish at present between movement and change.)

II

But neither does time exist without change; for when the state of our minds does not change at all, or we have not noticed its changing, we do not think that time has elapsed, any more than those who are fabled to sleep among the heroes in Sardinia do when they are awakened; for they connect the earlier 'now' with the later and make them one, cutting out the interval because of their failure to notice it. So, just as, if the 'now' were not different but one and the same, there would not have been time, so too when its difference escapes our notice the interval does not seem to be time. If, then, the non-realization of the existence of time happens to us when we do not distinguish any change, but the mind seems to stay in one indivisible state, and when we perceive and distinguish we say time has elapsed, evidently time is not independent of movement and change. It is evident, then, that time is neither movement nor independent of movement.

We must take this as our starting-point and try to discover—since we wish to know what time is—what exactly it has to do with movement.

Now we perceive movement and time together; for even when it is dark and we are not being affected through the body, if any movement takes place in the mind we at once suppose that some time has indeed elapsed; and not only that but also, when some time is thought to have passed, some movement also along with it seems to have taken place. Hence time is either movement or something that belongs to movement. Since then it is not movement, it must be the other.

But what is moved is moved from something to something, and all magnitude is continuous. Therefore the movement goes with the magnitude. Because the magnitude is continuous, the movement too is continuous, and if the movement, then the time; for the time that has passed is always thought to be as great as the movement.

The distinction of before and after holds primarily, then, in place; and there in virtue of relative position. Since then before and after hold in magnitude, they must hold also in movement, these corresponding to those. But also in time the distinction of before and after must hold; for time and movement always correspond with each other. The before and after in motion is identical in substratum with motion yet differs from it in being, and is not identical with motion.

But we apprehend time only when we have marked motion, marking it by before and after; and it is only when we have perceived before and after in motion that we say that time has elapsed. Now we mark them by judging that one thing is different from another, and that some third thing is intermediate to them. When we think of the extremes as different from the middle and the mind pronounces that the 'nows' are two, one before and one after, it is then that we say that there is time, and this that we say is time. For what is bounded by the 'now' is thought to be time—we may assume this.

When, therefore, we perceive the 'now' as one, and neither as before and after in a motion nor as the same element but in relation to a 'before' and an 'after', no time is thought to have elapsed, because there has been no motion either. On the other hand, when we do perceive a 'before' and an 'after', then we say that there is time. For time is just this—number of motion in respect of 'before' and 'after'.

Hence time is not movement, but only movement in so far as it admits of enumeration. An indication of this: we discriminate the more or the less by number, but more or less movement by time. Time then is a kind of number. (Number, we must note, is used in two ways— both of what is counted or countable and also of that with which we count. Time, then, is what is counted, not that with which we count: these are different kinds of thing.)

Just as motion is a perpetual succession, so also is time. But every simultaneous time is the same; for the 'now' is the same in substratum— though its being is different—and the 'now' determines time, in so far as time involves the before and after.

The 'now' in one sense is the same, in another it is not the same. In so far as it is in succession, it is different (which is just what its being now was supposed to mean), but its substratum is the same; for motion, as was said, goes with magnitude, and time, as we maintain, with motion. Similarly, then, there corresponds to the point the body which is carried along, and by which we are aware of the motion and of the before and after involved in it. This is an identical *substratum* (whether a point or a stone or something else of the kind), but it is different in definition—as the sophists assume that Coriscus' being in the Lyceum is a different thing from Coriscus' being in the market-place. And the body which is carried along is different, in so far as it is at one time here and at another there. But the 'now' corresponds to the body that is carried along, as time corresponds to the mention. For it is by means of the body that is carried along that we become aware of the before and after in the motion, and if we regard these as countable we get the 'now'. Hence in these also the 'now' as substratum remains the same (for it is what is before and after in movement), but its being is different; for it is in so far as the before and after is that we get the 'now'. This is what is most knowable; for motion is known because of that which is moved, locomotion because of that which is carried. For what is carried is a 'this', the movement is not. Thus the 'now' in one sense is always the same, in another it is not the same; for this is true also of what is carried.

Clearly, too, if there were no time, there would be no 'now', and vice versa. Just as the moving body and its locomotion involve each other mutually, so too do the number of the moving body and the number of its locomotion. For the number of the locomotion is time, while the 'now' corresponds to the moving body, and is like the unit of number.

Time, then, also is both made continuous by the 'now' and divided at it. For here too there is a correspondence with the locomotion and the moving body. For the motion or locomotion is made one by the thing which is moved, because *it* is one—not because it is one in substratum (for there might be pauses in the movement of such a thing)—but because it is one in definition; for this determines the movement as 'before' and 'after'. Here, too, there is a correspondence with the point; for the point also both connects and terminates the length—it is the beginning of one and the end of another. But when you take it in this way, using the one point as two, a pause is necessary, if the same point is to be the beginning and the end. The 'now' on the other hand, since the body carried is moving, is always different.

Hence time is not number in the sense in which there is number of the same point because it is beginning and end, but rather as the extremities of a line form a number, and not as the parts of the line do so, both for the reason given (for we can use the middle point as two, so that on that analogy time might stand still), and further because obviously the 'now' is no *part* of time nor the section any part of the movement, any more than the points are parts of the line—for it is two *lines* that are *parts* of one line.

In so far then as the 'now' is a boundary, it is not time, but an attribute of it; in so far as it numbers, it is number; for boundaries being only to that which they bound, but number (e.g. ten) is the number of these horses, and belongs also elsewhere.

It is clear, then, that time is number of movement in respect of the before and after, and is continuous since it is an attribute of what is continuous.

III

The smallest number, in the strict sense, is two. But of number as concrete, sometimes there is a minimum, sometimes not: e.g. of a line, the smallest in respect of *multiplicity* is two (or, if you like, one), but in respect of *size* there is no minimum; for every line is divided *ad infinitum*. Hence it is so with time. In respect of number the minimum is one (or two); in point of extent there is no minimum.

It is clear, too, that time is not described as fast or slow, but as many or few and as long or short. For as continuous it is long or short and as a number many or few; but it is not fast or slow—any more than any number with which we count is fast or slow.

Further, there is the same time everywhere at once, but not the same time before and after; for while the present change is one, the change which has happened and that which will happen are different. Time is not number with which we count, but the number of things which are counted; and this according as it occurs before or after is always different, for the 'nows' are different. And the number of a hundred horses and a hundred men is the same, but the things numbered are different—the horses for the men. Further, as a movement can be one and the same again and again, so too can time, e.g. a year or a spring or an autumn.

Not only do we measure the movement by the time, but also the time by the movement, because they define each other. The time marks the movement, since it is its number, and the movement the time. We describe the time as much or little, measuring it by the movement, just as we know the number by what is numbered, e.g. the number of the horses by one horse as the unit. For we know how many horses there are by the use of the number; and again by using the one horse as unit we know the number of the horses itself. So it is with the time and the movement; for we measure the movement by the time and vice versa. It is reasonable that this should happen; for the movement goes with the distance and the time with the movement, because they are quanta and continuous and divisible. The movement has these attributes because the distance is of this nature, and the time has them because of the movement. And we measure both the distance by the movement and the movement by the distance; for we say that the road is long, if the journey is long, and that this is long, if the road is long— the time, too, if the movement, and the movement, if the time.

Time is a measure of motion and of being moved, and it measures the motion by determining a motion which will measure the whole motion, as the cubit does the length by determining an amount which will measure out the whole. Further to be in time means, for movement, that both it and its essence are measured by time (for simultaneously it measures both the movement and its essence, and this is what being in time means for it, that its essence should be measured).

Clearly, then, to be in time has the same meaning for other things also, namely, that their being should be measured by time. To be in time is one of two things: to exist when time exists, and as we say of some things that they are 'in number'. The latter means either what is a part or mode of number—in general, something which belongs to number—or that things have a number.

Now, since time is number, the 'now' and the before and the like are in time, just as unit and odd and even are in number, i.e. in the sense that the one set belongs to number, the other to time. But things are in time as they are in number. If this is so, they are contained by time as things in number are contained by number and things in place by place.

Plainly, too, to be in time does not mean to coexist with time, any more than to be in motion or in place means to coexist with motion or place. For if 'to be in something' is to mean this, then all things will be in anything, and the world will be in a grain; for when the grain is, then also is the world. But this is accidental, whereas the other is necessarily involved: that which is in time necessarily involves that there is time when *it* is, and that which is in motion that there is motion when *it* is.

Since what is in time is so in the same sense as what is in number is so, a time greater than everything in time can be found. So it is necessary that all the things in time should be contained by time, just like other things also which are in anything, e.g. the things in place by place.

A thing, then, will be affected by time, just as we are accustomed to say that time wastes things away, and that all things grow old through time, and that people forget owing to the lapse of time, but we do not say the same of getting to know or of becoming young or fair. For time is by its nature the cause rather of decay, since it is the number of change, and change removes what is.

Hence, plainly, things which are always are not, as such, in time; for they are not contained by time, nor is their being measured by time. An indication of this is that none of them is *affected* by time, which shows that they are not in time.

Since time is the measure of motion, it will be the measure of rest too. For all rest is in time. For it does not follow that what is in time is moved, though what is in motion is necessarily moved. For time is not motion, but number of motion; and what is at rest can be in the number of motion. Not everything that is not in motion can be said to be at rest—but only that which can be moved, though it actually is not moved, as was said above.

To be in number means that there is a number of the thing, and that its being is measured by the number in which it is. Hence if a thing is in time it will be measured by time. But time will measure what is moved and what is at rest, the one *qua* moved, the other *qua* at rest; for it will measure their motion and rest respectively.

Hence what is moved will not be measured by the time simply in so far as it has quantity, but in so far as its *motion* has quantity. Thus none of the things which are neither moved nor at rest are in time; for to be in time is to be measured by time, while time is the measure of motion and rest.

Plainly, then, neither will everything that does not exist be in time, i.e. those non-existent things that cannot exist, as the diagonal's being commensurate with the side.

Generally, if time is the measure of motion in itself and of other things accidentally, it is clear that a thing whose being is measured by it will have its being in rest or motion. Those things therefore which are subject to perishing and becoming—generally, those which at one time exist, at another do not—are necessarily in time; for there is a greater time which will extend both beyond their being and beyond the time which measures their being. Of things which do not exist but are contained by time some were, e.g. Homer once was, some will be, e.g. a future event; this depends on the direction in which time contains them; if on both, they have both modes of existence. As to such things as it does not contain in any way, they neither were nor are nor will be. These are those non-existents whose opposites always are, as the incommensurability of the diagonal always is—and this will not be in time. Nor will the commensurability, therefore; hence this eternally is not, because it is contrary to what eternally is. A thing whose contrary is not eternal can be and not be, and it is of such things that there is coming to be and passing away.

IV

The 'now' is the link of time, as has been said (for it connects past and future time), and it is a limit of time (for it is the beginning of the one and the end of the other). But this is not obvious as it is with the point, which is fixed. It divides potentially, and in so far as it is dividing the 'now' is always different, but in so far as it connects it is always the same, as it is with mathematical lines. For the intellect it is not always one and the same point, since it is other and other when one divides the line; but in so far as it is one, it is the same in every respect.

So the 'now' also is in one way a potential dividing of time, in another the termination of both parts, and their unity. And the dividing and the uniting are the same thing and in the same reference, but in essence they are not the same.

So one kind of 'now' is described in this way: another is when the time of something is *near*. He will come now, because he will come to-day; he has come now, because he came to-day. But the things in the *Iliad* have not happened now, nor is the flood now—not that the time from now to them is not continuous, but because they are not near.

'At some time' means a time determined in relation to the first of the two types of 'now', e.g. at some time Troy was taken, and at some time there will be a flood; for it must be determined with reference to the 'now'. There *will* thus be a determinate time from this 'now' to that, and there *was* such in reference to the past event. But if there be no time which is not 'sometime', everytime will be determined.

Will time then fail? Surely not, if motion always exists. Is time then always different or does the same time recur? Clearly, it is the same with time as with motion. For if one and the same motion sometimes recurs, it will be one and the same time, and if not, not.

Since the 'now' is an end and a beginning of time, not of the same time however, but the end of that which is past and the beginning of that which is to come, it follows that, as the circle has its convexity and its concavity, in a sense, in the same thing, so time is always at the beginning and at an end. And for this reason it seems to be always different; for the 'now' is not the beginning and the end of the same thing; if it were, it would be at the same time and in the same respect two opposites. And time will not fail; for it is always at a beginning.

'Just now' refers to the part of future time which is near the indivisible present 'now' (When are you walking?—Just now; because the time in which he is going to do so is near), and to the part of past time which is not far from the 'now' (When are you walking?—I have been walking just now). But to say that Troy has just now been taken—we do not say that, because it is too far from the 'now'. 'Lately', too, refers to the part of past time which is near the present 'now'. 'When did you go?' 'Lately', if the time is near the existing now. 'Long ago' refers to the distant past.

'Suddenly' refers to what has departed from its former condition in a time imperceptible because of its smallness; but it is the nature of *all* change to alter things from their former condition. In time all things come into being and pass away; for which reason some called it the wisest of all things, but the Pythagorean Paron called it the most stupid, because in it we also forget; and his was the truer view. It is clear then that it must be in itself, as we said before, a cause of destruction rather than of coming into being (for change, in itself, makes things depart from their former condition), and only accidentally of coming into being, and of being. A sufficient evidence of this is that nothing comes into being without itself moving somehow and acting, but a thing can be destroyed even if it does not move at all. And this is what, as a rule, we chiefly mean by a thing's being destroyed by time. Still, time does not work even this change; but this sort of change too happens to occur in time.

We have stated, then, that time exists and what it is, and in how many ways we speak of the 'now', and what 'at some time', 'lately', 'just now', 'long ago', and 'suddenly' mean.

V

These distinctions having been drawn, it is evident that every change and everything that moves is in time; for the distinction of faster and slower exists in reference to all change, since it is found in every instance. In the phrase 'moving faster' I refer to that which changes before another into the condition in question, when it moves over the same interval and with a regular movement; e.g. in the case of locomotion, if both things move along the circumference of a circle, or both along a straight line; and similarly in all other cases. But what is *before* is in time; for we say 'before' and 'after' with reference to the distance from the 'now', and the 'now' is the boundary of the past and the future; so that since 'nows' are in time, the before and the after will be in time too; for in that in which the 'now' is, the distance from the 'now' will also be. But 'before' is used contrariwise with reference to past and to future time; for in the past we call 'before' what is farther from the 'now', and 'after'. So that since the 'before' is in time, and every movement involves a 'before', evidently every change and every movement is in time.

It is also worth considering how time can be related to the soul; and why time is thought to be in everything, both in earth and in sea and in heaven. Is it because it is an attribute, or state, of movement (since it is the number of movement) and all these things are movable (for they are all in place), and time and movement are together, both in respect of potentiality and in respect of actuality?

Whether if soul did not exist time would exist or not, is a question that may fairly be asked; for if there cannot be some one to count there cannot be anything that can be counted either, so that evidently there cannot be number; for number is either what has been, or what can be, counted. But if nothing but soul, or in soul reason, is qualified to count, it is impossible for there to be time unless there is soul, but only that of which time is an attribute, i.e. if *movement* can exist without soul. The before and after are attributes of movement, and time is these *qua* countable.

One might also raise the question what sort of movement time is the number of. Must we not say 'of *any* kind'? For things both come into being in time and pass away, and grow, and are altered, and are moved locally; thus it is of each movement *qua* movement that time is the number. And so it is simply the number of continuous movement, not of any particular kind of it.

But other things as well may have been moved now, and there would be a number of each of the two movements. Is there another time, then, and will there be two equal times at once? Surely not. For a time that is both equal and simultaneous is one and the same time, and even those that are not simultaneous are one in kind; for if there were dogs, and horses, and seven of each, it would be the same number. So, too, movements that have simultaneous limits have the same time, yet the one may in fact be fast and the other not, and one may be locomotion and the other alteration; still the time of the two changes is the same if it is both equal and simultaneous; and for this reason, while the movements are different and separate, the time is everywhere the same, because the *number* of equal and simultaneous movements is everywhere one and the same.

Now there is such a thing as locomotion, and in locomotion there is included circular movement, and everything is counted by some one thing homogeneous with it, units by a unit, horses by a horse, and similarly times by some definite time, and, as we said, time is measured by motion as well as motion by time (this being so because by a motion definite in time the quantity both of the motion and of the time is measured): if, then, what is first is the measure of everything homogeneous with it, regular circular motion is above all else the measure, because the number of this is the best known. Now neither alteration nor increase nor coming into being can be regular, but locomotion can be. This also is why time is thought to be the movement of the sphere, viz. because the other movements are measured by this, and time by this movement.

This also explains the common saying that human affairs form a circle, and that there is a circle in all other things that have a natural movement and coming into being and passing away. This is because all other things are discriminated by time, and end and begin as though conforming to a cycle; for even time itself is thought to be a circle. And this opinion again is held because time is a measure of this kind of locomotion and is itself measured by the circular movement; for apart from the measure nothing else is observed in what is measured; the whole is jut a plurality of measures.

It is said rightly, too, that the number of the sheep and of the dogs is the same *number* if the two numbers are equal, but not the same *decad* or the same *ten;* just as the equilateral and the scalene are not the same *triangle,* yet they are the same *figure,* because they are both triangles. For things are called the same so-and-so if they do not differ by a differentia of that thing, but not if they do; e.g. triangle differs from triangle by a differentia of triangle, therefore they are different triangles; but they do not differ by a differentia of figure, but are in one and the same division of it. For a figure of one kind is a circle and a figure of another kind a triangle, and a triangle of one kind is equilateral and a triangle of another kind scalene. They are the same figure, then, and that is a triangle, but not the same triangle. Therefore the number of the two groups also is the same number (for their number does not differ by a differentia of number), but it is not the same decad; for the things of which it is asserted differ; one group are dogs, and the other horses.

We have now discussed time—both time itself and the matters appropriate to the consideration of it.

9

Plotinus,
"Time and Eternity,"
from the *Enneads*

Plotinus (204–270), the greatest of the Neo-Platonists, studied in Alexandria and taught in Rome, where he collected his ideas in a book called the Enneads. *His work influenced St. Augustine and many other theologians. His treatise on eternity and time (*Ennead III.5*) is presented here in its entirety.*

I

Eternity and Time; two entirely separate things, we explain, 'the one having its being in the everlasting Kind, the other in the realm of Process, in our own Universe'; and, by continually using the words and assigning every phenomenon to the one or the other category, we come to think that, both by instinct and by the more detailed attack of thought, we hold an adequate experience of them in our minds without more ado.

When, perhaps, we make the effort to clarify our ideas and close into the heart of the matter we are at once unsettled: our doubts throw us back upon ancient explanations; we choose among the various theories, or among the various interpretations of some one theory, and so we come to rest, satisfied, if only we can counter a question with an approved answer, and glad to be absolved from further inquiry.

Now, we must believe that some of the venerable philosophers of old discovered the truth; but it is important to examine which of them really hit the mark and by what guiding principle we can ourselves attain to certitude.

What, then, does Eternity really mean to those who (thus casually) describe it as something different from Time? We begin with Eternity, since, when the standing Exemplar is known, its representation in

MacKenna translation.

image—which Time is understood to be—will be clearly apprehended—though it is of course equally true, admitting this relationship
of Time as image to Eternity the original, that if we chose to begin by
identifying Time we could thence proceed upwards by Recognition
(the Platonic Anamnesis) and become aware of the Kind which it
images.

II

What definition are we to give of Eternity?

Can it be identified with the (divine or) Intellectual Substance itself?

This would be like identifying Time with the Universe of Heavens
and Earth—an opinion, it is true, which appears to have had its adher-
ents. No doubt we conceive, we know, Eternity as something most
august; most august, too, is the Intellectual Kind; and there is no
possibility of saying that the one is more majestic than the other;—
the Absolute One may be left out of account, since not even majesty can
be predicated of it;—there is therefore a certain excuse for identifying
Eternity with the Intellectual World, all the more since the Intellectual
Substance and Eternity have the one scope and content.

Still; by the fact of representing the one as contained within the
other, by making Eternity a predicate to the Intellectual Existents—
'the Nature of the Exemplar', we read, 'is eternal'—we cancel the
identification; Eternity becomes a separate thing, something surrounding that Nature or lying within it or present to it. And the majestic
quality of both does not prove them identical: it might be transmitted
from the one to the other. So, too, Eternity and the Divine Nature
envelop the same entities, yes; but not in the same way: the Divine
may be thought of as enveloping parts, Eternity as embracing its content
in an unbroken whole, with no implication of part, but merely from
the fact that all eternal things are so by conforming to it.

May we, perhaps, identify Eternity with Repose-There as Time has
been identified with Movement-Here?

This would bring on the counter-question whether Eternity is presented to us as Repose in the general sense or as the Repose that
envelops the Intellectual Essence.

On the first supposition we can no more talk of Repose being eternal
than of Eternity being eternal: to be eternal is to participate in an
outside thing, Eternity.

Further, if Eternity is Repose, what becomes of Eternal Movement, which, by this identification, would become a thing of Repose?

Again, the concept of Repose scarcely seems to include that of perpetuity—I am speaking, of course, not of perpetuity in the time-order (which might follow on absence of movement) but of that which we have in mind when we speak of Eternity.

If, on the other hand, Eternity is identified with the Repose of the divine Essence, all the other categories of the divine are put outside of Eternity.

Besides, the conception of Eternity requires not merely Repose but also unity—and, in order to keep it distinct from Time, a unity excluding interval—but neither that unity nor that absence of interval enters into the conception of Repose as such.

Lastly, this unchangeable Repose in unity is a predicate asserted of Eternity, which, therefore, is not itself Repose, the absolute, but a participant in Repose.

III

What, then, can this be, this something in virtue of which we declare the entire divine Realm to be Eternal, everlasting? We must come to some understanding of this perpetuity with which Eternity is either identical or in conformity.

It must be at once something in the nature of unity and yet a notion compact of diversity, or (more exactly) a Kind, a Nature, that waits upon the Existents of that Other World, either associated with them or known in and upon them, they collectively being this Nature which, with all its unity, is yet diverse in power and essence. Considering this multifarious power, we declare it to be Essence or Being in so far as it is in some sense a subject or substratum; where we see life we think of it as Movement; where all is unvaried self-identity we call it Repose; and we know it as, at once, Difference and Identity when we recognize that all is unity with variety.

Then we reconstruct; we sum all into a collected unity once more, a sole Life in the Supreme; we concentrate Diversity and all the endless production of act: thus we know Identity, a concept or, rather, a Life never varying, not becoming what previously it was not, the thing immutably itself, broken by no interval; and knowing this, we know Eternity.

We know it as a Life changelessly motionless and ever holding the

Universal content in actual presence; not this now and now that other, but always all; not existing now in one mode and now in another, but a consummation without part or interval. All its content is in immediate concentration as at one point; nothing in it ever knows development: all remains identical within itself, knowing nothing of change, for ever in a Now, since nothing of it has passed away or will come into being, but what it is now, that it is ever.

Eternity, therefore—while not the Substratum (not the essential foundation of the Divine or Intellectual Principle)—may be considered as the radiation of this Substratum: it exists as the announcement of the Identity in the Divine, of that state—of being thus and not otherwise—which characterizes what has no futurity but eternally is.

What future, in fact, could bring to that Being anything which it now does not possess; and could it come to be anything which it is not once for all?

There exists no source or ground from which anything could make its way into that standing present; any imagined entrant will prove to be not alien but already integral. And as it can never come to be anything at present outside it, so, necessarily, it cannot include any past; what can there be that once was in it and now is gone? Futurity, similarly, is banned; nothing could be yet to come to it. Thus no ground is left for its existence but that it be what it is.

That which neither has been nor will be, but simply possesses being; that which enjoys stable existence as neither in process of change nor having ever changed—that is Eternity. Thus we come to the definition: the Life—instantaneously entire, complete, at no point broken into period or part—which belongs to the Authentic Existent by its very existence, this is the thing we were probing for—this is Eternity.

IV

We must, however, avoid thinking of it as an accidental from outside grafted upon that Nature: it is native to it, integral to it.

It is discerned as present essentially in that Nature like everything else that we can predicate There—all immanent, springing from that Essence and inherent to that Essence. For whatsoever has primal Being must be immanent to the Firsts and be a First—Eternity equally with the beauty that is among them and of them and equally with the truth that is among them.

Some of the predicates reside, as it were, in a partial phase of the All-Being; others are inherent in the All taken as a totality, since that Authentic All is not a thing patched up out of external parts, but is authentically an all because its parts are engendered by itself. It is like the truthfulness in the Supreme which is not an agreement with some outside fact or being but is inherent in each member about which it is the truth. To an authentic All it is not enough that it be everything that exists: it must possess all-ness in the full sense that nothing whatever is absent from it. Then nothing is in store for it: if anything were to come, that thing must have been lacking to it, and it was, therefore, not All. And what, of a Nature contrary to its own, could enter into it when it is (the Supreme and therefore) immune? Since nothing can accrue to it, it cannot seek change or be changed or ever have made its way into Being.

Engendered things are in continuous process of acquisition; eliminate futurity, therefore, and at once they lose their being; if the non-engendered are made amenable to futurity they are thrown down from the seat of their existence, for, clearly, existence is not theirs by their nature if it appears only as a being about to be, a becoming, an advancing from stage to stage.

The essential existence of generated things seems to lie in their existing from the time of their generation to the ultimate of time after which they cease to be: but such an existence is compact of futurity, and the annulment of that futurity means the stopping of the life and therefore of the essential existence.

Existence for the (generated) All must similarly consist in a goal to be attained: for this reason it keeps hastening towards its future, dreading to rest, seeking to draw Being to itself by a perpetual variety of production and action and by its circling in a sort of ambition after Essential Existence.

And here we have, incidentally, lighted upon the cause of the Circuit of the All; it is a movement which seeks perpetuity by way of futurity.

The Primals, on the contrary, in their state of blessedness have no such aspiration towards anything to come: they are the whole, now; what life may be thought of as their due, they possess entire; they, therefore, seek nothing, since there is nothing future to them, nothing external to them in which any futurity could find lodgement.

Thus the perfect and all-comprehensive essence of the Authentic Existent does not consist merely in the completeness inherent in its members; its essence includes, further, its established immunity from all lack with the exclusion, also, of all that is without Being—for not only must all things be contained in the All and Whole, but it can contain nothing that is, or was ever, non-existent—and this State and Nature of the Authentic Existent is Eternity: in our very word, Eternity means Ever-Being ($\alpha\iota\acute{\omega}\nu = \grave{\alpha}\varepsilon\iota\ \acute{o}\nu$).

V

This Ever-Being is realized when upon examination of an object I am able to say—or rather, to know—that in its very Nature it is incapable of increment or change; anything that fails by that test is no Ever-Existent or, at least, no Ever-All-Existent.

But is perpetuity enough in itself to constitute an Eternal?

No: the object must, further, include such a Nature-Principle as to give the assurance that the actual state excludes all future change, so that it is found at every observation as it always was.

Imagine, then, the state of a being which cannot fall away from the vision of this but is for ever caught to it, held by the spell of its grandeur, kept to it by virtue of a nature itself unfailing—or even the state of one that must labour towards Eternity by directed effort, but then to rest in it, immovable at any point, assimilated to it, co-eternal with it, contemplating Eternity and the Eternal by what is Eternal within the self.

Accepting this as a true account of an eternal, a perdurable Existent—one which never turns to any Kind outside itself, that possesses life complete once for all, that has never received any accession, that is now receiving none and will never receive any—we have, with the statement of a perduring Being, the statement also of perdurance and of Eternity: perdurance is the corresponding state arising from the (divine) substratum and inherent in it; Eternity (the Principle as distinguished from the property of everlastingness) is that substratum carrying that state in manifestation.

Eternity, thus, is of the order of the supremely great; intuition identifies it with God: it may fitly be described as God made manifest, as God declaring what He is, as existence without jolt or change, and therefore as also the firmly living.

And it should be no shock that we find plurality in it; each of the Beings of the Supreme is multiple by virtue of unlimited force; for to be limitless implies failing at no point, and Eternity is pre-eminently the limitless since (having no past or future) it spends nothing of its own substance.

Thus a close enough definition of Eternity would be that it is a life limitless in the full sense of being all the life there is and a life which, knowing nothing of past or future to shatter its completeness, possesses itself intact for ever.

VI

Now the Principle thus stated, all good and beauty, and everlasting, is centred in The One, sprung from It, and pointed towards It, never straying from It, but ever holding about It and in It and living by Its law; and it is in this reference, as I judge, that Plato—finely, and by no means inadvertently but with profound intention—wrote those words of his, 'Eternity stable in Unity'; he wishes to convey that Eternity is not merely something circling on its traces into a final unity, but has (instantaneous) Being about the One as the unchanging Life of the Authentic-Existent. This is certainly what we have been seeking: this Principle, at rest within the One, is Eternity; possessing this stable quality, being itself at once the absolute self-identical and none the less the active manifestation of an unchanging Life set towards the Divine and dwelling within It, untrue, therefore, neither on the side of Being nor on the side of Life—this will be Eternity (the Real-Being we have sought).

Truly to be comports never lacking existence and never knowing variety in the mode of existence: Being is, therefore, self-identical throughout, and, therefore, again is one undistinguishable thing. Being can have no this and that; it cannot be treated in terms of intervals, unfoldings, progression, extension; there is no grasping any first or last in it.

If, then, there is no first or last in this Principle, if existence is its most authentic possession and its very self, and this in the sense that its existence is Essence or Life—then, once again, we meet here what we have been discussing, Eternity.

Observe that such words as 'always, never, sometimes' must be taken as mere conveniences of exposition: thus 'always'—used in the sense not of time but of incorruptibility and endlessly complete scope—might set up the false notion of stage and interval. We might perhaps prefer to speak of 'Being', without any attribute; but since this term is applicable to Essence and some writers have used the word Essence for things of process, we cannot convey our meaning to them without introducing some word carrying the notion of perdurance.

There is, of course, no difference between Being and Everlasting Being; just as there is none between a philosopher and a true philosopher: the attribute 'true' came into use because there arose what masqueraded as philosophy; and for similar reasons 'everlasting' was adjointed to 'Being', and 'Being' to 'everlasting', and we have (the tautology of) 'Everlasting Being'. We must take this 'Everlasting' as expressing no more than Authentic Being: it is merely a partial expression of a potency which ignores all interval or term and can look forward to nothing by way of addition to the All which it possesses. The Principle of which this is the statement will be the All-Existent, and, as being all, can have no failing or deficiency, cannot be at some one point complete and at some other lacking.

Things and beings in the Time order—even when to all appearance complete, as a body is when fit to harbour a soul—are still bound to sequence; they are deficient to the extent of that thing, Time, which they need: let them have it, present to them and running side by side with them, and they are by that very fact incomplete; completeness is attributed to them only by an accident of language.

But the conception of Eternity demands something which is in its nature complete without sequence; it is not satisfied by something measured out to any remoter time or even by something limitless, but, in its limitless reach, still having the progression of futurity: it requires something immediately possessed of the due fullness of Being, something whose Being does not depend upon any quantity (such as instalments of time) but subsists before all quantity.

Itself having no quantity, it can have no contact with anything quantitative since its Life cannot be made a thing of fragments, in contradiction to the partlessness which is its character; it must be without parts in the Life as in the essence.

The phrase 'He was good' (used by Plato of the Demiurge) refers to a conception of the All; the Transcendent, he explains, did not originate in Time: so that also this Universe has had no temporal beginning; and if we speak of something 'before' it, that is only in the sense of the Cause from which it takes its Eternal Existence. Plato used the word merely for the convenience of exposition, and later corrects it as inappropriate to the order vested with the Eternity he conceives and affirms.

VII

Now comes the question whether, in all this discussion, we are not merely helping to make out a case for some other order of Beings and talking of matters alien to ourselves.

But how could that be? What understanding can there be failing some point of contact? And what contact could there be with the utterly alien?

We must then have, ourselves, some part or share in Eternity.

Still, how is this possible to us who exist in Time?

The whole question turns on the distinction between being in Time and being in Eternity, and this will be best realized by probing to the nature of Time. We must, therefore, descend from Eternity to the investigation of Time, to the realm of Time: till now we have been taking the upward way; we must now take the downward—not to the lowest levels but within the degree in which Time itself is a descent from Eternity.

If the venerable sages of former days had not treated of Time, our method would be to begin by linking to (the idea of) Eternity (the idea of) its Next (its inevitable downward or outgoing subsequent in the same order), then setting forth the probable nature of such a Next and proceeding to show how the conception thus formed tallies with our own doctrine.

But, as things are, our best beginning is to range over the most noteworthy of the ancient opinions and see whether any of them accord with ours.

Existing explanations of Time seem to fall into three classes:

Time is variously identified with what we know as Movement, with a moved object, and with some phenomenon of Movement: obviously it cannot be Rest or a resting object or any phenomenon of rest, since, in its characteristic idea, it is concerned with change.

Of those that explain it as Movement, some identify it with any and every Movement, others with that of the All. Those that make it a moved object would identify it with the orb of the All. Those that conceive it as some phenomenon of Movement treat it, severally, either as a period or as a standard of measure or, more generally, as an accompaniment, whether of Movement in general or of ordered Movement.

VIII

Movement Time cannot be—whether a definite act of moving is meant or a united total made up of all such acts—since movement, in either sense, takes place in Time. And, of course, if there is any movement not in Time, the identification with Time becomes all the less tenable.

In a word, Movement must be distinct from the medium in which it takes place.

And, with all that has been said or is still said, one consideration is decisive: Movement can come to rest, can be intermittent; Time is continuous.

We will be told that the Movement of the All is continuous (and so may be identical with Time).

But, if the reference is to the Circuit of the heavenly system, this Circuit takes place in Time, and the time taken by the total Circuit is twice the time taken by half the Circuit; whether we count the whole or only the first half, it is nevertheless the same movement of the heavenly system.

Further, the fact that we hear of the Movement of the outermost sphere being the swiftest confirms our theory. Obviously, it is the swiftest of movements by taking the lesser time to traverse the greater space—the very greatest—all other moving things are slower by taking a longer time to traverse a mere segment of the same extension: in other words, Time is not this movement.

And, if Time is not even the movement of the Cosmic Sphere much less is it the sphere itself, though that has been identified with Time on the ground of its being in motion.

Is it, then, some phenomenon or connexion of Movement?

Let us, tentatively, suppose it to be extent, or duration, of Movement.

Now, to begin with, Movement, even continuous, has no unchanging extent (as Time the equable has), since—to take only motion in space— it may be faster or slower; there must, therefore, be some unit of standard outside it, by which these differences are measurable, and this outside standard would more properly be called Time. And failing such a measure, which extent would be Time, that of the fast or of the slow—or rather which of them all, since these speed-differences are limitless?

Is it the extent of the ordered Movement?

Again, this gives us no unit since the movement is infinitely variable; we would have, thus, not Time but Times.

The extent of the Movement of the All, then?

If this means extent as inherent in the movement itself, we have Movement pure and simple (and not Time). Admittedly, Movement answers to measure—in two ways. First there is space; the movement is commensurate with the area it passes through, and this area is its extent. But this gives us, still, space only, not Time. Secondly, the circuit, considered apart from distance traversed, has the extent of its continuity, of its tendency not to stop but to proceed indefinitely: but this is merely amplitude of Movement; search it, tell its vastness, and, still, Time has no more appeared, no more enters into the matter, than when one certifies a high pitch of heat; all we have discovered is Motion in ceaseless succession, like water flowing ceaselessly, motion and extent of motion.

Succession or repetition gives us Number—dyad, triad, &c.—and the extent traversed is a matter of Magnitude; thus we have Quantity of Movement—in the form of number, dyad, triad, decade, or in the form of extent apprehended in what we may call the amount of the Movement: but, the idea of Time we have not. That definite Quantity is (not Time but) merely something occurring within Time, for, otherwise Time is not everywhere but is something belonging to Movement which thus would be its substratum or basic-stuff: once more, then, we would be making Time identical with Movement; for the extent of Movement is not something outside it but is simply its continuousness, and we need not halt upon the difference between the momentary and the continuous, which is simply one of manner and degree. The extended movement and its extent are not Time; they are in Time. Those that explain Time as extent of Movement must mean not the extent of the movement itself but something which determines its extension, something with which the movement keeps pace in its course. But what this something is, we are not told; yet it is, clearly, Time, that in which all Movement proceeds. This is what our discussion has aimed at from the first: 'What, essentially, is Time?' It comes to this: we ask 'What is Time?' and we are answered, 'Time is the extension of Movement in Time'!

On the one hand Time is said to be an extension apart from and outside that of Movement; and we are left to guess what this extension may be: on the other hand, it is represented as the extension of Move-

ment; and this leaves the difficulty what to make of the extension of
Rest—though one thing may continue as long in repose as another in
motion, so that we are obliged to think of one thing, Time, that covers
both Rest and Movements, and, therefore, stands distinct from either.

What then is this thing of extension? To what order of beings does
it belong?

It obviously is not spatial, for place, too, is something outside it.

IX

'A Number, a Measure, belonging to Movement?'

'Measure' is more plausible since Movement is a continuous thing;
but let us consider.

To begin with, we have the doubt which met us when we probed
its identification with extent of Movement: is Time the measure of any
and every Movement?

Have we any means of calculating disconnected and lawless Movement? What number or measure would apply? What would be the
principle of such a Measure?

One Measure for movement slow and fast, for any and every movement: then that number and measure would be like the decade, by
which we reckon horses and cows, or like some common standard for
liquids and solids. If Time is this kind of Measure, we learn, no doubt,
of what objects it is a Measure—of Movements—but we are no nearer
understanding what it is in itself.

Or: we may take the decade and think of it, apart from the horses
or cows, as a pure number; this gives us a measure which, even though
not actually applied, has a definite nature. Is Time, perhaps, a Measure
in this sense?

No: to tell us no more of Time in itself than that it is such a number
is merely to bring us back to the decade we have already rejected, or
to some similar abstract figure.

If, on the other hand, Time is (not such an abstraction but) a Measure
possessing a continuous extent of its own, it must have quantity, like
a footrule; it must have magnitude; it will, clearly, be in the nature of
a line traversing the path of Movement. But, itself thus sharing in the
movement, how can it be a Measure of Movement? Why should the
one of the two be the measure rather than the other? Besides, an
accompanying measure is more plausibly considered as a measure of
the particular movement it accompanies than of Movement in general.

Further, this entire discussion assumes continuous movement, since the accompanying principle, Time, is itself unbroken (but a full explanation implies justification of Time in repose).

The fact is that we are not to think of a measure outside and apart, but of a combined thing, a measured Movement, and we are to discover what measures it.

Given a Movement measured, are we to suppose the measure to be a magnitude?

If so, which of these two would be Time, the measured movement or the measuring magnitude? For Time (as measure) must be either the movement measured by magnitude, or the measuring magnitude itself, or something using the magnitude like a yard-stick to appraise the movement. In all three cases, as we have indicated, the application is scarcely plausible except where continuous movement is assumed; unless the movement proceeds smoothly, and even unintermittently and as embracing the entire content of the moving object, great difficulties arise in the identification of Time with any kind of measure.

Let us, then, suppose Time to be this 'measured Movement', measured by quantity. Now the Movement if it is to be measured requires a measure outside itself; this was the only reason for raising the question of the accompanying measure. In exactly the same way the measuring magnitude, in turn, will require a measure, because only when the standard shows such and such an extension can the degree of movement be appraised. Time then will be, not the magnitude accompanying the Movement, but that numerical value by which the magnitude accompanying the Movement is estimated. But that number can be only the abstract figure which represents the magnitude, and it is difficult to see how an abstract figure can perform the act of measuring.

And, supposing that we discover a way in which it can, we still have not Time, the measure, but a particular quantity of Time, not at all the same thing: Time means something very different from any definite period: before all question as to quantity is the question as to the thing of which a certain quantity is present.

Time, we are told, is the number outside Movement and measuring it, like the tens applied to the reckoning of the horses and cows but not inherent in them: we are not told what this Number is; yet, applied or not, it must, like that decade, have some nature of its own.

Or 'is it that which accompanies a Movement and measures it by its successive stages'; but we are still left asking what this thing recording the stages may be.

In any case, once a thing—whether by point or standard or any other means—measures succession, it must measure according to time: this number appraising movement degree by degree must, therefore, if it is to serve as a measure at all, be something dependent upon time and in contact with it: for, either, degree is spatial, merely—the beginning and end of the Stadium, for example—or in the only alternative, it is a pure matter of Time: the succession of early and late is stage of Time, Time ending upon a certain Now or Time beginning from a Now.

Time, therefore, is something other than the mere number measuring Movement, whether Movement in general or ordered Movement.

Further: why should the mere presence of a number give us Time—a number measuring or measured; for the same number may be either—if Time is not given us by the fact of Movement itself, the movement which inevitably contains in itself a succession of stages? To make the number essential to Time is like saying that magnitude has not its full quantity unless we can estimate that quantity.

Again, if Time is, admittedly, endless, how can number apply to it?

Are we to take some portion of Time and find its numerical statement? That simply means that Time existed before number was applied to it.

We may, therefore, very well think that it existed before the Soul or Mind that estimates it—if, indeed, it is not to be thought to take its origin from the Soul—for no measurement by anything is necessary to its existence; measured or not, it has the full extent of its being.

And suppose it is to be true that the Soul is the appraiser, using Magnitude as the measuring standard, how does this help us to the conception of Time?

X

Time, again, has been described as some sort of a sequence upon Movement, but we learn nothing from this, nothing is said, until we know what it is that produces this sequential thing; probably the cause and not the result would turn out to be Time.

And, admitting such a thing, there would still remain the question whether it came into being before the movement, with it, or after it; and, whether we say before or with or after, we are speaking of order in Time: and thus our definition is, 'Time is a sequence upon movement *in Time*'!

Enough. Our main purpose is to show what Time is, not to refute false definition. To traverse point by point the many opinions of our many predecessors would mean a history rather than an identification; we have treated the various theories as fully as is possible in a cursory review: and, notice, that which makes Time the Measure of the All-Movement is refuted by our entire discussion and, especially, by the observations upon the Measurement of Movement in general, for all the argument—except, of course, that from irregularity—apples to the All as much as to particular Movement.

We are, thus, at the stage where we are to state what Time really is.

XI

To this end we must go back to the state we affirmed of Eternity, unwavering Life, undivided totality, limitless, knowing no divagation, at rest in unity and intent upon it. Time was not yet: or at least it did not exist for the Eternal Beings. It is we that must create Time out of the concept and nature of progressive derivation, which remained latent in the Divine Beings.

How Time emerged we can scarcely call upon the Muses to relate since they were not in existence then—perhaps not even if they had been; though the Cosmos itself, when once engendered, could no doubt tell us best how Time arose and became manifest. Something thus the story must run:

Time at first—in reality before that 'first' was produced by desire of succession—Time lay, though not yet as Time, in the Authentic Existent together with the Cosmos itself; the Cosmos also was merged in the Authentic and motionless within it. But there was an active principle there, one set on governing itself and realizing itself (= the All-Soul), and it chose to aim at something more than its present: it stirred from its rest, and the Cosmos stirred with it. 'And we (the active principle and the Cosmos), stirring to a ceaseless succession, to a next, to the discrimination of identity and the establishment of ever new difference, traversed a portion of the outgoing path and produced an image of Eternity, produced Time.'

For the Soul contained an unquiet faculty, always desirous of translating elsewhere what it saw in the Authentic Realm, and it could not bear to retain within itself all the dense fullness of its possession.

A seed is at rest; the nature-principle within, uncoiling outwards,

makes way towards what seems to it a large life; but by that partition
it loses; it was a unity self-gathered, and now, in going forth from
itself, it fritters its unity away; it advances into a weaker greatness. It
is so with this faculty of the Soul, when it produces the Cosmos known
to sense—the mimic of the Divine Sphere, moving not in the very
movement of the Divine but in its similitude, in an effort to reproduce
that of the Divine. To bring this Cosmos into being, the Soul first laid
aside its eternity and clothed itself with Time; this world of its fashioning it then gave over to be a servant to Time, making it at every point
a thing of Time, setting all its progressions within the bournes of Time.
For the Cosmos moves only in Soul—the only Space within the range
of the All open to it to move in—and therefore its Movement has
always been in the Time which inheres in Soul.

Putting forth its energy in act after act, in a constant progress of
novelty, the Soul produces succession as well as act; taking up new
purposes added to the old it brings thus into being what had not existed
in that former period when its purpose was still dormant and its life
was not as it since became: the life is changed and that change carries
with it a change of Time. Time, then, is contained in differentiation
of Life; the ceaseless forward movement of Life brings with it unending
Time; and Life as it achieves its stages constitutes past Time.

Would it, then, be sound to define Time as the Life of the Soul in
movement as it passes from one stage of act or experience to another?

Yes; for Eternity, we have said, is Life in repose, unchanging, self-
identical, always endlessly complete; and there is to be an image of
Eternity—Time—such an image as this lower All presents of the
Higher Sphere. Therefore over against that higher Life there must be
another life, known by the same name as the more veritable Life of
the Soul; over against that Movement of the Intellectual Soul there
must be the movement of some partial phase; over against that Identity,
Unchangeableness and Stability there must be that which is not constant in the one hold but puts forth multitudinous acts; over against
that Oneness without extent or interval there must be an image of
oneness, a unity of link and succession; over against the immediately
Infinite and All-comprehending, that which tends, yes, to infinity but by
tending to a perpetual futurity; over against the Whole in concentration,
there must be that which is to be a whole by stages never final. The
lesser must always be working towards the increase of its Being; this
will be its imitation of what is immediately complete, self-realized,

endless without stage: only thus can its Being reproduce that of the Higher.

Time, however, is not to be conceived as outside of Soul; Eternity is not outside of the Authentic Existent: nor is it to be taken as a sequence or succession to Soul, any more than Eternity is to the Divine. It is a thing seen upon Soul, inherent, coeval to it, as Eternity to the Intellectual Realm.

XII

We are brought thus to the conception of a Natural-Principle—Time—a certain expanse (a quantitative phase) of the Life of the Soul, a principle moving forward by smooth and uniform changes following silently upon each other—a Principle, then, whose Act is (not one like that of the Supreme but) sequent.

But let us conceive this power of the Soul to turn back and withdraw from the life-course which it now maintains, from the continuous and unending activity of an ever-existent Soul not self-contained or self-intent but concerned about doing and engendering: imagine it no longer accomplishing any Act, setting a pause to this work it has inaugurated; let this outgoing phase of the Soul become once more, equally with the rest, turned to the Supreme, to Eternal Being, to the tranquilly stable.

What would then exist but Eternity?

All would remain in unity; how could there be any diversity of things? What earlier or later would there be, what futurity? What ground would lie ready to the Soul's operation but the Supreme in which it has its Being? Or, indeed, what operative tendency could it have even to That since a prior separation is the necessary condition of tendency?

The very sphere of the Universe would not exist; for it cannot antedate Time: it, too, has its Being and its Movement in Time; and if it ceased to move, the Soul-Act (which is the essence of Time) continuing, we could measure the period of its Repose by that standard outside it.

If, then, the Soul withdrew, sinking itself again into its primal unity, Time would disappear: the origin of Time, clearly, is to be traced to the first stir of the Soul's tendency towards the production of the sensible Universe with the consecutive act ensuing. This is how 'Time'—as we read—'came into Being simultaneously with' this All:

the Soul begot at once the Universe and Time; in that activity of the Soul this Universe sprang into being; the activity is Time, the Universe is a content of Time. No doubt it will be urged that we read also of 'the orbit of the Stars being Times': but do not forget what follows; 'the stars exist', we are told, 'for the display and delimitation of Time', and 'that there may be a manifest Measure'. No indication of Time could be derived from (observation of) the Soul; no portion of it can be seen or handled, so it could not be measured in itself, especially when there was as yet no knowledge of counting; therefore the Demiurge (in the Timaeus) brings into being night and day; in their difference is given Duality—from which, we read, arises the concept of Number.

We observe the tract between a sunrise and its return and, as the movement is uniform, we thus obtain a Time-interval upon which to support ourselves, and we use this as a standard. We have thus a measure of Time. Time itself is not a measure. How would it set to work? And what kind of thing is there of which it could say, 'I find the extent of this equal to such and such a stretch of my own extent?' What is this 'I'? Obviously something by which measurement is known. Time, then, serves towards measurement but is not itself the Measure: the Movement of the All will be measured according to Time, but Time will not, of its own nature, be a Measure of Movement: primarily a Kind to itself, it will incidentally exhibit the magnitudes of that movement.

And the reiterated observation of Movement—the same extent found to be traversed in such and such a period—will lead to the conception of a definite quantity of Time past.

This brings us to the fact that, in a certain sense, the Movement, the orbit of the universe, may legitimately be said to measure Time— in so far as that is possible at all—since any definite stretch of that circuit occupies a certain quantity of Time, and this is the only grasp we have of Time, our only understanding of it: what that circuit measures—by indication, that is—will be Time, manifested by the Movement but not brought into being by it.

This means that the measure of the Spheric Movement has itself been measured by a definite stretch of that Movement and therefore is something different; as measure, it is one thing and, as the measured, it is another; (its being measure or) its being measured cannot be of its essence.

We are no nearer knowledge than if we said that the foot-rule measures Magnitude while we left the concept Magnitude undefined;

or, again, we might as well define Movement—whose limitlessness puts it out of our reach—as the thing measured by Space; the definition would be parallel since we can mark off a certain space which the Movement has traversed and say the one is equivalent to the other.

XIII

The Spheral Circuit, then, performed in Time, indicates it: but when we come to Time itself there is no question of its being 'within' something else: it must be primary, a thing 'within itself'. It is that in which all the rest happens, in which all movement and rest exist smoothly and under order; something following a definite order is necessary to exhibit it and to make it a subject of knowledge—though not to produce it—it is known by order whether in rest or in motion; in motion especially, for Movement better moves Time into our ken than rest can, and it is easier to estimate distance traversed than repose maintained.

This last fact has led to Time being called a measure of Movement when it should have been described as something measured by Movement and then defined in its essential nature; it is an error to define it by a mere accidental concomitant and so to reverse the actual order of things. Possibly, however, this reversal was not intended by the authors of the explanation; but, at any rate, we do not understand them; they plainly apply the term Measure to what is in reality the measured and leave us unable to grasp their meaning: our perplexity may be due to the fact that their writings—addressed to disciples acquainted with their teaching—do not explain what this thing, measure or measured object, is in itself.

Plato does not make the essence of Time consist in its being either a measure or a thing measured by something else.

Upon the point of the means by which it is known, he remarks that the Circuit advances an infinitesimal distance for every infinitesimal segment of Time, so that from that observation it is possible to estimate what the Time is, how much it amounts to: but when his purpose is to explain its essential nature he tells us that it sprang into Being simultaneously with the Heavenly system, a reproduction of Eternity, its image in motion, Time necessarily unresting as the Life with which it must keep pace: and 'coeval with the Heavens' because it is this same Life (of the Divine Soul) which brings the Heavens also into Being; Time and the Heavens are the work of the one Life.

Suppose that Life, then, to revert—an impossibility—to perfect unity: Time, whose existence is in that Life, and the Heavens, no longer maintained by that Life, would end at once.

It is the height of absurdity to fasten on the succession of earlier and later occurring in the life and movement of this sphere of ours, to declare that it must be some definite thing and to call it Time, while denying the reality of the more truly existent Movement, that of the Soul, which has also its earlier and later: it cannot be reasonable to recognize succession in the case of the Soulless Movement—and so to associate Time with that—while ignoring succession and the reality of Time in the Movement from which the other takes its imitative existence; to ignore, that is, the very Movement in which succession first appears, a self-actuated movement which, engendering its own every operation, creates the sequence by which each instant no sooner comes into existence than it passes into the next.

But: we treat the Cosmic Movement as overarched by that of the Soul and bring it under Time; yet we do not set under Time that Soul-Movement itself with all its endless progression: what is our explanation of this paradox?

Simply, that the Soul-Movement has for its Prior (not Time but) Eternity which knows neither its progression nor its extension. The descent towards Time begins with this Soul-Movement; it made Time and harbours Time as a concomitant to its Act.

And this is how Time is omnipresent: that Soul is absent from no fragment of the Cosmos just as our Soul is absent from no particle of ourselves. As for those who pronounce Time a thing of no substantial existence, of no reality, they clearly belie God Himself whenever they say 'He was' or 'He will be': for the existence indicated by the 'was and will be' can have only such reality as belongs to that in which it is said to be situated: but this school demands another style of argument.

Meanwhile we have a supplementary observation to make.

Take a man walking and observe the advance he has made; that advance gives you the quantity of movement he is employing: and when you know that quantity—represented by the ground traversed by his feet, for, of course, we are supposing the bodily movement to correspond with the pace he has set within himself—you know also the movement that exists in the man himself before the feet move.

You must relate the body, carried forward during a given period of Time, to a certain quantity of Movement causing the progress and to the Time it takes, and that again to the Movement, equal in extension, within the man's soul.

But the Movement within the Soul—to what are you to refer that?

Let your choice fall where it may, from this point there is nothing but the unextended: and this is the primarily existent, the container to all else, having itself no container, brooking none.

And, as with Man's Soul, so with the Soul of the All.

Is Time, then, within ourselves as well?

Time is in every Soul of the order of the All-Soul, present in like form in all; for all the Souls are the one Soul.

And this is why Time can never be broken apart, any more than Eternity which, similarly, under diverse manifestations, has its Being as an integral constituent of all the eternal Existences.

10

J. M. E. McTaggart,
"The Unreality of Time,"
from *Mind*

McTaggart (1866–1925), British metaphysician and follower of Hegel, taught at Trinity College, Cambridge. The following article anticipated Chapter 33 of his principal work, The Nature of Existence, *published in 1927.*

It doubtless seems highly paradoxical to assert that Time is unreal, and that all statements which involve its reality are erroneous. Such an assertion involves a far greater departure from the natural position of mankind than is involved in the assertion of the unreality of Space or of the unreality of Matter. So decisive a breach with that natural position is not to be lightly accepted. And yet in all ages the belief in the unreality of time has proved singularly attractive.

In the philosophy and religion of the East we find that this doctrine is of cardinal importance. And in the West, where philosophy and religion are less closely connected, we find that the same doctrine continually recurs, both among philosophers and among theologians. Theology never holds itself apart from mysticism for any long period, and almost all mysticism denies the reality of time. In philosophy, again, time is treated as unreal by Spinoza, by Kant, by Hegel, and by Schopenhauer. In the philosophy of the present day the two most important movements (excluding those which are as yet merely critical) are those which look to Hegel and to Mr. Bradley. And both of these schools deny the reality of time. Such a concurrence of opinion cannot be denied to be highly significant—and is not the less significant because the doctrine takes such different forms, and is supported by such different arguments.

I believe that time is unreal. But I do so for reasons which are not, I think, employed by any of the philosophers whom I have mentioned, and I propose to explain my reasons in this paper.

Mind, xvii (1908).

Positions in time, as time appears to us *prima facie*, are distinguished in two ways. Each position is Earlier than some, and Later than some, of the other positions. And each position is either Past, Present, or Future. The distinctions of the former class are permanent, while those of the latter are not. If M is ever earlier than N, it is always earlier. But an event, which is now present, was future and will be past.

Since distinctions of the first class are permanent, they might be held to be more objective, and to be more essential to the nature of time. I believe, however, that this would be a mistake, and that the distinction of past, present and future is as *essential* to time as the distinction of earlier and later, while in a certain sense, as we shall see, it may be regarded as more *fundamental* than the distinction of earlier and later. And it is because the distinctions of past, present and future seem to me to be essential for time, that I regard time as unreal.

For the sake of brevity I shall speak of the series of positions running from the far past through the near past to the present, and then from the present to the near future and the far future, as the A series. The series of positions which runs from earlier to later I shall call the B series. The contents of a position in time are called events. The contents of a single position are admitted to be properly called a plurality of events. (I believe, however, that they can *as* truly, though not *more* truly, be called a single event. This view is not universally accepted, and it is not necessary for my argument.) A position in time is called a moment.

The first question which we must consider is whether it is essential to the reality of time that its events should form an A series as well as a B series. And it is clear, to begin with, that we never *observe* time except as forming both these series. We perceive events in time as being present, and those are the only events which we perceive directly. And all other events in time which, by memory or inference, we believe to be real, are regarded as past or future—those earlier than the present being past, and those later than the present being future. Thus the events of time, as observed by us, form an A series as well as a B series.

It is possible, however, that this is merely subjective. It may be the case that the distinction introduced among positions in time by the A series—the distinction of past, present and future—is simply a constant illusion of our minds, and that the real nature of time only contains the distinction of the B series—the distinction of earlier and later. In that case we could not *perceive* time as it really is, but we might be able to *think* of it as it really is.

This is not a very common view, but it has found able supporters. I believe it to be untenable, because, as I said above, it seems to me that the A series is essential to the nature of time, and that any difficulty in the way of regarding the A series as real is equally a difficulty in the way of regarding time as real.

It would, I suppose, be universally admitted that time involves change. A particular thing, indeed, may exist unchanged through any amount of time. But when we ask what we mean by saying that there were different moments of time, or a certain duration of time, through which the thing was the same, we find that we mean that it remained the same while other things were changing. A universe in which nothing whatever changed (including the thoughts of the conscious beings in it) would be a timeless universe.

If, then, a B series without an A series can constitute time, change must be possible without an A series. Let us suppose that the distinction of past, present and future does not apply to reality. Can change apply to reality? What is it that changes?

Could we say that, in a time which formed a B series but not an A series, the change consisted in the fact that an event ceased to be an event, while another event began to be an event? If this were the case, we should certainly have got a change.

But this is impossible. An event can never cease to be an event. It can never get out of any time series in which it once is. If N is ever earlier than O and later than M, it will always be, and has always been, earlier than O and later than M, since the relations of earlier and later are permanent. And as, by our present hypothesis, time is constituted by a B series alone, N will always have a position in a time series, and has always had one.[1] That is, it will always be, and has always been, an event, and cannot begin or cease to be an event.

Or shall we say that one event M merges itself into another event N, while preserving a certain identity by means of an unchanged element, so that we can say, not merely that M has ceased and N begun,

1. It is equally true, though it does not concern us on the hypothesis which we are now considering, that whatever is once in an A series is always in one. If one of the determinations past, present, and future can ever be applied to N, then one of them always has been and always will be applicable, though of course not always the same one.

but that it is M which has become N? Still the same difficulty recurs. M and N may have a common element, but they are not the same event or there would be no change. If therefore M changes into N at a certain moment, then, at that moment, M has ceased to be M, and N has begun to be N. But we have seen that no event can cease to be, or begin to be, itself, since it never ceases to have a place as itself in the B series. Thus one event cannot change into another.

Neither can the change be looked for in the numerically different moments of absolute time, supposing such moments to exist. For the same arguments will apply here. Each such moment would have its own place in the B series, since each would be earlier or later than each of the others. And as the B series indicate permanent relations, no moment could ever cease to be, nor could it become another moment.

Since, therefore, what occurs in time never begins or ceases to be, or to be itself, and since, again, if there is to be change it must be change of what occurs in time (for the timeless never changes), I submit that only one alternative remains. Changes must happen to the events of such a nature that the occurrence of these changes does not hinder the events from being events, and the same events, both before and after the change.

Now what characteristics of an event are there which can change and yet leave the event the same event? (I use the word characteristic as a general term to include both the qualities with the event possesses, and the relations of which it is a term—or rather the fact that the event is a term of these relations.) It seems to me that there is only one class of such characteristics—namely, the determination of the event in question by the terms of the A series.

Take any event—the death of Queen Anne, for example—and consider what change can take place in its characteristics. That it is a death, that it is the death of Anne Stuart, that it has such causes, that it has such effects—every characteristic of this sort never changes. "Before the stars saw one another plain" the event in question was a death of an English Queen. At the last moment of time—if time has a last moment—the event in question will still be a death of an English Queen. And in every respect but one it is equally devoid of change. But in one respect it does change. It began by being a future event. It became every moment an event in the nearer future. At last it was present. Then it became past, and will always remain so, though every moment it becomes further and further past.

Thus we seem forced to the conclusion that all change is only a change of the characteristics imparted to events by their presence in the A series, whether those characteristics are qualities or relations.

If these characteristics are qualities, then the events, we must admit, would not be always the same, since an event whose qualities alter is, of course, not completely the same. And, even if the characteristics are relations, the events would not be completely the same, if—as I believe to be the case—the relation of X to Y involves the existence in X of a quality of relationship to Y.[2] Then there would be two alternatives before us. We might admit that events did really change their nature, in respect of these characteristics, though not in respect of any others. I see no difficulty in admitting this. It would place the determinations of the A series in a very unique position among the characteristics of the event, but on any theory they would be very unique characteristics. It is usual, for example, to say that a past event never changes, but I do not see why we should not say, instead of this, "a past event changes only in one respect—that every moment it is further from the present than it was before". But although I see no intrinsic difficulty in this view, it is not the alternative I regard as ultimately true. For if, as I believe, time is unreal, the admission that an event in time would change in respect of its position in the A series would not involve that anything really did change.

Without the A series then, there would be no change, and consequently the B series by itself is not sufficient for time, since time involves change.

The B series, however, cannot exist except as temporal, since earlier and later, which are the distinctions of which it consists, are clearly time-determinations. So it follows that there can be no B series where there is no A series, since where there is no A series there is no time.

But it does not follow that, if we subtract the determinations of the A series from time, we shall have no series left at all. There is a series— a series of the permanent relations to one another of those realities which in time are events—and it is the combination of this series with the A determinations which gives time. But this other series—let us

---

2. I am not asserting, as Lotze did, that a relation between X and Y consists of a quality in X and a quality in Y—a view which I regard as quite indefensible. I assert that a relation Z between X and Y *involves* the existence in X of the quality "having the relation Z to Y" so that a difference of relations always involves a difference in quality, and a change of relations always involves a change of quality.

call it the C series—is not temporal, for it involves no change, but only an order. Events have an order. They are, let us say, in the order M, N, O, P. And they are therefore *not* in the order M, O, N, P, or O, N, M, P, or in any other possible order. But that they have this order no more implies that there is any change than the order of the letters of the alphabet, or of the Peers on the Parliament Roll, implies any change. And thus those realities which appear to us as events might form such a series without being entitled to the name of events, since that name is only given to realities which are in a time series. It is only when change and time come in that the relations of this C series become relations of earlier and later, and so it becomes a B series.

More is wanted, however, for the genesis of a B series and of time than simply the C series and the fact of change. For the change must be in a particular direction. And the C series, while it determines the order, does not determine the direction. If the C series runs M, N, O, P, then the B series from earlier to later cannot run M, O, N, P, or M, P, O, N, or in any way but two. But it can run either M, N, O, P (so that M is earliest and P latest) or else P, O, N, M (so that P is earliest and M latest). And there is nothing either in the C series or in the fact of change to determine which it will be.

A series which is not temporal has no direction of its own, though it has an order. If we keep to the series of the natural numbers, we cannot put 17 between 21 and 26. But we keep to the series, whether we go from 17, through 21, to 26, or whether we go from 26, through 21, to 17. The first direction seems the more natural to us, because this series has only one end, and it is generally more convenient to have that end as a beginning than as a termination. But we equally keep to the series in counting backward.

Again, in the series of categories in Hegel's dialectic, the series prevents us from putting the Absolute Idea between Being and Causality. But it permits us either to go from Being, through Causality, to the Absolute Idea, or from the Absolute Idea, through Causality, to Being. The first is, according to Hegel, the direction of proof, and is thus generally the most convenient order of enumeration. But if we found it convenient to enumerate in the reverse direction, we should still be observing the series.

A non-temporal series, then, has no direction in itself, though a person considering it may *take* the terms in one direction or in the other, according to his own convenience. And in the same way a person who contemplates a time-order may contemplate it in either direction.

I may trace the order of events from the Great Charter to the Reform Bill, or from the Reform Bill to the Great Charter. But in dealing with the time series we have not to do merely with a change in an external contemplation of it, but with a change which belongs to the series itself. And this change has a direction of its own. The Great Charter came before the Reform Bill, and the Reform Bill did not come before the Great Charter.

Therefore, besides the C series and the fact of change there must be given—in order to get time—the fact that the change is in one direction and not in the other. We can now see that the A series, together with the C series, is sufficient to give us time. For in order to get change, and change in a given direction, it is sufficient that one position in the C series should be Present, to the exclusion of all others, and that this characteristic of presentness should pass along the series in such a way that all positions on the one side of the Present have been present, and all positions on the other side of it will be present. That which has been present is Past, that which will be present is Future.[3] Thus to our previous conclusion that there can be no time unless the A series is true of reality, we can add the further conclusion that no other elements are required to constitute a time-series except an A series and a C series.

We may sum up the relations of the three series to time as follows: The A and B series are equally essential to time, which must be distinguished as past, present and future, and must likewise be distinguished as earlier and later. But the two series are not equally fundamental. The distinctions of the A series are ultimate. We cannot explain what is meant by past, present and future. We can, to some extent, describe them, but they cannot be defined. We can only show their meaning by examples. "Your breakfast this morning," we can say to an inquirer, "is past; this conversation is present; your dinner this evening is future." We can do no more.

The B series, on the other hand, is not ultimate. For, given a C series of permanent relations of terms, which is not in itself temporal, and therefore is not a B series, and given the further fact that the

---

3. This account of the nature of the A series is not valid, for it involves a vicious circle, since it uses "has been" and "will be" to explain Past and Future. But, as I shall endeavour to show later on, this vicious circle is inevitable when we deal with the A series, and forms the ground on which we must reject it.

terms of this C series also form an A series, and it results that the terms of the C series become a B series, those which are placed first, in the direction from past to future, being earlier than those whose places are further in the direction of the future.

The C series, however, is as ultimate as the A series. We cannot get it out of anything else. That the units of time do form a series, the relations of which are permanent, is as ultimate as the fact that each of them is present, past, or future. And this ultimate fact is essential to time. For it is admitted that it is essential to time that each moment of it shall either be earlier or later than any other moment; and these relations are permanent. And this—the B series—cannot be got out of the A series alone. It is only when the A series, which gives change and direction, is combined with the C series, which gives permanence, that the B series can arise.

Only part of the conclusion which I have now reached is required for the general purpose of this paper. I am endeavouring to base the unreality of time, not on the fact that the A series is more fundamental than the B series, but on the fact that it is as essential as the B series— that the distinctions of past, present and future are essential to time, and that, if the distinctions are never true of reality, then no reality is in time.

This view, whether it is true or false, has nothing surprising in it. It was pointed out above that time, as we perceive it, always presents these distinctions. And it has generally been held that this is a real characteristic of time, and not an illusion due to the way in which we perceive it. Most philosophers, whether they did or did not believe time to be true of reality, have regarded the distinctions of the A series as essential to time.

When the opposite view has been maintained, it has generally been, I believe, because it was held (rightly, as I shall try to show later on) that the distinctions of present, past and future cannot be true of reality, and that consequently, if the reality of time is to be saved, the distinction in question must be shown to be unessential to time. The presumption, it was held, was for the reality of time, and this would give us a reason for rejecting the A series as unessential to time. But of course this could only give a presumption. If the analysis of the notion of time showed that, by removing the A series, time was destroyed, this line of argument would be no longer open, and the unreality of the A series would involve the unreality of time.

I have endeavoured to show that the removal of the A series *does* destroy time. But there are two objections to this theory, which we must now consider.

The first deals with those time-series which are not really existent, but which are falsely believed to be existent, or which are imagined as existent. Take, for example, the adventures of Don Quixote. This series, it is said, is not an A series. I cannot at this moment judge it to be either past, present or future. Indeed I know that it is none of the three. Yet, it is said, it is certainly a B series. The adventure of the galley-slaves, for example, is later than the adventure of the windmills. And a B series involves time. The conclusion drawn is that an A series is not essential to time.

The answer to this objection I hold to be as follows. Time only belongs to the existent. If any reality is in time, that involves that the reality in question exists. This, I imagine, would be universally admitted. It may be questioned whether all of what exists is in time, or even whether anything really existent is in time, but it would not be denied that, if anything is in time, it must exist.

Now what is existent in the adventures of Don Quixote? Nothing. For the story is imaginary. The acts of Cervantes' mind when he invented the story, the acts of my mind when I think of the story—these exist. But then these form part of an A series. Cervantes' invention of the story is in the past. My thought of the story is in the past, the present, and—I trust—the future.

But the adventures of Don Quixote may be believed by a child to be historical. And in reading them I may by an effort of the imagination contemplate them as if they really happened. In this case, the adventures are believed to be existent or imagined as existent. But then they are believed to be in the A series, or imagined as in the A series. The child who believes them historical will believe that they happened in the past. If I imagine them as existent, I shall imagine them as happening in the past. In the same way, if any one believed the events recorded in Morris's *News from Nowhere* to exist, or imagined them as existent, he would believe them to exist in the future or imagine them as existent in the future. Whether we place the object of our belief or our imagination in the present, the past, or the future, will depend upon the characteristics of that object. But somewhere in our A series it will be placed.

Thus the answer to the objection is that, just as a thing is in time, it is in the A series. If it is really in time, it is really in the A series. If it is believed to be in time, it is believed to be in the A series. If it is imagined as in time, it is imagined as in the A series.

The second objection is based on the possibility, discussed by Mr. Bradley, that there might be several independent time-series in reality. For Mr. Bradley, indeed, time is only appearance. There is no real time at all, and therefore there are not several real series of time. But the hypothesis here is that there should be within reality several real and independent time-series.

The objection, I imagine, is that the time-series would be all real, while the distinction of past, present, and future would only have meaning within each series, and could not, therefore, be taken as ultimately real. There would be, for example, many presents. Now, of course, many points of time can be present (each point in each time-series is a present once), but they must be present successively. And the presents of the different time-series would not be successive, since they are not in the same time. (Neither would they be simultaneous, since that equally involves being in the same time. They would have no time-relation whatever.) And different presents, unless they are successive, cannot be real. So the different time-series, which are real, must be able to exist independently of the distinction between past, present, and future.

I cannot, however, regard this objection as valid. No doubt, in such a case, no present would be *the* present—it would only be the present of a certain aspect of the universe. But then no time would be *the* time—it would only be the time of a certain aspect of the universe. It would, no doubt, be a real time-series, but I do not see that the present would be less real than the time.

I am not, of course, asserting that there is no contradiction in the existence of several distinct A series. My main thesis is that the existence of *any* A series involves a contradiction. What I assert here is merely that, supposing that there could be any A series, I see no extra difficulty involved in there being several such series independent of one another, and that therefore there is no incompatibility between the essentiality of an A series for time and the existence of several distinct times.

Moreover, we must remember that the theory of a plurality of time-series is a mere hypothesis. No reason has ever been given why we should believe in their existence. It has only been said that there is no reason why we should disbelieve in their existence, and that therefore they may exist. But if their existence should be incompatible with something else, for which there is positive evidence, then there would be a reason why we should disbelieve in their existence. Now there is, as I have tried to show, positive evidence for believing that an A series is essential to time. Supposing therefore that it were the case (which, for the reasons given above, I deny) that the existence of a plurality of time-series was incompatible with the essentiality for time of the A series, it would be the hypothesis of a plurality of times which should be rejected, and not our conclusion as to the A series.

I now pass to the second part of my task. Having, as it seems to me, succeeded in proving that there can be no time without an A series, it remains to prove that an A series cannot exist, and that therefore time cannot exist. This would involve that time is not real at all, since it is admitted that, the only way in which time can be real is by existing.

The terms of the A series are characteristics of events. We say of events that they are either past, present, or future. If moments of time are taken as separate realities, we say of them also that they are past, present, or future. A characteristic may be either a relation or a quality. Whether we take the terms of the A series as relations of events (which seems the more reasonable view) or whether we take them as qualities of events, it seems to me that they involve a contradiction.

Let us first examine the supposition that they are relations. In that case only one term of each relation can be an event or a moment. The other term must be something outside the time-series.[4] For the relations of the A series are changing relations, and the relation of terms of the time-series to one another do not change. Two events are exactly in the same places in the time-series, relatively to one another, a million years before they take place, while each of them is taking place, and when they are a million years in the past. The same is true of the relation of moments to each other. Again, if the moments of time are to be distinguished as separate realities from the events which happen in them, the relation between an event and a moment is unvarying. Each event is in the same moment in the future, in the present, and in the past.

The relations which form the A series then must be relations of

4. It has been maintained that the present is whatever is simultaneous with the assertion of its presentness, the future whatever is later than the assertion of its futurity, and the past whatever is earlier than the assertion of its pastness. But this theory involves that time exists independently of the A series, and is incompatible with the results we have already reached.

events and moments to something not itself in the time-series. What this something is might be difficult to say. But, waiving this point, a more positive difficulty presents itself.

Past, present, and future are incompatible determinations. Every event must be one or the other, but no event can be more than one. This is essential to the meaning of the terms. And, if it were not so, the A series would be insufficient to give us, in combination with the C series, the result of time. For time, as we have seen, involves change, and the only change we can get is from future to present, and from present to past.

The characteristics, therefore, are incompatible. But every event has them all. If M is past, it has been present and future. If it is future, it will be present and past. If it is present, it has been future and will be past. Thus all the three incompatible terms are predictable of each event, which is obviously inconsistent with their being incompatible, and inconsistent with their producing change.

It may seem that this can easily be explained. Indeed it has been impossible to state the difficulty without almost giving the explanation, since our language has verb-forms for the past, present, and future, but no form that is common to all three. It is never true, the answer will run, that M *is* present, past and future. It *is* present, *will be* past, and *has been* future. Or it *is* past, and *has been* future and present, or again *is* future and *will be* present and past. The characteristics are only incompatible when they are simultaneous, and there is no contradiction to this in the fact that each term has all of them successively.

But this explanation involves a vicious circle. For it assumes the existence of time in order to account for the way in which moments are past, present and future. Time then must be pre-supposed to account for the A series. But we have already seen that the A series has to be assumed in order to account for time. Accordingly the A series has to be pre-supposed in order to account for the A series. And this is clearly a vicious circle.

What we have done is this—to meet the difficulty that my writing of this article has the characteristics of past, present and future, we say that it is present, has been future, and will be past. But "has been" is only distinguished from "is" by being existence in the past and not in the present, and "will be" is only distinguished from both by being existence in the future. Thus our statement comes to this—that the event in question is present in the present, future in the past, past in the future. And it is clear that there is a vicious circle if we endeavour to assign the characteristics of present, future and past by the criterion of the characteristics of present, past and future.

The difficulty may be put in another way, in which the fallacy will exhibit itself rather as a vicious infinite series than as a vicious circle. If we avoid the incompatibility of the three characteristics by asserting that M is present, has been future, and will be past, we are constructing a second A series, within which the first falls, in the same way in which events fall within the first. It may be doubted whether any intelligible meaning can be given to the assertion that time is in time. But, in any case, the second A series will suffer from the same difficulty as the first, which can only be removed by placing it inside a third A series. The same principle will place the third inside a fourth, and so on without end. You can never get rid of the contradiction, for, by the act of removing it from what is to be explained, you produce it over again in the explanation. And so the explanation is invalid.

Thus a contradiction arises if the A series is asserted of reality when the A series is taken as a series of relations. Could it be taken as a series of qualities, and would this give us a better result? Are there three quali-ties—futurity, presentness, and pastness, and are events continually changing the first for the second, and the second for the third?

It seems to me that there is very little to be said for the view that the changes of the A series are changes of qualities. No doubt my anticipation of an experience M, the experience itself, and the memory of the experience are three states which have different qualities. But it is not the future M, the present M, and the past M, which have these three different qualities. The qualities are possessed by three distinct events—the anticipation of M, the experience M itself, and the memory of M, each of which is in turn future, present, and past. Thus this gives no support to the view that the changes of the A series are changes of qualities.

But we need not go further into this question. If the characteristics of the A series were qualities, the same difficulty would arise as if they were relations. For, as before, they are not compatible, and, as before, every event has all of them. This can only be explained, as before, by saying that each event has them successively. And thus the same fallacy would have been committed as in the previous case.[5]

5. It is very usual to present Time under the metaphor of a spatial movement. But is it to be a movement from past to future, or from future to past? If the

We have come then to the conclusion that the application of the A series to reality involves a contradiction, and that consequently the A series cannot be true of reality. And, since time involves the A series, it follows that time cannot be true of reality. Whenever we judge anything to exist in time, we are in error. And whenever we perceive anything as existing in time—which is the only way in which we ever do perceive things—we are perceiving it more or less as it really is not.

We must consider a possible objection. Our ground for rejecting time, it may be said, is that time cannot be explained without assuming time. But may this not prove—not that time is invalid, but rather that time is ultimate? It is impossible to explain, for example, goodness or truth unless by bringing in the term to be explained as part of the explanation, and we therefore reject the explanation as invalid. But we do not therefore reject the notion as erroneous, but accept it as something ultimate, which, while it does not admit of explanation, does not require it.

But this does not apply here. An idea may be valid of reality though it does not admit of a valid explanation. But it cannot be valid of reality if its application to reality involves a contradiction. Now we began by pointing out that there was such a contradiction in the case of time— that the characteristics of the A series are mutually incompatible and yet all true of every term. Unless this contradiction is removed, the idea of time must be rejected as invalid. It was to remove this contradiction that the explanation was suggested that the characteristics belong

---

A series is taken as one of qualities, it will naturally be taken as a movement from past to future, since the quality of presentness has belonged to the past states and will belong to the future states. If the A series is taken as one of relations, it is possible to take the movement either way, since either of the two related terms can be taken as the one which moves. If the events are taken as moving by a fixed point of presentness, the movement is from future to past, since the future events are those which have not yet passed the point, and the past are those which have. If presentness is taken as a moving point successively related to each of a series of events, the movement is from past to future. Thus we say that events come out of the future, but we say that we ourselves move towards the future. For each man identifies himself especially with his present state, as against his future or his past, since the present is the only one of which he has direct experience. And thus the self, if it is pictured as moving at all, is pictured as moving with the point of presentness along the stream of events from past to future.

to the terms successively. When this explanation failed as being circular, the contradiction remained unremoved, and the idea of time must be rejected, not because it cannot be explained, but because the contradiction cannot be removed.

What has been said already, if valid, is an adequate ground for rejecting time. But we may add another consideration. Time, as we have seen, stands and falls with the A series. Now, even if we ignore the contradiction which we have just discovered in the application of the A series to reality, was there ever any positive reason why we should suppose that the A series *was* valid of reality?

Why do we believe that events are to be distinguished as past, present and future? I conceive that the belief arises from distinctions in our own experience.

At any moment I have certain perceptions. I have also the memory of certain other perceptions, and the anticipation of others again. The direct perception itself is a mental state qualitatively different from the memory or the anticipation of perceptions. On this is based the belief that the perception itself has a certain characteristic when I have it, which is replaced by other characteristics when I have the memory or the anticipation of it—which characteristics are called presentness, pastness, and futurity. Having got the idea of these characteristics we apply them to other events. Everything simultaneous with the direct perception which I have now is called present, and it is even held that there would be a present if no one had a direct perception at all. In the same way acts simultaneous with remembered perceptions or anticipated perceptions are held to be past or future, and this again is extended to events to which none of the perceptions I now remember or anticipate are simultaneous. But the origin of our belief in the whole distinction lies in the distinction between perceptions and anticipations or memories of perceptions.

A direct perception is present when I have it, and so is what is simultaneous with it. In the first place this definition involves a circle, for the words "when I have it," can only mean "when it is present". But if we left out these words, the definition would be false, for I have many direct presentations which are at different times, and which cannot, therefore, all be present, except successively. This, however, is the fundamental contradiction of the A series, which has been already considered. The point I wish to consider here is different.

The direct perceptions which I now have are those which now fall within my "specious present". Of those which are beyond it, I can only have memory or anticipation. Now the "specious present" varies in length according to circumstances, and may be different for two people at the same period. The event M may be simultaneous both with X's perception Q and Y's perception R. At a certain moment Q may have ceased to be part of X's specious present. M, therefore, will at that moment be past. But at the same moment R may still be part of Y's specious present. And, therefore, M will be present, at the same moment at which it is past.

This is impossible. If, indeed, the A series was something purely subjective, there would be no difficulty. We could say that M was past for X and present for Y, just as we could say that it was pleasant for X and painful for Y. But we are considering attempts to take time as real, as something which belongs to the reality itself, and not only to our beliefs about it, and this can only be so if the A series also applies to the reality itself. And if it does this, then at any moment M must be present or past. It cannot be both.

The present through which events really pass, therefore, cannot be determined as simultaneous with the specious present. It must have a duration fixed as an ultimate fact. This duration cannot be the same as the duration of all specious presents, since all specious presents have not the same duration. And thus an event may be past when I am experiencing it as present, or present when I am experiencing it as past. The duration of the objective present may be the thousandth part of a second. Or it may be a century, and the accessions of George IV. and Edward VII. may form part of the same present. What reason can we have to believe in the existence of such a present, which we certainly do not observe to be a present, and which has no relation to what we do observe to be a present?

If we escape from these difficulties by taking the view, which has sometimes been held, that the present in the A series is not a finite duration, but a mere point, separating future from past, we shall find other difficulties as serious. For then the objective time in which events are will be something utterly different from the time in which we perceive them. The time in which we perceive them has a present of varying finite duration, and, therefore, with the future and the past, is divided into three durations. The objective time has only two durations, separated by a present which has nothing but the name in common with the present of experience, since it is not a duration but a point. What is there in our experience which gives us the least reason to believe in such a time as this?

And so it would seem that the denial of the reality of time is not so very paradoxical after all. It was called paradoxical because it seemed to contradict our experience so violently—to compel us to treat so much as illusion which appears *primâ facie* to give knowledge of reality. But we now see that our experience of time—centring as it does about the specious present—would be no less illusory if there were a real time in which the realities we experience existed. The specious present of our observations—varying as it does from you to me—cannot correspond to the present of the events observed. And consequently the past and future of our observations could not correspond to the past and future of the events observed. On either hypothesis—whether we take time as real or as unreal—everything is observed in a specious present, but nothing, not even the observations themselves, can ever *be* in a specious present. And in that case I do not see that we treat experience as much more illusory when we say that nothing is ever in a present at all, than when we say that everything passes through some entirely different present.

Our conclusion, then, is that neither time as a whole, nor the A series and B series, really exist. But this leaves it possible that the C series does really exist. The A series was rejected for its inconsistency. And its rejection involved the rejection of the B series. But we have found no such contradiction in the C series, and its invalidity does not follow from the invalidity of the A series.

It is, therefore, possible that the realities which we perceive as events in a time-series do really form a non-temporal series. It is also possible, so far as we have yet gone, that they do *not* form such a series, and that they are in reality no more a series than they are temporal. But I think—though I have no room to go into the question here—that the former view, according to which they really do form a C series, is the more probable.

Should it be true, it will follow that in our perception of these realities as events in time, there will be some truth as well as some error. Through the deceptive form of time, we shall grasp some of their true relations. If we say that the events M and N are simultaneous, we say that they occupy the same position in the time-series. And there will be some truth in this, for the realities, which we perceive as the events M and N, do really occupy the same position in a series, though it is not a temporal series.

Again, if we assert that the events M, N, O, are all at different times, and are in that order, we assert that they occupy different positions in the time-series, and that the position of N is between the positions of M and O. And it will be true that the realities which we see as these events will be in a series, though not in a temporal series, and that their positions in it will be different, and that the position of the reality which we perceive as the event N will be between the positions of the realities which we perceive as the events M and O.

If this view is adopted, the result will so far resemble those reached by Hegel rather than those of Kant. For Hegel regarded the order of the time-series as a reflexion, though a distorted reflexion, of something in the real nature of the timeless reality, while Kant does not seem to have contemplated the possibility that anything in the nature of the noumenon should correspond to the time order which appears in the phenomenon.

But the question whether such an objective C series does exist, must remain for future discussion. And many other questions press upon us which inevitably arise if the reality of time is denied. If there is such a C series, are positions in it simply ultimate facts, or are they determined by the varying amounts, in the objects which hold those positions, of some quality which is common to all of them? And, if so, what is that quality, and is it a greater amount of it which determines things to appear as later, and a lesser amount which determines them to appear as earlier, or is the reverse true? On the solution of these questions it may be that our hopes and fears for the universe depend for their confirmation or rejection.

And, again, is the series of appearances in time a series which is infinite or finite in length? And how are we to deal with the appearance itself? If we reduce time and change to appearance, must it not be to an appearance which changes and which is in time, and is not time, then, shown to be real after all? This is doubless a serious question, but I hope to show hereafter that it can be answered in a satisfactory way.

11

Michael Dummett, "A Defense of McTaggart's Proof of the Unreality of Time," from the *Philosophical Review*

Michael Dummett, one of the most distinguished contemporary philosophers and the leading contributor to the contemporary debate about realism and anti-realism, is Wykeham Professor of Logic at the University of Oxford. His works include Frege: Philosophy of Language, The Interpretation of Frege's Philosophy, *and* Truth and Other Enigmas.

McTaggart's celebrated argument to prove that time is unreal runs as follows. There are two kinds of temporal fact concerning events: (a) that an event M is past, present, or future; (b) that an event M is before, at the same time as, or after another event N. Now facts of kind (a) cannot be reduced to facts of kind (b); and if there were no facts of kind (a), there would not genuinely be any time at all. For time essentially involves change: but change comes in only in connection with facts of kind (a). With facts of kind (b) there is no change at all: if an event M precedes an event N, it always will be true that M preceded N, and it always was true that M would precede N. There is change only in virtue of the fact that we can say of some event M, for example, that it has ceased to be future and is now present, and will cease to be present and become past.

But, McTaggart argues, the predicates "past," "present," and "future" involve a contradiction: for on the one hand they are incompatible predicates, and on the other to every event all three apply (or at least two of them). Someone will naturally reply that the predicates which apply are not the simple "past," "present," and "future," but rather, for example, "*will be* past," "*is* present," and "*was* future," and that these three predicates are not incompatible. But, McTaggart claims,

The Philosophical Review, Oct. (1960) lxix.

this move advances us no further. Instead of three, we now have nine predicates, each of which still applies to every event and some of which are incompatible, for example, the predicates "was past" and "will be future." Admittedly the objector may again reply that the predicates which really apply to the same event are "is going to have been past" and "was going to be future" and that these are again compatible. But McTaggart can counter this move as before, and so on indefinitely.

It is not at once clear where the victory lies. Every contradiction McTaggart points to the objector can dispel, but at every stage *a* contradiction remains. On examination, however, we see that the objector has not found an adequate reply to McTaggart's argument. Let us call "past," "present," and "future" "predicates of first level." If, as McTaggart suggests, we render "was future" as "future in the past," and so forth, then, we have the nine predicates of second level:

$$
\begin{Bmatrix} \text{past} \\ \text{present} \\ \text{future} \end{Bmatrix} \text{ in the } \begin{Bmatrix} \text{past} \\ \text{present} \\ \text{future} \end{Bmatrix}
$$

Similarly there are twenty-seven predicates of third level:

$$
\begin{Bmatrix} \text{past} \\ \text{present} \\ \text{future} \end{Bmatrix} \text{ in the } \begin{Bmatrix} \text{past} \\ \text{present} \\ \text{future} \end{Bmatrix} \text{ in the } \begin{Bmatrix} \text{past} \\ \text{present} \\ \text{future} \end{Bmatrix}
$$

and so on. But at any level the three predicates

$$
\begin{Bmatrix} \text{past} \\ \text{present} \\ \text{future} \end{Bmatrix} \text{ in the present in the present in the } \ldots \text{ in the present}
$$

are equivalent to the first-level predicates "past," "present," and "future," so that if there is a contradiction connected with the predicates of first level, the contradiction is not removed by ascending in the hierarchy.

An objection of a different kind has sometimes been raised. It has been argued that McTaggart's argument is vitiated by being in terms of events. It is quite unnecessary, the objection runs, for our language to contain expressions denoting events or devices for generalizing about events; everything we want to say could be said using only names of and generalizations about the objects which figure in the events. This view involves some difficulties (for example, whether every event consists of something happening to an object) and needs to be supplemented by an account of how the introduction of events as entities gives rise to McTaggart's paradox; but in any case it fails as an objection to McTaggart's argument, since this argument could have been stated as cogently, if not as elegantly, in terms of objects. Time involves change, and if there is change, then, at least on the present view, some objects must have different predicates applying to them at different times; here indeed we may have to count "is no more" and "is not yet" as predicates. But this just means that to one and the same object incompatible predicates apply; for example, the paper was white and is yellow, so the incompatible predicates "white" and "yellow" apply to the paper.

One has a strong natural impression that McTaggart's argument is a sophism based on a blindness to the obvious properties of token-reflexive expressions. A token-reflexive expression is one like "I," "here," "now," whose essential occurrence in a sentence renders that sentence capable of bearing different truth-values according to the circumstances of its utterance—by whom, when, and where it is uttered, to whom it is addressed, with what gestures it is accompanied, and so forth. Then it seems that an adequate objection to McTaggart may run as follows. If we say of a predicate in which a token-reflexive expression occurs essentially that it "applies" to an entity if there are any circumstances in which it may truly be asserted of that entity, and if we call two such predicates "incompatible" when there exist no circumstances in which they can both be truly asserted of any one entity, then it is possible for two incompatible predicates to apply to one and the same entity. It seems therefore that we may conclude that McTaggart has not really unearthed a contradiction at all.

This objection is intended as a reformulation of the first, unsuccessful objection which we considered. The first objector held that a contradiction which arose at any level of our hierarchy could be resolved by ascending one level. From the standpoint of the present objection, what the first objector was trying to do was specify the circumstances in which the predicate was asserted of the event, he failed because his specification was itself by means of a token-reflexive expression, and hence he succeeded only in constructing new predicates of the same type, by means of which the same pseudo-paradox could be generated.

It is because people suppose that McTaggart can be refuted by some such objection as that which we are now considering that they do not take him very seriously, but I believe that this solution rests on a grave misunderstanding. If it gave a correct account of the matter, then only stupidity could explain McTaggart's failure to use a quite analogous argument to show the unreality of space and the unreality of personality. Every place can be called both "here" and "there," both "near" and "far," and every person can be called both "I" and "you": yet "here" and "there," "near" and "far," "I" and "you" are incompatible. It would be no use for an objector to say that London is nearby far away, but far away nearby, or that it is "here" there but "there" here, since it can also be called "nearby nearby" and " 'here' here," and so on. Similarly, it would be no use an objector saying "You are 'you' to me,, but 'I' to you," because everyone can be called both " 'you' to you" and " 'I' to you." McTaggart does not, however, display the slightest inclination to apply his argument in this way to space or to personality: indeed, in arguing for the unreality of time, he repeatedly contrasts space with time. It follows that the refutation we are considering must have missed an essential part of his argument.

McTaggart's argument is divided into two parts. In part one he attempts to establish that there would be no time if there were no facts of kind (a), on the ground that time involves change and change is possible only if there are facts of kind (a). Part two attempts to show that the existence of facts of kind (a) involves a contradiction. Part two depends upon part one: it is because the analogue of part one does not hold for space or for personality that the analogue of part two for space or for personality has no force. We must therefore beware of passing over part one with little attention, for it contains the heart of the argument.

To see what it means to say that there would be no time if there were no facts of kind (a), we may ask what it means to deny the analogue of this for space. Facts of kind (a) are facts into the statement of which temporally token-reflexive expressions enter essentially. By contrast, the use of spatially token-reflexive expressions is not essential to the description of objects as being in a space. That is, I can describe an arrangement of objects in space although I do not myself have any position in that space. An example would be the space of my visual field. In that space there is no here or there, no near or far: I am not in that space. We can, I think, conceive, on the strength of this analogy, of a being who could perceive objects in our three-dimensional physical space although he occupied no position in that space. He would have no use for any spatially token-reflexive expressions in giving a description of the physical universe, and yet that description might be a perfectly correct description of the objects of the universe as arranged in space.

McTaggart is saying that on the other hand a description of events as taking place *in time* is impossible unless temporally token-reflexive expressions enter into it, that is, unless the description is given by someone who is himself in that time. Suppose someone who can observe all events which take place in our universe, or some region of it, during some period of time. We may first suppose that he observes them successively, that he cannot choose which events he will next observe but can observe them only in the order in which they take place. Then even if he knows both what he has observed and what he is going to observe, he cannot give a complete description of his observations without the use of temporally token-reflexive expressions. He can give a complete narration of the sequence of events, but there would remain to be answered the question, "And which of these events is happening *now?*" We can indeed avoid this by putting the observer's thoughts and utterances into the description, but now we have merely made the original observer part of the region observed, and the point may be made again for an observer who gives a description of this enlarged region.

If instead we now imagine the observer as able to survey the whole course of events at once, or at least as able to observe the events at will in whatever order he chooses, then we can conceive of him as observing a static-dimensional configuration, one dimension of which represents time. (Of course, this is not quite accurate, since not every event which takes place in time is a physical event.) It is now clear, however, that what he observes can only be a model of the sequence of events in our three-dimensional space, not that sequence of events itself. We can, of course, make a static three-dimensional representation of the course of events over a finite period of time on a changing two-dimensional surface. But it makes no sense to suppose that that course of events is identical with some static three-dimensional configuration. This is evident from the fact that there is an element of convention in the three-dimensional representation: we lay it down that the axes are to be chosen in a certain way, that such-and-such an axis represents time, and that such-and-such a direction along this axis represents the direction earlier-to-later; these conventions cannot be shown in the model. This remains true even if there in fact is such a three-dimensional configuration.

Imagine a cylinder made of glass with irregular internal coloring like a child's marble. A two-dimensional surface, in shape roughly a shallow cone without its base, moves through the cylinder so that its vertex travels at a uniform rate relative to the axis of the cylinder, the base of the cone remaining perpendicular to this axis. If we now replace the cylinder and the surface of the cone by their analogues in four-dimensional space, we get something like what we are sometimes inclined to conceive that our world must in fact be like. That is, we are sometimes inclined to suppose that what we observe at any one time is a three-dimensional segment of a static four-dimensional physical reality; but as we travel through the four-dimensional structure we observe different three-dimensional segments at different times. But of course the fourth dimension can no more be identified with time than the road down which someone travels can be identified with the time that passes as he travels down it. If our hypothetical observer observes only the four-dimensional configuration without observing our movement—the movement of our consciousness—through it, like someone observing the road but blind to the traveler, he does not see all that happens. But if he also observes our passage through it, what he is observing is no longer static, and he will again need token-reflexive expressions to report what he observes.

Granted, then, that part one of McTaggart's argument establishes that what is in time cannot be fully described without token-reflexive expressions, how does part two enable us to pass from this to the assertion that time is unreal? Might not part one of the argument be taken rather as demonstrating the reality of time in a very strong sense, since it shows that time cannot be explained away or reduced to anything else? In particular, does not the objection we considered—that McTaggart's attempt to uncover a contradiction rested on a neglect of the obvious properties of token-reflexive expressions—at least invalidate part two of the argument?

I think the point is that McTaggart is taking it for granted that reality must be something of which there exists in principle a complete description. I can make drawings of a rock from various angles, but if I am asked to say what the real shape of the rock is, I can give a description of it as in three-dimensional space which is independent of the angle from which it is looked at. The description of what is really there, as it really is, must be independent of any particular point of view. Now if time were real, then since what is temporal cannot be completely described without the use of token-reflexive expressions, there would be no such thing as the complete description of reality. There would be one, as it were, maximal description of reality in which the statement "The event *M* is happening" figured, others which contained the statement "The event *M* happened," and yet others which contained "The event *M* is going to happen."

I personally feel very strongly inclined to believe that there must be a complete description of reality; more properly, that of anything which is real, there must be a complete—that is, observer-independent—description. Hence, since part one of McTaggart's argument is certainly correct, his conclusion appears to follow that time is unreal. But this conclusion seems self-refuting in something of the way in which, as McTaggart himself points out, the view that evil is an illusion is self-refuting: that is, if there is no evil, the illusion that there is evil is certainly evil. To say that time is unreal is to say that we apprehend relations between events or properties of objects as temporal when they are not really temporal at all. We have therefore to conceive of these events or objects as standing to one another in some non-temporal relation which we mistake for the temporal one. But just what does our "apprehension of these relations as temporal" consist in? Which apprehension is McTaggart thinking of—I mean, the apprehension at which time? Clearly, even if the world is really static, our apprehension of it changes. It does not help to say that we are even mistaken about what we think we see, because the fact would remain that we still make different such mistakes at different times.

If this last piece of reasoning, to the effect that the belief that time is unreal is self-refuting, is correct, then McTaggart's argument shows that we must abandon our prejudice that there must be a complete description of reality. This prejudice is one that lies very deep in many people. I shall not here attempt to explore it further, to find out whether it can be supported or what mistakes, if any, it rests on. It is enough if I have succeeded in showing that it is to this prejudice that McTaggart is implicitly appealing, and that it is this which must be extirpated if his conclusion is not to be accepted, and above all that his argument is not the trivial sophism which it at first appears.

12

Paul Horwich,
"The Moving Now,"
from *Asymmetries in Time*

Paul Horwich, Professor of Philosophy at M.I.T., was trained in both physics and philosophy. Apart from Asymmetries in Time, *he has written* Probability and Evidence *and* Truth.

1. The 'moving now' conception of time

The quintessential property of time, it may seem, is the difference between the past and the future. And here I don't just mean that the past and the future are separate regions, or that the past and future directions along the continuum of instants are opposite to one another, bur rather that these two directions are somehow fundamentally un-alike. This idea is fostered by the desire to explain pervasive temporally asymmetric phenomena, such as causation, knowledge, decay, and the phenomenological feeling of 'moving into the future'. And it is reflected in the use of such phrases as "time's arrow" and in our inclination to say that time "goes" in one direction and not the other. Despite the fact that these expressions have an air of metaphor about them, they clearly imply *anisotropy*—that is, a significant lack of symmetry between the two directions of the temporal continuum. We tend to believe, in short, that time *itself* is temporally asymmetric.

This view of time contrasts with our attitude towards space. We can pick any straight line and define two opposite directions along it. Although the directions are numerically distinct from one another, we would regard them as essentially similar. We wouldn't expect the result of an experiment to depend on the direction in which our apparatus is pointing. Thus we suppose that space is isotropic. Not that the supposition is taken to be *necessarily* true. Aristotelian space, for exam-ple, is anisotropic in that directions toward and away from the center of the universe are ascribed quite different causal properties: fire naturally goes one way, and earth another. Similarly it should not be surprising if the question of time's anisotropy proves to be an empirical, contingent matter.

Often, however, those who proclaim the anisotropy of time are not motivated by scientific considerations but are gripped by a certain metaphysical picture. They have in mind that time is more than just a fixed sequence of events ordered by such relations as *later than* and *simultaneous with*, but that it also contains a peculiar property—being *now*—which moves gradually along the array in the direction from past to future. This idea is sometimes combined with a further metaphysical doctrine: namely, that there is an ontological distinction between the past and the future—a distinction that can be represented in a tree model of reality, in which the past consists of a fixed, definite course of events and the future contains nothing but a manifold of branching possibilities. These alleged aspects of time—which I shall describe in more detail as we proceed—are thought to especially distinguish it from space, which possesses no such features. Recent advocates of this sort of view include Broad (1938), Taylor (1965), Gale (1969), Geach (1972), and Schlesinger (1980). On the other hand, there are many philosophers—for example, Russell (1903), Williams (1951), Smart (1955), and Grünbaum (1963)—who reject the 'moving *now*' conception and think that the past and future have exactly the same ontological status. They maintain that the word "now" is an indexical expression (on a par with "here" and "I") whose special function is to designate whatever time happens be the time at which the word-token is uttered. On this account, the thought that an event E is first in the future, will become present, and then fade into the past does not presuppose a 'moving *now*', but it implies merely that E is later than the time at which that thought is entertained, simultaneous with some subsequent time, and earlier than times after that.

Our job in this chapter will be to try to settle these issues—that is, to decide whether there really is any objective feature of the world that corresponds to the idea of a 'moving *now*' and to assess the merits of the tree model. To this end I shall begin by describing and defending McTaggart's (1908) notorious proof that there is no such thing as the 'moving *now*.' But I won't endorse his entire line of thought. McTaggart argues that the 'moving property' theory of *now* is self-contradictory, but he thinks that this conception is nevertheless essential to time. He concludes therefore that time does not exist and that, though "now" indeed functions as an indexical, it refers not to times but rather to other entities that are somewhat like instants of time but only pale substitutes for them. I shall support McTaggart's rejection of the 'moving *now*' but not his further claim that genuine time could not exist without it. We shall see that the best defense against McTaggart's attack on the 'moving *now*' involves a commitment to the tree model of reality. Therefore, in exposing and undermining the antifatalistic and the verificationist motivations for that ontological picture, I hope to reinforce McTaggart's criticism of the 'moving *now*'.

After reaching these conclusions, I shall try to explain why we are nevertheless so captivated by the 'moving *now*' conception. And in the next chapter we shall see that the metaphysical asymmetries suggested by the 'moving *now*' and the tree model are not needed for time to be anisotropic. Even if those ideas are wholly incorrect, there remains the possibility that time is intrinsically asymmetric in virtue of some purely physical, empirical phenomenon.

To begin with, it is worth a moment's digression to note that although McTaggart follows Leibniz (the Leibniz/Clarke correspondance; see Alexander 1956) in trying to prove *a priori* that time does not exist, their two arguments are totally unrelated. This is because Leibniz and McTaggart disagree radically about the sort of thing time would have to be, in order to be real. For Leibniz, real time would be a substance—a Newtonian continuum of thinglike instants at which events are located, ordered by the relation *later than*. But according to McTaggart, something quite different would have to be involved for time to exist: namely, a property, *being now*, which glides along the continuum of instants in the future direction. Moreover there is no need, in his view, for substantial instants. It would suffice if there were merely states of the world ordered by the relation, *later than*, just so long as the property, *now*, moves through these states, singling out progressively later and later ones, as shown in figure 1.

In McTaggart's terminology temporal locations may be specified in terms of two alternative systems of coordinates: the *A*-series, which locates an event relative to *now* (as being in the distant past, the recent past, the present, tomorrow, etc.), and the *B*-series, which locates an event relative to other events (as earlier than *F*, or simultaneous with *G*, etc.). His view is that time requires that there be a *B*-series, which in turn requires an *A*-series; but that the *A*-series is self-contradictory. Thus Leibniz and McTaggart are arguing against the instantiation of different conceptions of time. Leibniz tries to show that a continuum of

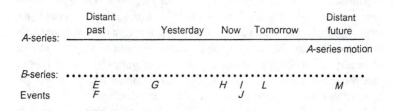

Figure 1

instants cannot exist because it would violate the principles of Sufficient Reason and Identity of Indiscernibles. McTaggart contends that the 'moving *now*' model of time is indispensible yet incoherent.

2. McTaggart's argument for the unreality of time

The outline of McTaggart's proof is as follows:

1. Events are located in a *B*-series (ordered with respect to *later than*), only if time exists.
2. Time exists, only if there is genuine change.
3. There is genuine change in the world, only if events are located in a real *A*-series.

THEREFORE:

i. Events are ordered with respect to *later than*, only if they are located in a real *A*-series.

4. If events are located in a real *A*-series, then each event acquires the absolute properties *past*, *now*, and *future*.
5. There is a contradiction in supposing that any event has any two of these absolute properties.

THEREFORE:

ii. A real *A*-series cannot exist.

THEREFORE:

(M) Events are not ordered with respect to *later than*.

Evidently this is a perfectly valid argument: there is nothing wrong with the deductive reasoning by which the preliminary conclusions, i and ii, are derived from their respective premises, and by which McTaggart's final conclusion, (M), is then drawn. It remains, however, to justify these premises. Let us consider what may be said on their behalf.

1. *Events are located in a B-series, only if time exists.* In order to see that McTaggart's first premise is correct, one must remember that it is not time in the Newtonian sense—an array of thinglike instants—whose reality is in question. Rather, the consequent of (1)—time exists—is supposed to be construed in a very broad way, as something like 'the world exhibits temporality'. And in that case, premise 1 becomes a trivial truth.

2. *Time exists, only if there is genuine change.* It might seem as though there could be time without change. For consider the scenarios schematized in figure 2. Cases like these are good candidates for time without

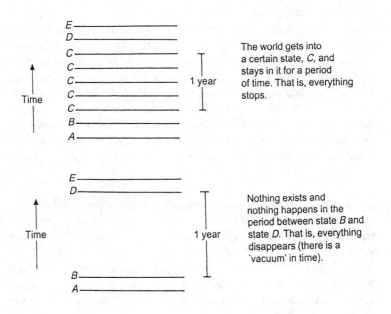

Figure 2

change, and many philosophers who believe there could be time without change (e.g., Shoemaker 1969) have thought that it would suffice to show that worlds like those can occur. Such possibilities, however, are not what McTaggart is intent to deny. His view is that even in those cases there is still, contrary to first appearances, change of a certain kind taking place: namely, states *A* and *B* are receding further and further into the past, and *D* is approaching the present. The *now* is in motion.

According to McTaggart, this sort of change is not only necessarily present if time passes, but also it is the only sort of *genuine* change that there could be. Consider, for example, a hot poker, which gradually cools in the period from $t1$ to $t2$. McTaggart denies that its being hot at $t1$ and cold at $t2$ constitutes a genuine change. For, he says, it was and will be true throughout the history of the universe that this poker is hot at $t1$ and cold at $t2$. Those facts are eternal; they always were, and always will obtain. That kind of variation with respect to time no more qualifies as genuine change than a variation of the temperature along the poker's length. What is required for genuine change, on the other hand, is that the sum total of facts at one time be not the same as the sum total of facts at another time.

Here, by the way, is the place at which I would quarrel with McTaggart's proof, although the rationale for digging in at exactly this point will become clear only in retrospect. When we see what he has in mind by "genuine change", this will undermine whatever initial inclination we may have had to agree that the reality of time requires such a thing. In other words, McTaggart's demonstration, in the second part of his argument, that 'genuine change' is self-contradictory should not persuade us that time is unreal but, rather, should force us to acknowledge that time does not require 'genuine change' after all.

3. *There is genuine change in the world, only if events are located in a real A-series.* A variation in the facts would not occur if time consisted in the *B*-series alone. For the *B*-series is a fixed ordering of events with respect to one another (and with respect to instants of time, if there are such entities). Therefore the *B*-series provides only for temporal facts like 'the poker is hot at t1', which, if it obtains at all, obtains forever. Genuine change can come about only in virtue of the relative motion of the *A*- and the *B*-series, in which the *now* moves gradually in the direction from earlier to later. This generates genuine changes

of the following kind: *E* is in the distant future, *E* is in the near future, *E* is now, *E* is in the past, and so on.

Note that there are certain metaphysically innocuous construals of the terms "past", "now", and "future" that must be rejected by McTaggart, since they would not imply a real *A*-series. Consider, for example, the use of "now" in sentences such as "*E* is now (present) at *t*". This usually means "*E* occurs at *t*", which is a *B*-series fact. Similarly "*E* is past at *t*" means "*E* is earlier than *t*", and "*E* is future at *t*" means "*E* is later than *t*". Past, present, and future have become *relative* properties, whose exemplification is accommodated by the *B*-series.

Alternatively, suppose that "now" is an indexical expression, like "here" and "I", whose referent depends on the context of utterance. In particular, "now" would rigidly pick out the time, whatever it happens to be, at which the word is used. And suppose that at *t*1 I truthfully say "*E* is now", and at *t*2 I say "*E* is not now". Each of these utterences expresses facts, and each of the facts obtains throughout all time. One might be tempted to dispute this claim. One might doubt that "*E* is now", said at *t*1, expresses a fact that obtains at *t*2, since that sentence uttered at *t*2 would be false. But this would be a non sequitur because the sentence does not say the same thing at the two different times. The word "now", used at *t*1, simply provides a way of referring to the time *t*1. And the fact expressed by the first remark—though perhaps not the same as the fact expressed by "*E* is at *t*1"—is just as permanent. Consequently McTaggart holds that for there to be genuine change and a real *A*-series, "past", "present", and "future" can be neither relational predicates nor indexicals.

So far McTaggart has tried to show that time requires the existence of a genuinely moving *now*. And, as I have already said, this preliminary conclusion may be resisted. The remainder of his argument is a demonstration that the 'moving *now*' conception is self-contradictory. This is part of his reasoning that I believe is correct and important.

4. *If events are located in a real A-series, then each event acquires the absolute properties past, now, and future.* A real *A*-series entails that for every event such as *E*, there is a fact, included in the totality of facts that constitutes the universe, consisting of *E*'s having the quality of *presentness*, that is,

E is (or, *E* is now)

but also the universe must contain the facts

> *E* will be (or, *E* is future)

and

> *E* was (or, *E* is past)

Given what is meant by "a real *A*-series," such facts are not relations between events and times. They are not, in other words, the exemplification of merely *relative* properties, which can both apply and fail to apply to the same event relative to different frames of reference. Rather, such facts consist in the exemplification by events of absolute properties.

5. *There is a contradiction in supposing that any event possesses any two of these absolute properties.* Past, present, and future (which are equivalent to 'earlier than now', 'now', and 'later than now') are incompatible attributes. Therefore the supposition that one event has them all involves a contradiction. That is to say, it is impossible that the history of the universe contain the three facts: *E* is past, *E* is now, *E* is future.

One will be tempted to object, as follows. There is a contradiction only if the *A*-series qualities are attributed *simultaneously* to *E*; but such simultaneous attribution is not required by the existence of the *A*-series; rather, its existence entails only that each of the *A*-series qualities apply to *E* at some time or other. That is to say, McTaggart's premise 4 will be satisfied even if the *A*-series determinations are acquired *successively*, and in that case no contradiction arises. In other words, the requirement described in premise 4 may be met by the existence of the facts

> *E* is future at *t*1
> *E* is present at *t*2
> *E* is past at *t*3

which are quite compatible. There is no need to take premise 4 to imply that all the *A*-series determinations would have to apply at the same time.

However, one must beware of resolving the contradiction in ways that involve eliminating any real *A*-series. And this is exactly what has just happened. For the meanings of "future", "present", and "past" in the preceding sentences are "later than", "simultaneous with", and "earlier than". The facts described are generated by the *B*-series. Genuine change has been lost in the reformulation. To preserve genuine change—to have a real *A*-series—it is not enough that there be a variation in *relative* presentness from one time to another (like the variation in the velocity of an object relative to different reference frames). Rather, there must be variation of facts. Thus it is necessary to construe premise 4 in such a way that the transitions from '*E* will be' to '*E* is' to '*E* was' are transitions between mutually exclusive, absolute states.

At this point McTaggart's opponent might well complain that revealing such a variation of facts was precisely the intention behind his reformulation of premise 4. The idea, he says, was *not* to transform *past, present,* and *future* into mere relations (which admittedly only succeeds in eliminating the *A*-series) but rather to suggest that the facts "*E* is past", and so on, might themselves obtain only relative to a temporal perspective. In other words, the premise 4 should have been formulated more perspicuously with the following sentences:

> The fact that *E is future* obtains at $t1$
> The fact that *E is present* obtains at $t2$
> The fact that *E is past* obtains at $t3$

Thus there *is*, after all, a variation, from one time to another, as to which facts obtain.

In response to this suggestion, however, we are justified in resisting the crucial assumption that the italicized internal sentences express facts. For a strong case can be made that this last formulation of premise 4 trades on an idiosyncratic and unmotivated conception of *fact*. After all, we do not regard

> *X* is to the left of *Y*

and

> *X* is not to the left of *Y*

as explicit descriptions of facts. Rather, we suppose that whenever such claims are true, they are partial accounts of facts whose explicit descriptions take the form

> X is to the left of Y relative to Z

and

> X is not to the left of Y relative to W

Similarly one does not say that the facts, fully articulated, include

> It is raining

and

> It is not raining

But rather, for example,

> It is raining in Manchester

and

> It is not raining in Florida

The general point is that we reserve the term "fact" for those aspects of reality whose explicit descriptions are sentences that are true *simpliciter*—and not merely true relative to some context or point of view, and false relative to others. Consequently, if we are going to say that "E is past" is sometimes true and sometimes false, then unless some good reason is given to depart from our usual conception of fact, we should not countenance this sentence as an explicit characterization of a fact. The real facts, as we said initially, are described by sentences of the form "E is past at t", in which pastness has been transformed into a relation.

These remarks do not absolutely preclude the idea that facts may be relative: that is, dependent on a frame of reference. The point is, rather, that such a perspectival view of reality would require a radical change in our conception of fact, and that any such revision would call for some independent motivation. So far, in our discussion of this problem, no reason to abandon the usual notion of fact has been offered. And this is why the response to McTaggart that we are now considering is inadequate as it stands. However, that is not to say that no such argument for perspectivalism *could* be given. Indeed, a strategy to that end, based on verificationist considerations, is suggested by Dummett (1960). I shall take it up in the next section, in connection with Aristotle's tree model of reality.

I have been arguing that McTaggart's contradiction is not avoided by the supposition that the futurity, presentness, and pastness of *E* obtain relative to three times, *t*1, *t*2, and *t*3. Notice that it is equally futile to try to escape his conclusion by rendering the facts as follows:

> *E* is future, in the past
> *E* is now, in the present
> *E* is past, in the future

In the first place, this strategy is subject to the same criticism as before: the initial occurrences of "future", "present", and "past" have been transformed into relative properties. So these sentences can be re-formulated as

> *E* is later than past times
> *E* is simultaneous with the present time
> *E* is earlier than future times

which do not entail the existence of the facts required by a real *A*-series. And in the second place, such second-order temporal attributions are just as problematic, from McTaggart's point of view, as the first-order ones. For they are compatible with one another only if we assume that the *past, present,* and *future* are disjoint regions of time (or of events). And that assumption is contrary to his requirement: that every event and time has the qualities of *past, present,* and *future.* This being so, we can derive from the first statement (supposing that "past" and "present" are coextensive)

> *E* is future, in the present

which conflicts with the second statement. Therefore the contradiction is not avoided by introducing second-order temporal attributions. This is because, from the fact that each of the first-order attributions must hold, it follows that each of the second-order attributions must hold. And they conflict just as blatantly as the first-order attributions.

The most common criticism of McTaggart's argument (e.g., Broad

1938; Prior 1967) is exactly the point just dealt with: to claim that consistency may be achieved by a reformulation in terms of higher-order temporal attributions. It is not appreciated that McTaggart himself considers and refutes this strategy. To repeat, he denies that his requirement that the world contain the facts

> E is past
> E is present
> E is future

is misstated when construed literally, in which case the facts are mutually inconsistent with one another; and therefore he denies that the required facts are accurate represented by, for example,

> E is past, in the future
> E is now, in the present
> E is future, in the past

For the operative occurrences of "past", "present", and "future" have been turned into relations. Therefore McTaggart denies that the initial contradiction is treated by introducing second-order attributions. Nevertheless he is quite happy to conduct the argument at the second level. For, from his first-order requirement, it follows that *every* second-order attribution must hold—and this is also a contradiction.

Thus McTaggart shows that a certain very tempting, 'moving *now*' conception of time is not actualized. But he does not succeed in proving that time is unreal, because the first part of his argument is not persuasive (Mellor 1981). In other words, we need not agree with him (premise 2) that it is essential to the reality of time that there be 'genuine change', in his sense. This claim is implausible and never really substantiated. If we are persuaded, as I think we should be, by the second part of his argument, we will conclude that there can be no 'real A-series' or 'genuine change'. Rather, change is always variation in one thing with respect to another, the totality of absolute facts about those functional relations remaining forever constant.

13

D. C. Williams,
"The Myth of Passage,"
from *The Journal of Philosophy*

D. C. Williams, the Harvard philosopher, was born in 1899. His best known works are The Ground of Induction *and* The Principles of Empirical Realism. *"The Myth of Passage" is his argument against the idea that time is a 'now' which moves.*

At every moment each of us finds himself the apparent center of the world, enjoying a little foreground of the here and now, while around him there looms, thing beyond thing, event beyond event, the plethora of a universe. Linking the furniture of the foreground are sets of relations which he supposes also to bind the things beyond and to bind the foreground with the rest. Noteworthy among them are those queerly obvious relations, peculiarly external to their terms, which compose the systems of space and time, modes of connection exhaustively specifiable in a scheme of four dimensions at right angles to one another. Within this manifold, for all that it is so firmly integrated, we are immediately struck by a disparity between the three-dimensional spread of space and the one dimension of time. The spatial dimensions are in a literal and precise sense perpendicular to one another, and the sub-manifold which they compose is isotropic, the same in all directions. The one dimension of time, on the other hand, although it has the same formal properties as each of the other three, is at least sensuously different from them as they are not from one another, and the total manifold is apparently not isotropic. Whereas an object can preserve the same shape while it is so shifted that its height becomes its breadth, we can not easily conceive how it could do so while being shifted so that its breadth becomes its duration.

The theory of the manifold, I think, is the one model on which we

From D. C. Williams, "The Myth of Passage," from *The Journal of Philosophy*, July, 1951. Reprinted with permission of *The Journal of Philosophy*.

can describe and explain the foreground of experience, or can intelligibly and credibly construct our account of the rest of the world, and this is so because in fact the universe is spread out in those dimensions. There may be Platonic entities which are foreign to both space and time; there may be Cartesian spirits which are foreign to space; but the homely realm of natural existence, the total of world history, is a spatio-temporal volume, of somewhat uncertain magnitude, chockablock with things and events. Logic, with its law of excluded middle and its tenseless operators, and natural science, with its secular world charts, concur inexorably with the vision of metaphysics and high religion that truth and fact are thus eternal.

I believe that the universe consists, without residue, of the spread of events in space-time, and that if we thus accept realistically the four-dimensional fabric of juxtaposed actualities we can dispense with all those dim non-factual categories which have so bedevilled our race: the potential, the subsistential, and the influential, the noumenal, the numinous, and the non-natural. But I am arguing here, not that there is nothing outside the natural world of events, but that the theory of the manifold is anyhow literally true and adequate to that world.

The chink in the armor of the theory is supposed to be on the side of time. Sir James Jeans regretted that time is mathematically attached to space by so "weird" a function as the square root of minus one,[1] and the very word "weird," being cognate with "*werden*," *to become,* is a monument to the uncanniness of our fourth dimension. Perhaps there exists an intellectualistic solipsist who grants the propriety of conceiving a temporal stretch of events, to wit, his own whole inner biography, while denying that the spatial scheme is a literal truth about anything. Most of the disparagers of the manifold, however, are of opposite bias. Often ready enough to take literally the spatial extension of the world, they dispute the codicil which rounds it out in the dimension of time. They do not intend this as a disparagement of time. On the contrary, they are what Wyndham Lewis (in *Time and Western Man*) called "time snobs." They plume themselves that by refusing to time the dimensional status they alone are "taking time seriously."

The partisans of time often take it with such Spartan seriousness that they deny existence to virtually all of it—to all of it, in short, but the infinitesimal pulse of the present. If we may interpret strictly some characteristic statements of Schopenhauer and the late Professor

1. *The Mysterious Universe,* New York, 1930, p. 118.

Mead,[2] for example, they would have it that the totality of being consists of the set of events which are simultaneous with the utterance "*now*," and most of the schools which are loosely called "romantic" would seem committed at heart to the same conclusion. This, of course, is incredible in point of psychology, for nobody can help believing at any moment that it has predecessors and successors. Also, it is incredible in point of logic, not just because induction tells us the contrary, but deductively, because a concrete object can no more exist with zero duration than with zero breadth and length.

One motive for the paradoxical philosophy of the present is the general romantic polemic against logic and the competence of concepts. The theory of the manifold is the logical account of events *par excellence*, the teeth by which the jaws of the intellect grip the flesh of occurrence. The Bergsonian, who thinks that concepts can not convey the reality of time because they are "static," and the Marxist who thinks that process defies the cadres of two-valued logic, have thus an incentive for denying, in effect, all of the temporal universe except the present flash and urge. To counter their attack, it is a nice and tempting question whether and how concepts are "static," and whether and how, in any case, a true concept must be similar to its object. But we can not here undertake the whole defense of the intellect against its most radical critics. We shall rather notice those two main motives for trimming down the time system which affect to utilize conceptual analysis and do not outright condemn it. One of them is an extreme sharpening of the positivistic argument from the egocentric predicament. For if it is impossible for my concepts to transcend experience in general, it may well be impossible for them to transcend the momentary experience in which they are entertained. Conversely, however, anybody who rejects the arguments for instantaneous solipsism, as most people do, must reject this argument for diminishing the manifold. The remaining motive is the finding of an intolerable anomaly in the statement that what was but has ceased, or what will be but has not begun, nevertheless *is*. Although equally cogent against the past and the future, this sort of reflection has generally been used, as by Aristotle, by certain neo-scholastics, by C. D. Broad, and by Professors Weiss and Hartshorne, to deny the reality only of the future, while preserving the past. I have

2. *Die Welt als Wille und Vorstellung*, Bk. 4, Sect. 54; *The Philosophy of the Present*, Chicago, 1932.

contended elsewhere[3] that the argument is in any case invalid, because
it mistakes for an ontological absolute the semantical accident that the
significance of Indo-European verbs is generally complicated by *tenses*.
Thus when I replace the colloquial "There will be a sea fight tomorrow"
with the logically proper "There is a sea fight tomorrow," I seem to
be making, not the innocuous assertion that there is a sea fight and it
is located in the world manifold one day later than the utterance, but
the contradiction that it is both on the same day with the utterance
and on the latter day. Strictly, of course, the statement today that there
is a sea fight tomorrow no more means that tomorrow's sea fight is
today than the statement, in New York, that there are pyramids in
Egypt, means that the pyramids are in New York.

Let us assume now provisionally that the theory of the manifold is
at least true as far as it goes. The temporalist must shorten his lines,
then, and insist that, even so, it is not adequate: the time axis is not
the whole story, is not "real time" not "the genuine creative flux." If
he means by this that the theory of temporal extension, along with the
spatial models provided by calendars, kymographs, and statistical time
charts, is in the last analysis fictitious, corresponding to nothing in the
facts, he is reverting, under a thin cloak of dissimulation, to the mere
rejection which we have agreed to leave aside. If he means, at the other
extreme, no more than that the theory and the models themselves are
not identical, either numerically or qualitatively, with the actual temporal succession which they represent, he is uttering a triviality which is
true of every theory or representation. If he means that the temporal
spread, though real and formally similar to a spatial spread, is qualitatively or intuitively very different from it, or lies in a palpably and
absolutely unique direction, he says something plausible and important
but not at all incompatible with the philosophy of the manifold. He is
most likely to mean, however, another proposition which is never more
than vaguely expressed: that over and above the sheer spread of events,
with their several qualities, along the time axis, which is analogous
enough to the spread of space, there is something extra, something
active and dynamic, which is often and perhaps best describe as "passage." This something extra I think is a myth: not one of those myths

---

3. "The Sea Fight Tomorrow," in *Structure, Method, and Meaning: Essays in
Honor of Henry M. Sheffer*, New York, 1951. The argument there is mainly
that the world of natural events anyhow embraces no less than the eternal
manifold; my argument below is mainly that it involves no more.

which foreshadow a difficult truth in a metaphorical way, but one which is fundamentally false, deceiving us about the facts, and blocking our understanding of them.

The literature of "passage" is immense, but it is naturally not very exact and lucid, and we can not be sure of distinguishing in it between mere harmless metaphorical phenomenology and the special metaphysical declaration which I criticize. But "passage," it would seem, is a character supposed to inhabit and glorify the present, "the passing present,"[4] "the moving present,"[5] the "travelling now."[6] It is "the passage of time as actual . . . given now with the jerky or whooshy quality of transience."[7] It is James's "passing moment."[8] It is what Broad calls "the transitory aspect" of time, in contrast with the "extensive."[9] It is Bergson's living felt duration. It is Heidegger's *Zeitlichkeit*. It is Tillich's "moment that is creation and fate."[10] It is "the act of becoming," the mode of potency which Mr. Hugh King finds properly appreciated only by Aristotle and Whitehead.[11] It is Eddington's "ongoing" and "the formality of taking place"[12] and Dennes's "surge of process."[13] It is the dynamic essence which Professor Ushenko believes that Einstein omits from the world.[14] It is the mainspring of McTaggart's "*A*-series"

4. William Dennes, "Time as Datum and as Construction," in *The Problem of Time*, Berkeley, 1935, p. 103.

5. Isabel Stearns, "Time and the Timeless," *Review of Metaphysics*, Vol. 4 (1950), p. 198.

6. George Santayana, *Realms of Being*, New York, 1942, p. 258.

7. Clarence Lewis, *An Analysis of Knowledge and Valuation*, La Salle, 1946, p. 19. This is pretty surely phenomenology, not metaphysics, but it is too good to omit.

8. *A Pluralistic Universe*, New York, 1928, p. 254.

9. *Examination of McTaggart's Philosophy*, Cambridge, 1938, Vol. II, Pt. I, p. 271.

10. Paul Tillich, *The Interpretation of History*, New York, 1936, p. 129.

11. Hugh R. King, "Aristotle and the Paradoxes of Zeno," this JOURNAL, Vol. XLVI (1949), pp. 657–670. This is an exceptionally ingenious, serious, and explicit statement of the philosophy which I am opposing.

12. *Space, Time, and Gravitation*, 1920, p. 51; *The Nature of the Physical World*, 1928, p. 68.

13. "Time as Datum and as Construction," pp. 91, 93.

14. A. P. Ushenko, *Power and Events*, Princeton, 1949, p. 146.

which puts movement in time,[15] and it is Broad's pure becoming.[16] Withal it is the flow and go of very existence, nearer to us than breathing, closer than hands and feet.

So far as one can interpret these expressions into a theory, they have the same purport as all the immemorial turns of speech by which we describe time as *moving*, with respect to the present or with respect to our minds. Time flows or flies or marches, years roll, hours pass. More explicitly we may speak as if the perceiving mind were stationary while time flows by like a river, with the flotsam of events upon it; or as if presentness were a fixed pointer under which the tape of happenings slides; or as if the time sequence were a moving-picture film, unwinding from the dark reel of the future, projected briefly on the screen of the present, and rewound into the dark can of the past. Sometimes, again, we speak as if the time sequence were a stationary plain or ocean on which we voyage, or a variegated river gorge down which we drift; or, in Broad's analogy, as if it were a row of housefronts along which the spotlight of the present plays. "The essence of nowness," Santayana says, "runs like fire along the fuse of time."[17] Augustine pictures the present passing into the past, where the modern pictures the present as invading the future,[18] but these do not conflict, for Augustine means that the *events* which were present become past, while the modern means that *presentness* encroaches on what was previously the future. Sometimes the surge of presentness is conceived as a mere moving illumination by consciousness, sometimes as a sort of vivification and heightening, like an ocean wave heaving along beneath a stagnant expanse of floating seaweed, sometimes as no less than the boon of existence itself, reifying minute by minute a limbo of unthings.

The doctrine of the moving present has some startling applications, notably in the idea of a time machine. The theory of the four-dimensional manifold seemed already an invitation to the notion of time travel, and the additional idea that we move with respect to time confirms it. For if I normally voyage through time in a single direction

---

15. *The Nature of Existence*, Vol. II, Book v, Chap. 33.

16. *Scientific Thought*, 1923, p. 67; *Examination of McTaggart*, p. 277.

17. *Realms of Being*, p. 491.

18. Augustine, *Confessions*, Book XI, Chap. 14; cf. E. B. McGilvary, "Time and the Experience of Time," in *An Anthology of Recent Philosophy*, ed. Robinson, New York, 1929.

at a fixed rate, I can hope to make a machine which will enable me to voyage slower or faster or backward.

Now, the most remarkable feature of all this is that while the modes of speech and thought which enshrine the idea of passage are universal and perhaps ineradicable, the instant one thinks about them one feels uneasy, and the most laborious effort can not construct an intelligible theory which admits the literal truth of any of them. McTaggart was driven to deny the reality of time because he believed that while time must combine the dimensional spread with the fact of passage, the *B*-series with the *A*-series, every attempt to reconcile the two ended in absurdity. Broad can only cling in the hope that a better reconciliation may yet be found. My present thesis would resolve the antinomy by rejecting the extra idea of passage as spurious altogether.

The obvious and notorious fault of the idea, as we have now localized it, is this. Motion is already defined and explained in the dimensional manifold as consisting of the presence of the same individual in different places at different times. It consists of bends or quirks in the world lines, or the space-time worm, which is the four-dimensioned totality of the individual's existence. This is motion in space, if you like; but we can readily define a corresponding "motion in time." It comes out as nothing more dramatic than an exact equivalent: "motion in time" consists of being at different times in different places. True motion then is motion at once in time and space. Nothing can "move" in time alone any more than in space alone, and time itself can not "move" any more than space itself. "Does this road go anywhere?" asks the city tourist. "No, it stays right along here," replies the countryman. Time "flows" only in the sense in which a line flows or a landscape "recedes into the west." That is, it is an ordered extension. And each of us proceeds through time only as a fence proceeds across a farm: that is, parts of our being, and the fence's, occupy successive instants and points, respectively. There is passage, but it is nothing extra. It is the mere happening of things, their strung-along-ness in the manifold. The term "the present" is the conventional way of designating the cross-section of events which are simultaneous with the uttering of the phrase, and "the present moves" only in that when similar words occur at successively different moments, they denote, by a twist of language, different cross-sections of the manifold. Time travel, then, is analyzable either as the banality that at each different moment we occupy a different moment from the one we occupied before, or the contradiction that at each different moment we occupy a different moment from the one which we are then occupying—that five minutes from now, for example, I may be a hundred years from now.[19]

The tragedy then of the extra idea of passage or absolute becoming, as a philosophical principle, is that it incomprehensibly doubles its world by re-introducing terms like "moving" and "becoming" in a sense which both requires and forbids interpretation in the preceding ways. For as soon as we say that time or the present or we move in the odd extra way which the doctrine of passage requires, we have no recourse but to suppose that this movement in turn takes time of a special sort: $time_1$ move at a certain rate in $time_2$, perhaps one $second_1$ per one $second_2$, perhaps slower, perhaps faster. Or, conversely, the moving present slides over so many seconds of $time_1$ in so many seconds of $time_2$. The history of the new moving present, in $time_2$, then composes a new and higher time dimension again, which cries to be vitalized by a new level of passage, and so on forever.

We hardly needed to point out the unhappy regress to which the idea to time's motion commits us, for any candid philosopher, as soon as he looks hard at the idea, must *see* that it is preposterous. "Taking place" is not a formality to which an event incidentally submits—it is the event's very being. World history consists of actual concrete happenings in a temporal sequence; it is not necessary or possible that happening should happen to them all over again. The system of the manifold is thus "complete" in something like the technical logical sense, and any attempted addition to it is bound to be either contradictory or supererogatory.

Bergson, Broad, and some of the followers of Whitehead[20] have tried to soften the paradoxes of passage by supposing that the present does not move across the total time level, but that it is the very fountain where the river of time gushes out of nothingness (or out of the power of God). The past, then, having swum into being and floated away, is

19. "He may even now—if I may use the phrase—be wandering on some plesiosaurus haunted oolitic coral reef, or beside the lonely saline seas of the Trinssic Age"—H. G. Wells, *The Time Machine*, epilogue. This book, perhaps the best yarn ever written, contains such early and excellent accounts of the theory of the manifold that it has been quoted and requoted by scientific writers.

20. Bergson's theory of the snowball of time may be thus understood: the past abides in the center while ever new presents accrete around it. For Broad, see *Scientific Thought*, p. 66, and on Whitehead see King, *loc. cit.*, esp. p. 663.

eternally real, but the future has no existence at all. This may be a more appealing figure but logically it involves the same anomalies of meta-happening and meta-time which we observed in the other version.

What, then, we must ask, were the motives which drove men to the staggering philosophy of passage? One of them, I believe, we can dispose of at once. It is the innocent vertigo which inevitably besets a creature whose thinking is strung out in time, as soon as he tries to think of the time dimension itself. He finds it easiest to conceive and understand purely geometrical structures. Motion is more difficult, and generally remains vague, while time *per se* is very difficult indeed, but being now identified as the principle which imports motion into space, it is put down as a kind of quintessential motion itself. The process is helped by the fact that the mere further-along-ness of successive segments, either of a spatial or of a temporal stretch, can quite logically be conceived as a degenerate sort of change, as when we speak of the flow of a line or say that the scenery changes along the Union Pacific.

A rather more serious excuse for the idea of passage is that it is supposed necessary and sufficient for adding to the temporal dimension that intrinsic *sense*, from earlier to later, in which it is supposed to differ radically from any dimension of space.[21] A meridian of longitude has only a direction, but a river has a "sense," and time is in this like the river. It is, as the saying goes, irreversible and irrevocable. It has a "directed tension."[22] The mere dimension of time, on the other hand, would seem to be symmetrical. The principle of absolute passage is bidden to rectify this symmetry with what Eddington called "time's arrow."

It might be replied that science does not supply an arrow for time because it has no need of it. But I think it plain that time does have a sense, from early to late. I only think that it can be taken care of on much less draconian principles than absolute passage. There is nothing in the dimensional view of time to preclude its being generated by a uniquely asymmetrical relation, and experience suggests powerfully that it is so generated. But the fact is that every real series has a "sense" anyhow. This is provided, if by nothing else, than by the sheer numerical identity and diversity of terms. In the line of individual things or events, $a, b, c, \ldots z$, whether in space or in time, the "sense" from a to z is

21. See, for example, Broad, *Scientific Thought*, p. 57.
22. Tillich, *op. cit.*, p. 245.

ipso facto other than the "sense" from *z* to *a*. Only because there is a difference between the ordered couple *a; z* and the couple *a; z* can we define the difference between a symmetrical and an asymmetrical relation. Only because there are already two distinguishable "ways" on a street, determined by its individual ends, can we decide to permit traffic to move one way and prohibit it the other. But a sufficient difference of sense, finally, would appear to be constituted, if nothing else offered, by the inevitably asymmetrical distribution of properties along the temporal line (or any other). The time-extended organization of living and conscious beings, in particular, has a special and asymmetrical "run," fore and aft. Eddington suggested that the arrow could be provided for the cosmos by the principle of entropy.[23] As for the irrevocability of past time, it seems to be no more than the trivial fact that the particular events of 1902, let us say, can not also be the events of 1952. Very similar events might be so, however, and if very few of them are, this is the fault of the concrete nature of things and not of any grudge on the part of time.[24]

The final motive for the attempt to consummate the fourth dimension of the manifold with the special perfection of passage is the vaguest but the most substantial and incorrigible. It is simply that we *find* passage, that we are immediately and poignantly involved in the jerk and whoosh of process, the felt flow of one moment into the next. Here is the focus of being. Here is the shore whence the youngster watches the golden mornings swing toward him like serried bright breakers from the ocean of the future. Here is the flood on which the oldster wakes in the night in shudder at its swollen black torrent cascading him into the abyss.

It would be futile to try to deny these experiences, but their correct description is another matter. If they are in fact consistent with our theory, they are no evidence against it; and if they are entailed by it, they are evidence in its favor. Since the theory was originally constructed to take account of them, it would be odd if they were inconsistent with it or even irrelevant to it. I believe that in fact they are neither, and

---

23. *The Nature of the Physical World*, Chap. 3. See Russell too. *An Inquiry Into Meaning and Truth*, New York, 1942, p. 122.

24. Dennes argues thus, *loc. cit.* The root of the tragedy is that our wills and feelings are pointed forward in time. We *want* a plethoric and repetitive future, while we seldom bemoan the deficiencies of the past or the southeast.

that the theory of the manifold provides the true and literal description of what the enthusiastic metaphors of passage have deceptively garbled.

The principal reason why we are troubled to accommodate our experience of time to the intellectual theory of time goes very deep in the philosophy of philosophy. It is that we must here scrutinize the undoctored fact of perception, on the one hand, and must imagine our way into a conceptual scheme, and envisage the true intrinsic being of its objects, on the other hand, and then pronounce on the numerical identity of the first with the second. This is a very rare requirement. Even such apt ideas as those of space and of physical objects, as soon as we contemplate them realistically, begin to embarrass us, so that we slip into the assumption that the real objects of the conceptions, if they exist at all, exist on a different plane or in a different realm from the sensuous spread and lumpiness of experience. The ideas of time and of the mind, however, do not permit of such evasion. Those beings are given in their own right and person, filling the foreground. Here for once we must fit the fact directly into an intellectual form, without benefit of precedent or accustomed criteria. First off, then, comparing the calm conceptual scheme with the turbid event itself, we may be repelled by the former, not because it is not true to the latter, but because it *is* not the latter. When we see that this kind of diversity is inevitable to every concept and its object, and hence is irrelevant to the validity of any, we demur because the conceptual scheme is indifferently flat and third personal, like a map, while the experienced reality is centripetal and perspectival, piled up and palpitating where we are, gray and retiring elsewhere. But this, of course, affecting the spread of time no more than that of space, is only because every occasion on which we compare the world map with experience has itself a single specific location, confronting part of the world, remote from the rest. The perspectivity of the view is exactly predictable from the map. The deception with respect to time is worse than with respect to space because our memories and desires run time-wise and not space-wise. The jerk and whoosh of this moment, which are simply the real occurrence of one particular batch of events, are no different from the whoosh and being of any other patch of events up and down the eternal time-stretch. Remembering some of the latter, however, and anticipating more, and bearing in mind that while they happen they are all called "the present," we mistakenly hypostatize *the* Present as a single surge of bigness which rolls along the time-axis. There is in fact no more a single rolling Now than there is a single rolling Here along a spatial line—a standing line of soldiers, for example, though each of them has his vivid presentment of his own Here.

Let us hug to us as closely as we like that there is real succession, that rivers flow and winds blow, that things burn and burst, that men strive and guess and die. All this is the concrete stuff of the manifold, the reality of serial happening, one event after another, in exactly the time spread which we have been at pains to diagram. What does the theory allege except what we find, and what do we find that is not accepted and asserted by the theory? Suppose a pure intelligence, bred outside of time, instructed in the nature of the manifold and the design of the human space-time worm, with its mnemic organization and the strands of world history which flank it, and suppose him incarnated among us: what could he have expected the temporal experience to be like except just about what he actually discovers it to be? How, in brief, could processes which endure and succeed each other along the time line appear as anything other than enduring and successive processes?

The theory of the manifold leaves abundant room for the sensitive observer to record any describable difference he may find, in intrinsic quality, relational texture, or absolute direction, between the temporal dimension and the spatial ones. He is welcome to mark it so on the map. The very singleness of the time dimension, over against the amalgamated three dimensions of space, may be an idiosyncrasy with momentous effects; its *fourthness*, so to speak, so oddly and immensely multiplying the degrees of freedom embodied in the familiar spatial complex, was bound to seem momentous too. The theory of the manifold has generally conceded or emphasized that time is unique in these and other respects and I have been assuming that it was right to do so. In the working out of this essay, however, I have come a little uneasily in the surmise that the idea of an absolute or intrinsic difference of texture of orientation is superfluous. For, regardless of whether there is such an underlying absolute disparity, it is plain that things, persons, and events, as a matter of natural fact, are strung along with respect to the time axis in patterns notably different from those in which they are deployed in space. The very concept of "things" or "individual substances" derives from a peculiar kind of coherence and elongation of clumps of events in the time direction. Living bodies in particular have a special organized trend timewise, a *conatus scae conservandi*, which nothing has in spatial section. Characteristic themes of causation run in the same direction, and paralleling all these, and accounting for their importance and obviousness to us, is the pattern of mental events, the stream of consciousness, with its mnemic cumulation and that sad anxiety to *keep going* futureward which contrasts strangely with our comparative indifference to our spatial girth. An easy interpretation would be that the world content is uniquely organized in the time direction because the time direction itself is aboriginally unique. Modern philosophical wisdom, however, consists mostly of trying the cart before the horse, and I find myself more than half convinced by the oddly repellent hypothesis that the peculiarity of the time dimension is not thus primitive but is wholly a resultant of those differences in the mere *de facto* run and order of the world's filling. It is then conceivable, though doubtless physically impossible, that one four-dimensional area of the manifold be slewed around at right angles to the rest, so that the time order of that area, as composed by its interior lines of strain and structure, runs parallel with a spatial order in its environment. It is conceivable, indeed, that a single whole human life should lie thwartwise of the manifold, with its belly plump in time, its birth at the east and its death in the west, and its conscious stream perhaps running alongside somebody's garden path.[25] It is part of the same proposal, I think, that the "sense" of time be similarly composed. It is conceivable too then that a human life be twisted, not 90° but 180°, from the normal temporal grain of the world. F. Scott Fitzgerald tells the story of Benjamin Button who was born in the last stages of senility and got younger all his life till he died a dwindling embryo.[26] Fitzgerald imagined the reversal to be so imperfect that Benjamin's stream of consciousness ran, not backward with his body's gross development, but in the common clockwise manner. We might better conceive a reversal of every cell twitch and electron whirl, and hence suppose that he experienced his own life stages in the same order as we do ours, but that he observed everyone around him moving backward from the grave to the cradle. I may be overbold to unveil such speculations,

25. I should expect the impact of the environment on such a being to be as wildly queer and out of step with the way he is put together, that his mental life must be a dragged-out monstrous delirium. Professor George Burch has suggested to me that it might be the mystic's timeless illumination. Whether these diagnoses are different I shall not attempt to say.

26. "The Curious Case of Benjamin Button," reprinted in *Pause to Wonder*, ed. Fischer and Humphries, New York, 1944, pp. 16–41.

since to some they will seem a warning of the dangers of any dimensional view. The more reasonable reflection, however, is that if even this extravagant version, a completely isotropic theory of space-time, can be squared pretty well with the experience and idea of passage, there can be no serious doubt of the adequacy of the more moderate theory which neither asserts nor denies that the manifold is isotropic.

The same fact of the grain and configuration of events which, if it does not constitute, certainly accompanies and underlines the "senses" of space and time, has other virtues which help to naturalize experience in the manifold. I think that it accounts for the apparent *rate* of happening, for example; for the span of the specious present; and for the way in which the future is comparatively malleable to our present efforts and correspondingly dark to our present knowledge.

As the dimensional theory accommodates what is true in the motion of passage, that is, the occurrence of events, in contrast with a mythical rearing and charging of time itself, so it accounts for what is true in the notions of "flux," "becoming," "emergence," "creative advance," and the rest. Having learned the trick of mutual translation between theory and experience, we see where the utter misrepresentation lies in the accusation that the dimensional theory denies that time is "real," or that it substitutes a safe and static world, a block universe, a petrified *fait accompli*, a *totum simul*, for the actuality of risk and change. Taking time with the truest seriousness, on the contrary, it calmly diagnoses "novelty" or "becoming," for example, as the occurrence of an entity, or kind of entity, at one time in the world continuum which does not occur at any previous time. No other sort of novelty than this, I earnestly submit, is discoverable or conceivable—or desirable. In practice, the modern sciences of the manifold have depicted it as a veritable caldron of force and action. Although the theory entails that it is true at every time that events occur at other times, it emphatically does not entail that all events happen at the same time or at every time, or at no time. It does not assert, therefore, that future things "already" exist or exist "forever." Emphatically also it does not, as is frequently charged, "make time a dimension of space,"[27] any more than it makes space a dimension of time.

27. This is asserted, perhaps not with literal intent, by Charles Hartshorne, *Man's Vision of God*, p. 140, and Paul Tillich, *op. cit.*, pp. 132, 248. It is close kin to Bergson's allegation that the principles of the manifold "spatializes" time.

The theory of the manifold, which is thus neutral with respect to the amount of change and permanence in the world, is surprisingly neutral also toward many other topics often broached as though they could be crucial between it and the extra idea of passage. It is neutral, so far, toward whether space and time are absolute and substantival in the Democritean and Newtonian way, or relative and adjectival in Spencer's and Whitehead's way, or further relativistic in Einstein's way. The theory of space does not, as Bergson pretended, have any preference for discontinuity over continuity, and the philosophy of the manifold is quite prepared to accept any verdict on whether space or time or both are continuous or discrete, as it is also on whether they are finite or infinite. Instead of "denying history," it preserves it, and is equally hospitable to all philosophies of history except such as themselves deny history by disputing the objectivity and irrevocability of historical truth. It does not care whether events eternally recur, or run along forever on the dead level as Aristotle thought, or enact the ringing brief drama of the Christian episode, or strive into the Faustian boundless. It is similarly neutral toward theories of causation and of knowledge. The world manifold of occurrences, each eternally determi*nate* at its own place and date, may and may not be so determ*ined* in its texture that what occurs at one juncture has its sufficient reason at others. If it does evince such causal connections, these may be either efficient (as apparently they are) or final (as apparently they are not). The core of the causal nexus itself may be, so far as the manifold is concerned, either a real connection of Spinoza's sort, or Whitehead's, or the scholastics', or the mere regular succession admitted by Hume and Russell. It was as much a mistake for Spinoza to infer, if he did, that the eternal manifold and strict causation entail one another, as it is for Whitehead, the scholastics, and Professors Ushenko and Weiss to infer the opposite (as they seem to), that "real time" and "real causation" entail one another.[28] The theory is similarly noncommittal toward metaphysical accounts of individual substances, which it can allow to be compounds of form and matter or mere sheaves of properties.

The theory of the manifold makes a man at home in the world to the extent that it guarantees that intelligence is not affronted at its first step into reality. Beyond that, the cosmos is as it is. If there is moral

28. See, for example, Whitehead, *Process and Reality*, New York, p. 363; Paul Weiss, *Nature and Man*, New York, 1947.

responsibility, if the will is free, if there is reasonableness in regret and hope in decision, these must be ascertained by more particular observations and hypotheses than the doctrine of the manifold. It makes no difference to our theory whether we are locked in an ice-pack of fate, or whirled in a tornado of chance, or are firm-footed makers of destiny. It will accept benignly either the Christian Creator, or the organic and perfect Absolute, or Hume's sandpile of sensation, or the fluid melée of contextualism, or the structured world process of materialism.

The service which the theory performs with respect to all these problems is other than dictating solutions of them. It is the provision of a lucent frame or arena where they and their solutions can be laid out and clearheadedly appraised in view of their special classes of evidence. Once under this kind of observation, for example, the theories of change which describe becoming as a marriage of being and not-being, or an interpenetration of the present with the future and the past, become repulsive, not because they conflict especially with the philosophy of the manifold, but because they plainly contradict them-selves. When we see that the problem how Achilles can overtake the tortoise is essentially the same as the problem how two lines can intersect one another obliquely, we are likely to be content with the simple mathematical intelligibility of both. When we see that the "change" of a leaf's color from day to day is of the same denomination as its "change" from inch to inch of its surface, we are less likely to hope that mysterious formulas about the actualization of the potential and the perdurance of a substratum are of any use in accounting for either of them.

If there is some appearance of didactic self-righteous-ness in my effort here to save the pure theory of the manifold from being either displaced or amended by what I think is the disastrous myth of passage, this is because I believe that the theory of the manifold is the very paradigm of philosophic understanding. This is so with respect to its content, since it grasps with a strong but delicate logic the most crucial and richest facts. It is so also with respect to its method, which is that of clarifying the obscure and assimilating the apparently diverse. Most of the effect of the prophets of passage, on the other hand, is to melt back into the primitive magma of confusion and plurality the best and sharpest instruments which the mind has forged. Some of those who do this have a deliberate preference for the melting pot of mystery as an end in itself. The others hope eventually to cast from it, no doubt, a finer metal and to forge a sharper point. I suggest to them, however, that if a tithe of the genius and industry which they spend on that ill-omened enterprise were spent on the refinement and imaginative use of the instrument we have, whatever difficulties still attend it would soon be dissipated.

14

W.V.O. Quine,
"Time,"
from *Word and Object*

W.V.O. Quine, born in 1908, taught for many years at Harvard. He is the most distinguished and influential contemporary American analytic philosopher. His major work is Word and Object. *In this passage he argues from a logical point of view that time is a dimension like space.*

Our ordinary language shows a tiresome bias in its treatment of time. Relations of date are exalted grammatically as relations of position, weight, and color are not. This bias is of itself an inelegance, or breach of theoretical simplicity. Moreover, the form that it takes—that of requiring that every verb form show a tense—is peculiarly productive of needless complications, since it demands lip service to time even when time is farthest from our thoughts. Hence in fashioning canonical notations it is usual to drop tense distinctions.

We may conveniently hold to the grammatical present as a form, but treat it as temporally neutral. One does this in mathematics and other highly theoretical branches of science without deliberate convention. Thus from "Seven of them remained and seven is an odd number" one unhesitatingly infers "An odd number of them remained," despite the palpable fallacy of the analogous inference from "George married Mary and Mary is a widow." One feels the "is" after "seven" as timeless, unlike the "is" after "Mary," even apart from any artifice of canonical notation.

Where the artifice comes is in taking the present tense as timeless always, and dropping other tenses. This artifice frees us to omit temporal information or, when we please, handle it like spatial information. "I will not do it again" becomes "I do not do it after now," where "do" is taken tenselessly and the future force of "will" is translated into a phrase "after now," comparable to "west of here." "I telephoned him

From W. V. O. Quine, *Word and Object,* © 1960, M.I.T. Press.

but he was sleeping" becomes "I telephone him then but he is sleeping then," where "then" refers to some time implicit in the circumstances of the utterance.

This adjustment lays inferences such as the above ones about seven and George conveniently open to logical inspection. The valid one about seven becomes, with present tenses read timelessly, "Seven of them then remain and seven is an odd number; therefore an odd number of them then remain." In this form the inference no longer has an invalid analogue about George and Mary, but only a valid one: "George marries before now Mary and Mary is a widow now; therefore George marries before now (one who is) a widow now." (Whether to write "marries before now" as here, or "then marries" in parallel to the example about seven, is merely a question whether to suppose that the sentences came on the heels of some reference to a specific past occasion. I have supposed so in the one example and not in the other.)

Such rephrasing of tense distorts English, though scarcely in an unfamiliar way; for the treating of time on a par with space is no novelty to natural science. Of the perplexities that are thus lessened, instances outside the domain of logical deduction are not far to seek. One is the problem of Heraclitus. Once we put the temporal extent of the river on a par with the spatial event, we see no more difficulty in stepping into the same river at two times than at two places. Furthermore the river's change of substance, at a given place from time to time, comes to be seen as quite on a par with the river's difference in substance at a given time from place to place; sameness of river is controverted no more on the one count than on the other.

The problem of Heraclitus was already under control, without help of the alignment of time with space; but intuitively the alignment helps. Similarly for perplexities of personal identity: the space-time view helps one appreciate that there is no reason why my first and fifth decades should not, like my head and feet, count as parts of the same man, however dissimilar. There need be no unchanging kernel to constitute me the same man in both decades, any more than there need be some peculiarly Quinian textural quality common to the protoplasm of my head and feet; though both are possible.[1]

Physical objects, conceived thus four-dimensionally in space-time, are not to be distinguished from events or, in the concrete sense of

1. Cf. Goodman, *Structure of Appearance*, p. 94.

the term, processes.[2] Each comprises simply the content, however heterogeneous, of some portion of space-time, however disconnected and gerrymandered. What then distinguishes material substances from other physical objects is a detail: if an object is a substance, there are relatively few atoms that lie partly in it (temporally) and partly outside.

Zeno's paradoxes, if they can be made initially puzzling, become less so when time is looked upon as spacelike. Typical ones consist essentially in dividing a finite distance into infinitely many parts and arguing that infinite time must be consumed in traversing them all. Seeing time in the image of space helps us appreciate that infinitely many periods of time can just as well add up to a finite period as can a finite distance be divided into infinitely many component distances.

Discussion of Zeno's paradoxes, as of much else, is aided by graphing time against distance. Note then that such graphs are quite literally a treatment of time as spacelike.

Just as forward and backward are distinguishable only relative to an orientation, so, according to Einstein's relativity principle, space and time are distinguishable only relative to a velocity. This discovery leaves no reasonable alternative to treating time as spacelike. But the benefits surveyed above are independent of Einstein's principle.[3]

Tense, then, is to give way to such temporal qualifies as "now," "then," "before t," "after t," and to these only as needed. These qualifiers may be systematized along economical lines, as follows.

Each specific time or epoch, of say an hour's duration, may be

---

2. They are what Strawson (*Individuals*, pp. 56 f.) has dismissed as *process-things*, "not to be identified either with the processes which things undergo *or* with the things which undergo them. . . . I was concerned to investigate . . . the categories we actually possess; and the category of process-things is one we neither have nor need." He supports his distinctions with examples of usage. Given his concern with usage conservation, I expect he is in the right. But our present concern is with canonical deviations.

3. Einstein's discovery and Minkowski's interpretation of it provided an essential impetus, certainly, to spatiotemporal thinking, which came afterward to dominate philosophical constructions in Whitehead and others. But the idea of paraphrasing tensed sentences into terms of eternal relations of things to times was clear enough before Einstein. See e.g. Russell, *Principles of Mathematics* (1903), p. 471. For further discussion of tense elimination see my *Elementary Logic*, pp. 6 f., 111–15, 155 ff.; Goodman, *Structure of Appearance*, pp. 296 ff.; Reichenbach, *Elements of Symbolic Logic*, pp. 284–298; Taylor; Williams, "The Sea Fight Tomorrow."

taken as an hour-thick slice of the four-dimensional material world, exhaustive spatially and perpendicular to the time axis. (Whether something is an epoch in this sense will depend on point of view, according to relativity theory, but its existence as an object will not.) We are to think of t as an epoch of any desired duration and any desired position along the time axis.[4] Then, where x is a spatiotemporal object, we can construe "x at t" as naming the common part of x and t. Thus "at" is taken as tantamount to the juxtapositive notation illustrated in the singular term "red wine." Red wine is red at wine.

We easily extend "at" to classes. Where z is mankind, z at t may be explained as the class $\hat{y}(Ex)(y = (x$ at $t)$ and $x \,\varepsilon\, z)$ of appropriate man stages.

We can treat the indicator words "now" and "then" on a par with "I" and "you," as singular terms. Just as the temporary and shifting objects of reference of "I" and "you" are people, those of "now" and "then" are times or epochs. "I now" and "I then" mean "I at now," and "I at then"; the custom just happens to be to omit the "at" here, as in "red wine."[5]

"Before" can be construed as a relative term predicable of times. Such constructions as "x is eating y before t" and "x is eating y after t" then come through thus:

$$(\exists u)\ (u \text{ is before } t \text{ and } x \text{ at } u \text{ is eating } y),$$

$$(\exists u)\ (t \text{ is before } u \text{ and } x \text{ at } u \text{ is eating } y).$$

In this example I have used the progressive aspect "is eating," in preference to "eats," because what is concerned is the state and not the disposition; contrast "Tabby eats mice." Temporal qualifications

4. The question of an instant, or epoch of no duration, is best set aside now.

5. In *Individuals*, p. 216. Strawson argues against viewing "now" as a singular term. His argument is that "now" sets no temporal boundaries. One possible answer might be to defend vagueness; another would be to construe the temporal boundaries as those of the shortest utterance of sentential form containing the utterance of "now" in question. The latter answer is in our present spirit of artificial regimentation, and we must note that the Strawson passage has a different context. I even share, in a way, an ulterior doctrine that he is there engaged in supporting, for I think it is of a piece with my reflections on the primacy of unanalyzed occasion sentences in the theory of radical translation and of infant learning.

apply to the latter as well, for there may have been a time when Tabby had no taste for mice, and a time may come when she will lose it. Thus we may say "Tabby now eats mice," "Tabby at t eats mice," as well as "Tabby at t is eating mice," but in the one case we report a phase in her evolving pattern of behavior while in the other we report an incident in her behavior.

15

O. K. Bouwsma,
"The Mystery of Time (Or, The Man Who
Did Not Know What Time Is),"
from *Philosophical Essays*

O. K. Bouwsma was a friend and follower of Wittgenstein. He wrote in the Introduction to his Philosophical Essays, *in which "The Mystery of Time" was reprinted, having originally appeared in* The Journal of Philosophy, *"I have long hesitated to assume the risk of the incalculable harm these essays might do but now in view of the likewise incalculable good they might do, I have tossed a coin and it came down just as I thought it would. It stood on its edge. And I knocked it down."*

The occasion of this essay is the remark of a student, which he made after a company of us had tried to assure him that if he knew how to answer such questions as: What time is it? and when were you born? and are you going soon? and were you always lazy? etc., then he would also know what time is. He protested, however, that though he certainly did know all these things, he still did not know what time is. Accordingly I want to study two cases of men who do not know what time is. The first is to be one which is exceedingly simple and which I want to use in order to exhibit a clear case of not knowing what time is. The second is a case which I have found baffling, and which is authentic. I think that I have succeeded in discovering in this case just what it is that the man who does not know what time is, does not know. In a middle part of this essay I have reviewed a small part of the language of time in order to show how rich this is in ramifications, which then one may, according to one's disposition, play in, as children do in a large and empty house, or which then one may lose oneself in, as older people

also do. What, in certain aspects, makes this a playground is what also
makes it a labyrinth.

I

Once upon a space there was a man who laid linoleum, a fantastical
fellow, who did not believe in clocks. He would get up from the floor,
his measuring foot in hand, and stare at the clock, laying down his
measure in this direction and that, round about the clock. Sometimes
he would move his hand through the air in the neighborhood of the
clock as though he were trying to feel something, a current or stream.
"Nothing there," he would mutter as he returned to his linoleum on
the floor, patting the linoleum, pleased to rest his hand on something
tangible. He'd go on taking measurements and at intervals he would
caress his measuring stick and would talk to it. A few minutes later
he would look up at the clock, almost angrily. The clock went on
ticking. At times he'd clench his fist. Whole mornings he would pass
in this way, making love to his foot-rule and fighting the clock. He
would speak scornfully of everything pertaining to the clock, calling it
an imposter. "Time," he would say, "time, seconds, minutes, hours,
days, knights and their ladies. Bah!" He was grim. Then he'd look at
his ruler. "Tell me, tell me, how many inches in an hour?" And he'd
look at the clock and come down hard on the next nail in the linoleum.

There have, of course, been other strange encounters with clocks
and watches. In the inventory which the Lilliputians made of what they
found in the pockets of Gulliver is the following note: "Out of the
right fob hung a great silver chain, with a wonderful kind of engine at
the bottom. We directed him to draw out whatever was fastened to
that chain; which appeared to be a globe, half silver, and half some
transparent metal: for on the transparent side we saw certain strange
figures circularly drawn, and thought we could touch them, till we
found our fingers stopped by that lucid substance. He put this engine
to our ears, which made an incessant noise like that of a watermill,
and we conjecture it is either some unknown animal, or the god that
he worships; but we are more inclined to the latter opinion, because
he assures us (if we understood him right, for he expressed himself
very imperfectly) that he seldom does anything without consulting it:
he called it his oracle, and said it pointed out the time for every action
of his life." Later the Emperor "was amazed at the continual noise it
made, and the motion of the minute hand, which he could easily

discern; for their sight is much more acute than ours; and asked the opinions of his learned men about him, which were various and remote, as the reader may well imagine without my repeating; although indeed I could not very perfectly understand them." But my only point now is to point out that the man who laid linoleum is not the first to have been mystified by a watch or clock. Besides I'm not through telling about him.

Of course, this man was not simply curious. He was quite disturbed. It was no joke. All his life he had been familiar with clocks. They had had ever so many times together until this "antic disposition" took hold of him. And so it was on the day of which I was speaking. In the evening he visited his friend the clockmaker, seated in the midst of his clock-works, taking tictation and tightening short-hands. He entered the clock-shop, glanced hurriedly about with both ears, and sat down. Not much was said at first. This was a clock-shop and two hundred clocks stared down at him. Pendulumonium! At eight o'clock the whole clock-works began to move, bells rang out from tiny clock-steeples, roosters crowed on tiny perches, cuckoos clock-cooed from tiny balconies, and eight assorted insects flew past a waiting bird as she gobbled up the hours. On the face of one trick clock, the minute hand was extended from the face of the clock, its fingers outspread with the end of the thumb resting on the tip of what seemed to be a nose raised in the center. Fortunately, he did not see this. But he did see and hear too much. He could bear it no longer. Most absurd thing! "Ach," he cried, getting up from his chair, "Your clocks! Your clocks! What do they mean, your clocks?" and he gave a short kick in the direction of the case set in order with clocks before him. The clocks went on ticking, tick, tick, not heeding.

"Come," he said, with marvelous self-control, "I see your clocks. Now show me time, not ages, not aeons, but just one minute, and then I'll believe in your clocks." And he handed him his foot-rule. The clock-maker smiled, embarrassed, and glanced at his clocks. Plainly he felt responsible, but he returned the foot-rule. "I'm in earnest," his friend continued. "Today I fought your clock. I threw my hammer at it. And missed. Look!" And he got down on his hands and knees and measured the long side of the linoleum in the clock-maker's shop. "There," he said. "I measured the linoleum. Here's my foot-rule. You saw how I laid it down, laid it down, again and again, and counted to twelve. There are twelve feet on this side. You see the linoleum and you see the foot-rule. Now, then, as I have just shown you, so now you show me twelve minutes of time. Twelve feet of linoleum, twelve minutes of time! If, for instance, you got down on your knees with the clock in your hand and measured the linoleum, and counted thirty-six minutes of linoleum, then, I should understand how you were using the clock and what you were measuring. Or if you rolled your clock from one edge of the linoleum to the other, and you counted the rolls, that too would suit me. There might be circular foot-rules. But how do you manage to get down on your hands and knees or whatever you do, and so hold time down flat, and pull it straight so that you can get your measurement? Linoleum, five minutes flat."

He was in dead earnest. The clock-maker rubbed the bristles on his chin and tried not to be afraid. He looked about him and looked into the faces of his clocks. There was no help there. In his desperation he picked up a clock and was about to get down on his knees with the clock in his measuring hand, when another of his clocks rang off and a cuckoo stepped out and cocked its little head in his direction. The clock-maker, crouched as he was on one knee, looked up and burst out laughing. He set the clock back on the shelf. The layer of linoleum did not smile. He looked grimly at the cuckoo still cocking its head and the whole hickory-dickory-dock shebang. Dumb clocks! And he thought of that man who had made the largest machine in the world, which could do nothing, which also could not measure linoleum. He frowned and he got the notion that clocks were designed to make fun of laying linoleum, as though laying linoleum consisted of nothing but raising two hands and counting up to twelve. He was getting angry. "Listen," said the clock-maker, "the clock isn't used in that way and time isn't like an edge of the linoleum. There are other forms of measure. You can't pour linoleum into a cup nor squeeze it out of an eye-dropper. Ten drops of linoleum! Trying to explain to someone what a twelve-foot length of linoleum is like, by showing him how an eye-dropper works—well, that won't do any good. You don't talk about pounds, ounces, and pence in giving a man change for a kilo-cycle. There are all sorts of measures." He paused. Then he brightened. "Did you ever read this line in Black: 'Can wisdom be put in a silver-rod or love in a golden-bowl?' You just try it." He felt that he was doing pretty well. He was rising in his own estimation and began to feel airy. "And here is a line from such another: 'I have measured out my life in coffee-spoons.' " Then he switched. "Ah," he said. "I think I can explain clocks to you. Do you know the hour-glass and the sun dial?" But it was too late. His friend was not listening. Ever since the idea of pouring linoleum and the idea of the eye-dropper had been mentioned, he was pre-occupied. He was talking to himself, asking: What is time? and pausing, and then going on: What is water? He was trying to get the hang of his own question and when he thought of water he felt much better. If only he could meet time, as he could meet water, dipping his delighting fingers into it, then he might yet be a friend of clocks. He got up, musing, waved his hand to the clock-maker, and then, looking about him, he waved to the clock too. "Good," he said, "If I can manage to figure time in liters, I'll shake hands with all of you," and he made a gesture as though he were about to shake hands with a clock. They all ticked back at him, speeding up their tempo, and fidgeting with their hands. At least so it seemed to him. "Keep quiet," he shouted, and a chorus of clocks shouted back to him: "We keep time." He rushed out.

He walked. As he passed the town-hall, he looked up at the great wheel in the tower. It began striking the hour and boomed down at him. He winced at every stroke, covered his ears, and walked faster. He hurried on to his friend, an expert in water-meters. His friend saw him coming. "Good!" he said to himself. "We'll play a game of bridge," an excellent game, by the way, for people so much occupied with water. They greeted each other, but it was soon evident that there was to be no game of bridge. His visitor began at once: "Listen, listen," he cried. "Will you show me the workings of your water-meter?" He gave no explanation and his friend asked no question. "Well," he said, and he showed him a model meter incased in glass, all its secrets open, its outsides transparent. His visitor studied it carefully, saw where the water runs into the water-meter and out again, and he read the chasing figures, 1, 2, 3, 4, . . . , and he saw that all was wet as it should be. It ticked like a clock and this especially pleased him. "Ah," he said, "I'm on the right track. I see the water and I see the measure-chamber, gulping and spilling measures of water, as the water flows. And there are the numbers." Satisfaction warmed his face. "Wonderful! Wonderful! Forty gallons, so many cubic feet of water, have run through the chamber while I watched the numbers goose-trot through the opening. Water plain as linoleum!" He felt thoroughly relaxed. This is what he wanted to see. Now for the clock. "If only I had a transparent clock, then I should see time flow as now I saw the water in this meter flow. Time meter! Time flows. Time like a river. " 'Time, like an everflowing stream.' " The more he saw and the more he said, the more he felt assured.

The water-meter master watched his friend curiously, but understood neither his excitement nor his words. He realized that there was some concern about a clock and about time, and he glanced at the old grandfather pendu-slumbering in the corner. Nothing striking about that! He was glad in any case that his water-meter had been useful. "What's the matter?" he asked. "Has your clock stopped?" His friend looked at him troubled. "Clock stopped? Clock stopped? Was it going somewhere?" And he looked serious. "No, indeed. My foot-rule is clogged. Can't tell time on your water-meter." He smiled. Obviously he was not going to explain. The other shook his head, slipped a cover over the water-meter, and drew out his watch. He handed it over to his friend, who looked at it, turning it over carefully, then he glanced in the direction of the water-meter. Then he returned it without a word. A minute or two later he said: "I must be going." And he left.

So the friend of linoleum went home. He walked up the stairs, trying to make a noise like a clock, ticking, just to work up his sympathies, hoping in this way to understand the clock. When he got to his room, he walked straight to the clock and sat down on the bed to examine it. He turned it upside down, and turned it round and round. He shook it and he squeezed it. He noticed the knobs and keys on the backside of it. He was taking time seriously, almost anxiously. He looked for an opening to discover where time comes in and he found one at the top just under the bell, and he held his hand over it, but the clock went on ticking and he felt no time on his hand. He shook the clock again, hoping to catch a few seconds seeping through the seams from the inside, but he saw only a fine spray of dust sifting down on the table. He was, however, in no mood to take time for that or that for time—though he was at first startled to see it, was for a moment hopeful. "Ah!" he exclaimed. But then he knew. Finally he decided to take the clock apart, to get a look inside. "Clocks keep time. Well, we'll see." And so, poor fellow, he undid the clock. He was not a bit surprised. The insides of the clock were not even wet. There was not a sparkle of temporal dew even in the spring. He sighed. He gathered the debris of his clock in his hands and laid it on a chair. And he could not imagine how time, had there really been some, could have escaped him. He had been so careful.

But this was not the end of his perplexity. He went on trying to puzzle out how the clock could be measuring something. In his most meticulous fashion he would say: "Well, perhaps the clock does measure something. Per hand from six to twelve is six units of the push of the turn of the index-thumb against the key that winds the spring that unwinds against the cog that moves with the wheel that goes tick." And then he would write this down and snuggle up to it, it was so reasonable. "So one o'clock is so much of the push of the index-thumb against the key spent in the progress of the hand from some point in the circumference of the face to another point in the circumference of the same face, semi-ambi-dextrous to the center." And so too the hour-glass measures sand. On other days he would review what he had said before. "Is push time? But why, then, does a man, when he looks at his watch, run for a bus?" And he would hold his head. And then he would come up with another theory. "Time," he would say, "is invisible, an invisible water, and it flows through clocks and is gulped and spilled in upsy-downsy containers, ticken upwards and ticken downwards, as the invisible flows." And this is right too, for is not time invisible? What a comfort in comparison with time linoleum is, so simple—and visible, too! And water, too. But his speculation was not always so gentle. There were times when he suspected clock-makers of a grand conspiracy, obviously, for profit, imposing their machines upon all the people and teaching them a language to go with it, and calling their watches and clocks time-pieces. And the people had now been taken in for some generations, so that though people knew very well what the insides of a clock are like, one seldom heard of anyone doing as he had done, investigating a clock to find out whether there was anything in it. "Time is an illusion, a mere appearance," he would say, "engineered by people who are giving us the works." He thought it un-American too.

II

In the preceding section, I have, as I indicated earlier, presented the simple case of a man who does not know what time is. It is obvious enough that he approaches the clock with the foot-rule, expecting to discover something vaguely like linoleum, and that later he approaches it with the expectation that it, the clock, works like a water-meter, and that something vaguely like water runs through the clock. Knowing what time is would in this case be something like feeling the drift of time against the surface or against the edge of one's foot-rule or like feeling something soft as a baby's breath in the palm of one's hand as one shakes the clock over it. Time tipping the edge of a foot-rule, time on one's hands! The explanation is, I think, also obvious. This man knows to begin with that we measure linoleum, water, and time. How much linoleum? How much water? How much time? He also knows how to measure linoleum, and discovers how to measure water. He understands the use of the foot-rule and also the use of the water-meter. Now, then, he tries to understand the clock and the use of the clock in terms of the foot-rule and the water-meter and their use. It is this comparison which leads to the idea of something like linoleum, and something like water, and it is something like linoleum and something like water that he looks for in the neighborhood of the clock. Finding nothing, he is troubled and says that he does not know what time is.

I have noticed in this explanation that we measure linoleum, water, and time. This means that there is an extensive parallel in the language of these. We use numbers in respect to each, and, of course, there are units. In measuring we do some things that are similar. We read off numbers on the foot-rule, on the face of the clock, on the face of the water-meter, and, of course, we add, subtract, etc. Naturally it doesn't follow that one can answer such questions as: How many square feet of linoleum in one hour? or how much water in five minutes? If someone insisted that he did not know what an hour is because he could not say how many square feet of linoleum there are in an hour, then, in any case, you would see what it was that he did not know. And so with how much water in five minutes. Now what I have noticed here is a relatively uninteresting illustration of the way in which the language of time is intertwined with the language of quite different contexts. This intertwining of the language gives rise to something like the experience one may have when a familiar street in one neighborhood leads one without one's being aware into a neighborhood which is of a quite different character. From the village into the Italian section, from this busy square into a street of quiet houses and gardens. A different world! This may be entertaining. It may also be quite confusing and distressing. "I'm lost. Where am I?" So too with the language of time. Stepping, as it were, on one word and pressing it hard, loosing it from its present context, one may suddenly find oneself stepping along in a different context, scarcely knowing where one is, and then thoroughly confusing neighborhoods. In the city the view of one bit of street by which one came into the different neighborhood may mislead one into supposing he hasn't left the other neighborhood at all and so he may continue to try to find his way within this neighborhood as he well might in the other. This is dizzying. It may be like trying to find your way in a strange house, in the middle of the night, when you are not enough awake to realize you are not at home. So you blink and bump your head.

In what immediately follows I am going to present an heterogeneous grouping of fragments of the intertwining of the language of time with the language or languages of other things. There will be nothing systematic about this. There will be fragments, sentences or phrases, which will be like short streets connecting neighborhoods. There will be others in which I enter the adjacent neighborhood. The point of this will be to provide further illustration of that aspect of language which, when taken in a certain absentminded way, may give one's head a permanent whirl, or when taken in a certain well-lit mindedness, may give one a ride not unlike that one gets in a fun-house.

Notice the variety and color: Once upon a time. He's behind time but four steps ahead of Jones. A long time ago. There's been a mix-up in time. A time interval. Can you tell time? I wouldn't if I could. Time is mean. Mean-time. The clock is striking the hour. Savagery in the belfry. Time passed. So did the milk-man. The time is up. Night fell. No wonder, it's so dark! In a twinkling. In the shake of a lamb's tail. Shorter than the shake of a puppy's tail. The turn of the century. The turn of the screw. The turn of a phrase. It will soon be time. What was it before? A month of Sundays. Five minutes late. Which five minutes? Times overlap. It seams so. He lives in the past. He dies in the future. Time is money. What's money? Money is groceries. Time is groceries. Right now. Wrong hereafter. Relativity of time and morals. On the hour. Shove over about five minutes. The crowded years. Squeeze in a little time. Time slips away. Between the hours of four and six. Ah! There you are! A stitch in time. A gap in the years. Time heals all things. Remove the stitches. The fulness of time. The fulness of skirts. Time takes its toll. Toll pays for highways. "Time hath a wallet at her back." Nevermore. Nevertheless. Always the same. The day is shot. "Who killed cock-robin?" Not yet? No, yet. Pause for a second. The second is late. No duel without a second. No duo without a second. Take your time. Why does he get a larger piece? Down the corridors of time. Electric light and running water for the first fifty years. "Looking backwards." A time capsule. For chronic diseases. To counter-act the acids of modernity. Chrono-Belcher. A secure tomorrow. Yesterday teetering on the verge of 12 p.m. The future "in a retrospective arrangement." The past teaches us. The lessons of the past. "There, that will teach you to keep your hands out of the fire." The past teaching all hands present to mind future fires. The best time of the year. The dancing hours. Compline hour. The hour of decision. Tossed coin. All heads saying, "Tails." Time to eat. Chronic gluttony. Stuffing yourself, gobbler. Fat as a tick. Spare me a tidbit, just a tasty interval. Time consuming. Just a minute for desert. Time to turn over a new leaf. From the palm in my hand to the tree taking leaf in the spring.

And now I should like to nimble-numble at a few of these "*Once upon a time.*" Indeed! Twice below a certain space we met. In the subway. You said: "Have you the time?" And I said: "I have fifty years." You pouted. It was about time you, a pout about. "*He's behind time.*" What a pity! He can never catch up. Time cannot be overtaken. No overtaking. And he with his future always just a jiffy ahead of him, and he crying, "Halt! Halt!" "*A long time ago.*" A far country. Go back in time some place, and live in those other people's presents. Go to bed in 1953 and get up in time to buy corn from Joseph in Egypt. "Is your name Benjamin?" "No, no, sir. I did not steal your silver-cup. I have just dreamed in from the U.S.A." He would not understand. "You are under arrest. You are an anachromist. When do you come from? How did you get out of your century?" Meeting Caesar there too, asking Joseph for a few husks and a bucket of ashes to celebrate the Ides of Kisley. "What language do you speak?" "Dico the Roman language," he says in his very best Egyptian which is English. "It was once going to be the most up-to-date, by jabberers, before the future returned." Joseph goes on filling sacks as though time had been renewed and tomorrow was still to come. "There's been a mix-up in time." Tangles in tense. A tense wood. Was issing and will and soon wassing. Ex post factos ante factoring. Eternal recurrence in a jumble. What are your whenabouts? "*The clock is striking the hour.*" A careless hour, loitering on the way to ten o'clock. Came in with chiming morning face, like snail, unwillingly to gong. Ten strokes on his pendulum. Doing time.

There are good times, corking good times, uncorking good times. ("A barrel of fun," "a barrel of monkeys.") There are bad times, perfect times, dandy times, nice times, high old times, hard times, grand times, gay times, sad times, rotten times, times that are out of joint. There's railroad time, Greenwich time, five-o'clock shadow on the sun-dial, exact time. We have, we make, we spend, we gain, we buy, we save, we sell, we put in, we waste, we while away ("wit a whittle whittle stick"). We give, we fill, we take out, we steal, we shorten, we squeeze out, we spare, we stretch, we lengthen, we cut, we halve, we keep, we hoard, we get, we take, we seize, we use, we watch, we pick up, we lack, we find, we need, we divide, we lose, we fritter away, we kill, we beat, we invest. What? Time. Time is money. Put time in the bank. Invest weekly. He, taking up his gun, said: "I'm going out to kill time." She shuddered. Expert marksman. Catching time on the wing. But time flies. Time runs, time flows, time creeps ("Tomorrow and tomorrow and tomorrow . . . to the last syllable. . ."), time never stops, time marches on (clopperty, clopperty, clop). Time waits for no man always at the same speed, twenty-fours every so many minutes.

Time is pressing. With a mangle, alas! ("And at my back I always hear.") Time withers. (Wrong. "Time cannot wither nor custom stale.") Time corrupts. The prey of time, the ravages of time. The prisoners of time. ("Stone walls . . . nor iron bars . . ." but. . . .) One solid hour. Packed with thrills. Room for only one more bubble. Time is a blabber. Time will tell. A lost week-end Found in the middle of no-when, a tiny island surrounded by something like water. Free time. "The gift of another day." The space of one week. How to compute the area of one week with two unknowables. My time is yours. I have a second. Let's split. A split second. Sounds like a cocoa-nut. Nothing inside. A light-year. A dark hour. Signs of the times: Neon, jitters, robins, whirring, falling leaves, squirrels hiding nuts. Working against time. ("Give me a lever long enough and a fulcrum strong enough. . ." and I'll stop everything.) Time hangs heavy. Ripe bananas. Seize the moment. By the scruff of the nick of time. A time-piece. "Slab of eternity." A chip off the old block universe. Times without number. Times with number: Three times three. In a trice. In a tricecycle, over and over and over. He came in on time. Time is faster than a horse.

The time is coming. (Have you had word? Travel plans.). The time is near. ("I can hear the whistle blowing.") The time is here. (Bring out the red carpet.) The time is going. (All aboard!) The time is gone. (Disappearing in the shadows.) Yesterday is but a shadow of its former self. You'd scarcely know it was the same day. So changed. Been through something. Do you remember the time? Indeed. I'd recognize it anywhere. Is it long since? My last haircut. Travel by memory. Make it in no time at all. See the world from a howdah decked out by your own "imagination." A week's work. Six working days, everybody else sitting around. Five-day week. Seventy-some in a year. The first day of the week fell on a Sunday. That's why Sunday walks bowed. Many happy returns of the day. Recurrence to suit wishes. Same day last year this year. Eat the same cake, burn the same candle at the other end. In one year and out of the other. A full day, brimming over, spilled. My time is exhausted. Breathless. Can't stand the pace. A blue Monday, a white Christmas, a black day in our history, "the violet hour," "rosy-fingered dawn," a golden age, the faded past, a green morning, dark ages, the mauve decade, a gray day, a pretty soon, a handsome present, a bright future. Time in assorted colors. Velvet night. What color is Tuesday? Tuesday is fat and florid.

There's no time like the present. There are no apples like the apples of my eye. There's no space like here. " 'There's no place like home.'" Never postpone today. Postpone tomorrow. When? Tomorrow. But I may not have the time. That's just the time to postpone. A sentence of five years. Parse it. An exercise for logicians who live a thousand years. A compound proposition. For ever and a day. A baker's dozen. A billion years. The story of the rocks. "Once upon a glacial morning, before the sun rose; there was no sun. . . ." The crucible of time. Hot. Rag-time.

A man on his way lost time. His watch also lost time. A double loss! Time lost cannot be recovered. Like spilled milk. Sop it up. Ten minutes in a wet towel. "Little Sheba." Another man found time, but not the time the other man lost. Ten minutes as good as new, unused, second-hand. Second-hand time goes faster. He also found one dime and he found some things impossible. When he said that he had found some things impossible, people would not believe him. They said no one could find things impossible, that there are no impossible things. Time, they allowed, was possible, and when they asked him where he found time, he said time was up and wouldn't say another word. They figured that what is up must come down and so they waited. Time would find them out. They winced at the thought. Then the man who found time turned, elbowing his way through time, he was virtually in time, and said to the man who had lost time, "My time is yours," and so finder shared with loser, the ten minutes he had found, breaking it into two five-minute time-pieces. They tick-talked to one another until time ran out on them. Surprised, they both exclaimed, "Where has the time gone?" One answered, "South, for the winter," but the other answered: "No, time is up again. It was high time, you know. It went past like that." And he pretended that he was a bird. "Of course," said the other, "Time flies, have you never heard of the mosquito fleet? but will time return?" "No," said the other, "Time is no homing pigeon." And they were very sad, as they both stood, looking up, watching time flapping its wings in the avisphere.

These are "the fragments I have shared" in order to prepare myself for what I propose to do in the next section. These fragments, you may remember, I intended as further illustration of the intertwining of the language of time with the language or languages of other things. Obviously this intertwining may be exploited sportingly. My interest is in the fact that there is this intertwining. And my interest comes about this way. There are cases in which this intertwining has serious consequences, and in which it is difficult to see both what the intertwining in a particular case is, and that the serious consequences do arise from such intertwining. The serious consequence I have in mind is that a man should say, "I do not know what time is."

III

In this section I want to study a second case of the man who does not know what time is, this case a bona-fide one, a case with which I have wrestled. The case is expressed in the following long sentence: "The great mystery of Time, were there no other; the illimitable, silent, never-resting thing called Time, rolling, rushing on, swift, silent, like an all-embracing ocean-tide, on which we and all the universe swim like exhalations, like apparitions which are and then are not; this is forever very literally a miracle, a thing to strike us dumb, for we have no word to speak about it." "The great mystery of Time." I propose now to try to understand just what it is that is the mystery of time by way of certain other mysteries. Time is not the only mystery. There is the mystery of the sea and there is the mystery of the sky and stars. There are, of course, minor mysteries such as the mystery of caves and of deep places. And man too, it is said, is a mystery, the greatest mystery of all. For the present I wish to consider the mystery of the sea and that of the sky and stars. I am no doubt led to these in particular by the language in which the mystery of time is expressed. I turn first to the mystery of the sea.

Consider, then, some thoughtful man in the days of Columbus or some days before Columbus, as he looks out to the west from some high rock on the shore of the great ocean. He ponders that endless expanse of water, water, water, and more water, on and on, water, wave upon wave, never-ending. Is there another shore? A shoreless sea! His eyes find no relief. There is only water. He stomps with his foot on the rock, with a relish for terra firma. He turns his gaze upon the hills behind him, his eyes resting there, a refuge from the terrors of endlessness. "Are there hills like these there?" and he fixes his eyes steadily on the west. He imagines himself winged like a bird, in flight over the water, arriving at another shore, strange peoples, palm trees, rich meadows, a better land, who knows? "Giants, perhaps, with walrus mustaches. And clusters of grapes borne between two upon a staff." This is not the first time he has stood upon this rock and mused upon the lands that are far away, washed by the water at his feet. There has been talk, too, hushed and wonder-full, with friends, and even some levity. "Come, let's get into my little boat and we'll find the other shore." All for smile's sake. They knew and he knew that they would not venture out in any boat, big or little. Another shore? Might not their boat suddenly be carried by the strong waters, tumbling into the abyss, far away from mama and the kitchen stove? Leviathan is no house-cat. And even were the sea set in a saucer and all were well in quiet weather, might not some storm carry them all over the edge like spilled coffee to spatter the floor of the fundament? And so the sea teased them but they did not dare to attempt to pluck out the heart of its mystery. "Three wise men of Gotham!" One man did, of course. And, whether in unquiet desperation (furious at the infinite) or in quiet confidence, he set sail to set his eyes to rest upon that other who-knows-whether shore. On Columbus day! "There is another shore." And he looked back, following the line of the wake of his boat, and he thought of that rock on that other other shore.

Here, then, is a simple case of mystery. Is there another shore? Are there people there? (Is Mars inhabited? No, not yet. But there is a little clover growing out of the rocks.) There are questions, and wist-fulness, and a certain helplessness. "We'll never find out." (What's at the end of the rainbow?) And then some brave sailor dares to face the terrors, and returns with a few gay feathers and an olive leaf and a piece of wampum. And that is the end of the mystery.

This is, however, by no means all of the mystery of the sea. Imagine the sea under a pale moon with clouds. Mystery has its own sky. "I should never have made the sun, but I should have made the moon. The sun is too bright." The moon is for vague and sweet wonder, the sea and waves in soft light and shadow. And things under the sea! The lost Atlantis, the submerged cathedral, Davy Jones' locker, lost ships, mermaids, and pirates' gold. "So is this great and wide sea, wherein are things creeping, innumerable, both small and great beasts." The sea is deep and is dark and wide, and swarms with tiny lights, the lanterns of little fishes. Oh! for a walk in that dark deep on the ocean floor to see the strange creatures like living gold and silver, treasures of the sea. The whale's home. "As we have seen, God came upon him in the whale, and swallowed him down to the living gulfs of doom, and with swift slantings tore him along 'into the midst of the seas,' where the eddying depths sucked him ten fathoms down, and 'the weeds were wrapped about his head' and all the watery world of woe bowled over him." "Ten fathoms down . . . the watery world of woe." And there are storms at sea and darkness and fog and rain and a thousand ships tossing under the stars. The Ancient Mariner, The Flying Dutchman, the man without a country, Captain Carlson on the broken ship!

And now notice this echo of the sentence which I quoted above: "The great mystery of the Sea, where there no other: the illimitable, noisy, never-resting thing we call The Sea, rolling, rushing on, swift, noisy, an all-embracing ocean, on which we and all the earth swim like exhalations, like apparitions which are and then are not; this is, forever, literally a miracle; a thing to strike us dumb,—for we have no word to speak about it."

This, I think, will not do. But I should like to notice the divergence in the following elaboration, engaging still the language in which the original sentence goes on about time. Imagine this mediation: "The great mystery of the sea, were there no other," and he, the man on the rock, shakes his head slowly, sighs, and looks out upon the water. And he thinks of the stars. "The illimitable." He begins counting the waves for as far as he can see. He gives up, and looks out beyond the last wave he counted. "Noisy." The waves break upon the shore. "Listen! You hear the grating roar." "Never-resting thing we call the sea." "Sophocles long ago heard it on the Aegean." Not one drop of water in all this expanse is still, nor has ever been. "Endlessly rocking," as water falls rise, and water-rises fall, rocking water. "Rolling, rushing on, swift." His eyes catch one line of surf cresting one high wave and they follow its rising tumult, faster, faster, as it pursues the wave before it, swifter, swifter, till it dashes in foam upon the shore. He shouts "Stay! Stay!" and braces himself as with his eyes to halt the wild sea-horses, which rise and leap over his command. Testing his power! (King Canute went home pretty well soaked.) Tide waits and waves wait for no man, nor for any man's word or eye. "An all-embracing ocean." Three-fourths of the earth's surface is water and all the land is an island, floating on that all-encompassing sea. "On which" we and all that is on the earth and all the land, swim like flotsam and then some, like "mire and dirt" cast up by the troubled sea. Our land rests at anchor at the mercy of impervious, reckless water, sustained and shaken by an incontinent sea into whose depths, at the stir of one wild shudder, any windy day, it may fall down, down, down, whales scampering, itself to be dissolved, water to water. "This is forever very literally a miracle; a thing to strike us dumb, for we have no word to speak about it."

Now I should like to comment on this. I tried in the first place to represent the mystery of the sea, its overwhelming extent, its depths and darkness, the lore of history and story, the great beasts and shining little fishes, strange, unknown to man. The sea is full of mystery. My intention was to see whether I could, having had a glimpse of the mystery of the sea, write about that mystery in the words in which the sentence goes on about the mystery of time. Time is illimitable. Well, so is the sea of overwhelming extent. For the purposes of wonder it is large enough. "Silent?" No, not silent, but, then, perhaps noise has its own mystery. "Never-resting?" Indeed! The sea never rests. "Rolling, rushing, swift?" Yes, sometimes more spectacularly even than time. "An all-embracing ocean-tide?" You could say so. There's water all around us. And we and the universe exhalations, apparitions, swimming? No. And this in any case does not enter into the mystery of the sea. And now if we say that time like the sea is very big and very restless, "mighty like a whale," is time's mystery further like the mystery of the sea? The sentence takes no account of the light of the moon shining pale on time, no account of lost cities, lost ships, lore of history and story, submerged in time. Where are they now? At the bottom of the sea of time. It takes no account of "things creeping, innumerable," "of small and great beasts" hidden in the folds of time, time stretched out like a curtain. So far, then, I think we can say that comparing the mystery of time to the mystery of the sea helps on the whole chiefly to see that they are not similar, that one cannot understand the mystery of time in this way. Tentatively, let us say that both time and the sea are of marvelous extent and that both are reckless.

There is another mystery, the mystery of the sky and stars. Mystery is, of course, bound up with the unknown, with wonder. The mystery of the sea is articulate, but the mystery of sky and stars is relatively inarticulate. There are no such questions as: Is there another shore?

If I go straight up, will I bump my head? The question, in any case, hasn't the right tone. The sky is not strewn with lost ships, with pirates' gold, with a lost Atlantis. If on occasion a great church were suddenly whirled off the earth into space and we saw it disappearing in the direction of a far star, intact, not a brick out of place, and if men now and then were caught in a draught, waved good-bye from a cloud, and we saw them ride off for a spree among the stars, or if we now and then saw or thought we saw in faintest outline the inter-stellar caravans moving swiftly, red and green lights flashing, before and after landing, then we should have something more like the mystery of the sea. Even such a question as: Is Mars inhabited? hasn't the right atmosphere, is generally unconnected with the mystery of the sky and stars. Wonder in this case is vague wonder. The sky and stars are too far away, and they have not swallowed, and have not hidden in their depths, treasure and the burnished lore of history and story. So our wonder has little substance. We do not look steadfastly at some star and ask: And are they singing a hymn in that church, high notes bouncing off the points of neighboring stars? Will Jonathan, who flew away yesterday, sift down a spray of star-dust to show Stella he hasn't forgotten?

Still, there is wonder.

Consider the verses:

> Twinkle, twinkle, little star!
> How I wonder what you are!
> Up above the world so high
> Like a diamond in the sky.

Little stars are cherished shining in the wonder of children and children's wonder twinkles in the winkles of the star.

And now this from a man who did not write nursery rhymes: "Two things there are fill the mind with ever new and increasing admiration and awe, the oftener and more steadily we reflect on them: the starry heavens above and the moral law within." "The more steadily we reflect on them!" Did Kant on his walk one day look into the sky and at one bright star and say: "How I wonder what you are!" I suppose not. He looked into "The starry heavens above," and reflected. And what were his words? Did he say: "And behold the height of the stars, how high they are," or "When I consider thy heavens, the work of thy fingers, the moon and stars which thou hast ordained, what is man that thou art mindful of him?" Only, I take it, as we connect the stars with man, for instance, or with God, is there any richness in this mystery of the stars. St. Augustine's feeling, not only towards the heavens, but also towards the earth and sea is expressed in the following passages:

> And what is this? I asked the earth; and it answered, "I am not He." And whatsoever are therein made the same confession. I asked the sea and the deeps, and the creeping things that lived and they replied, "We are not thy God; seek higher than we." I asked the breezy air, and the universal air with its inhabitants answered, "Anaximenes was deceived, I am not God." I asked the heavens, sun, moon, and stars: "Neither," say they, "are we the God whom thou seekest." And I answered unto all those things which stand about the door of my flesh: "Ye have told me concerning my God that ye are not He; tell me something about Him." And with a loud voice they exclaimed, "He made us." My questioning was my observing of them; and their beauty was their reply.

The mystery of the stars is, I take it, something special, bathed in a religious light. There are descriptions of the heavens which are, however, quite different. Notice:

> This most excellent canopy, the air, look you; this brave o'erhanging firmament, this majestical roof fretted with golden fire why it appears no other thing to me than a foul and pestilent congregation of vapors.

And this:

> And that inverted bowl they call the sky
> Whereunder crawling cooped we live and die,
> Lift not your hands to It for help for it
> As impotently moves as you and I.

And this:

> A wise man
> Watching the stars pass across the sky,
> Remarked:
> In the upper air the fireflies move more slowly.
>   Amy Lowell

And in these the note of mystery is gone.

Apart from the religious overtones, however, some men have spoken of the mystery of the heavens in a different vein, almost literally of that mystery as a form of consternation. It comes, I think, to something like this. There are forms of picture-puzzle arrangements of black dots, for instance, on a white background, and the puzzler is invited to make out the picture of an old man brushing his shoes or of a bear with his head in a jar. If he cannot make it out, then, of course, the arrangement remains a mystery. Now, then, it is supposed that if the stars were arranged all over the blue himmels in a network of squares, then there would be no mystery. No one would then be fascinated by the stars. It might in that case be very monotonous and anyone who suggested that the stars should be redistributed as if scattered out of a pepper-pot might be acclaimed as a fine architect of the new heavens. Nevertheless this deep-seated hankering for a pattern has this consequence, that when men now do look into the star-lit skies they are overwhelmed and baffled as by a puzzle which exceeds their capacities. They do, of course, find what relief they can in the big and little dipper and the lady in a chair, the arrow and the little fox and so on. The aim however is one picture and it is the frustration involved here which is expressed in the idea of the mystery. The fascination remains, even after one has given up. A variant of this idea is that when one looks into the sky he is tempted straightway to count them, this, perhaps, being one way of arranging them. But he cannot. Hence, the following comment of Burke:

> The number is certainly the cause. The apparent disorder augments the grandeur, for the appearance of care is highly contrary to our idea of magnificence. Besides the stars lie in such apparent confusion as makes it impossible on ordinary occasions to reckon them. This gives them the advantage of a certain infinity.

So it is in various ways the overspreading "heaven-tree of stars," the everlasting chandelier in the ceiling of the world feeds our wonder.

And now reflect: "The great mystery of the Heavens, were there no other; the illimitable, silent, never-resting thing called the Heavens, rolling, rushing on, swift, silent, like an all-embracing ocean-tide on which we and all the universe swim like exhalations, like apparitions which are and then are not, this is forever very literally a miracle; a thing to strike us dumb, for we have no word to speak about it." Will this do?

I am trying to understand "the mystery of Time," meaning by this that I am trying to understand the man who speaks of such a mystery. The clues to understanding him may be such other mysteries as we are acquainted with, and, of course, what he goes on to say. It is in this way that I came to remind myself of the mysteries of sea and sky. The language in which the author of the sentence writes of the mystery certainly encourages this. We have already seen that this may throw some light upon the mystery. Time is "an all-embracing ocean-tide." Strange sea! If one could paddle with one's feet on the bank of time as one can paddle on the bank of the sea, then, surely, a part of time would be laid. As it is, we know that we do paddle with our feet in the stream of time, but we cannot feel it. No one stubs his toe there against the current. As for what I have noted of the mystery of the heavens and stars, there is even less that is useful in understanding "the mystery of time." There is nevertheless something else which may be described as the mystery of the heavens which may be useful and which is analogous to the idea of "the strange sea." I should like to return to this, but before I do so, I want to study more closely the "description" of time in the sentence about the mystery.

It is clear that no one has come to think of time as like the sea or like the sky, by having seen both time and the sea or sky, as one might have come to think of the sky as like the sea. For we do see both sea and sky. But, then, the question is as to how we do come to think of time as like the sea. The answer is, I take it, simple enough. The same types of sentence which serve us in discussing time or in remarks about (?) time, serve us also in describing the sea. It is this similarity which gives rise to the illusion that time is a sea.

The sentences that I want to notice are these:

> Time is illimitable.
> Time is silent.
> Time never rests.
> Time rolls, rushes on.
> Time is all-embracing.

I propose with respect to each of these sentences, first of all to explain briefly the use of the sentence, and then to go on to show how by assimilating the meaning of the sentence to somewhat parallel sentences about the sea, we come up with the stirring meta-mystery of time. My explanation of the use of these sentences will very likely be incomplete and may be incorrect. My intention, however, is to exhibit the character of that use, sufficiently to distinguish its use from the analogous sentences about the sea.

Time is illimitable. What does this mean? Briefly, this means that for such expressions as "The first hour," "the last hour," "the beginning of time," "the end of time," we have, save in certain contexts such as "the first hour of the day," "during the last hour," no use. This involves further that we also have no use for such sentences as "there is no first hour" and "there is no last hour." We may all recollect how St. Augustine wrestled with this.

The temptation, however, to try to understand this in a different way is exceedingly strong. "If the roving thought of anyone should wander through the images of by-gone times," then one may go on as follows. Beyond the present moment, there is a next, and a next and a next. Tomorrow is coming, and next week, and January and 1955. And then? Then another decade, another century. And the same thing will be the case if you look behind you over this present moment's shoulder. There is the moment before and so on and so on. There is yesterday and last week and September and 1953. And then? Then the forties, and 1900. And, of course, you can go on indefinitely, tearing the leaves off old calendars and making new ones. A shoreless sea! Isn't this how it is at sea when you stand high and look over the water, the sea before you, wave upon wave, dimming into the waters of tomorrow and the waters of yesterday? Is not every man a Flying Dutchman until the sea of time swallows him? There is no shore, no harbor. Time is illimitable.

Time is silent. This is a remarkable detail, and is emphasized by repetition in the sentence quoted at the beginning of this part of the essay. Consider. Time passes. Listen! You could hear a pin drop. "Like a thief in the night." (Time is a thief. It steals your youth away. "Gather ye rose-buds while ye may." "Time, you old gypsy man!") Time passes. There's not a squeak. Helmholtz could not have heard it. The highest fidelity cannot capture it. On cat's paws! Keep your ear to space, catch an echo as time bangs against the earth's axis, a faint throbbing. The sea is not silent. As the waves pound one another, they roar; but time hasn't even a tiny cry. It is also true, of course, that time is not blue, does not smell of fish and tastes neither salty nor of lemon-ade. Why, then is a special point made of this, that time is silent? Well, I take it that if one has already got an impression of time as like the sea, and one has in mind too its restlessness and its rolling, then the silence of such a sea intensifies the mystery. Imagine a sea, a turbulent sea, silent as a picture. Is not that a strange sea?

I need, perhaps, not remark that, apart from conversations between two men, neither of whom knows what time is, the sentence: "Time is silent," has no point. Neither is space sour.

Time never rests. It's never an hour for more than sixty minutes. That's how it is with now, too. Now always comes in at the same time, now, that is, and moves on. Guests may stay on, but four o'clock leaves on schedule. Tomorrow is coming, moves in, moves on, is gone, joins yesterday. It will never come by this way again. Time does not stand still. Nor does tomorrow come in, move out, and then rest. It keeps on going and every day it's farther away. There is no siesta, no rest, for time. Time marches on. Time waits for nobody. "Sun, stand thou still upon Gibeon; and thou moon, in the valley of Ajalon," was not spoken to Time. Time goes on, unwearied, what endurance! unwearying, without a break. Perpetual motion. Nothing can keep time back. Time is irresistible. Put your foot out on the last of Monday to halt Tuesday, and Tuesday runs, subtly rilling, over and through your foot. Get your foot wedged in between 4:59 and 5:01 and see it carried away, disappearing in the mists of last week. King Canute, throwing time back, buckets full of today hitting him full in the face as he tries to make tomorrow stand still. Too much pressure. Build a wall to keep the future out of this year. Make a lunge, telescoping time, jamming 4000 years into a 1000-year space. The engineering feat of the millenniums. The latest advances in Chronodamnamics. Working against time. Hopeless! Time rolls, rushes on, pushed on by the wave of the future. Against the sea you can build a wall. The sea has a bed. It does not rest but can rest. But time has no bed. Its waves are dashed against no shore. There is no shore. The past recedes every day another day. The future advances every day another day. This is, shall we say, an eternal fact, as old as calendars.

So, in this case, there never will be a Columbus who will set sail to explore and to discover the shore from which the future starts out. The future, no matter how far into tomorrow-orroworrow he will have advanced, will already be on its way. Time will not be caught napping.

Time is all-embracing. Everything is in time. When is four o'clock? In time. When did Socrates live? In time. When will you keep still? In time. How can time hold so much? Time is very big. The fishes are in the water. The ships are in the sea. The stars are in the sky. The birds are in the air. And all things, fishes and water, and birds and air, and stars and sky are in time. Time is immense. Without water fish cannot swim. Without air birds cannot fly. Without sky the stars cannot shine. The water carries the fish, the air carries the birds. The sky carries the stars. Water, air, and sky are buoyant. And water and air and sky are themselves buoyant, buoyed, in buoyantest time. Time is all embracing, all-embuoyant. And if, now, everything is in time, is time also in all things? Are not all things time-embracing? Mutual love! It is so. Time permeates all things. Lift the tiny scales of little fishes, time is there. Examine the entrails of birds, time is there. Tiresias knew. And in the hottest regions of the stars, time is there. In the drop of water, in the breath of air, in a patch of sky, time is there. Time permeates all things. And now we can also understand the words: "on which we and all the universe swim." For as fish swim in the water and birds swim in the air and the stars swim in the sky, so all swimming in the water and all swimming in the air and all swimming in the sky are swimming in time, the sea, air, sky, of time. Time is a sea, an air, a sky.

And now, I think that we are near to plucking out the heart of the mystery of time. But we are still to explain the rest of that part of the sentence which begins: "on which we and all the universe swim." It goes on: "like exhalations, like apparitions which are and then are not." Time's exhalation, apparitions of time! For this purpose I should like to quote the following sentences from Sir Isaac Newton, from which it will, I think, be clear that the mystery of time is twin to the mystery of the aether.

> But to proceed to the hypothesis: It is to be supposed therein, that there is an aetherial medium, much of the same constitution with air, but far rarer, subtler, and more strongly elastic. . . . But it is not to be supposed that this medium is one uniform matter, but composed partly of the main phlegmatic body of aether, partly of other various aetherial spirits, much after the manner that air is compounded of the phlegmatic body of air, intermixed with various vapours and exhalations. For the electric and magnetic effuvia, and the gravitating principle seem to argue such variety. Perhaps the whole frame of nature may be nothing but various contextures of some certain aetherial spirits or vapours, condensed as it were by precipitation, much after that manner that vapours are condensed into water, or exhalations into grosser substances, though not so easily condensable; and after condensation wrought into various forms, at first by the immediate hand of the creator, and ever since by the power of nature, which by virtue

of the command, increase and multiply, became a complete imitation of the copy set by the Protoplast. Thus, perhaps, may things be originated from aether.

So the aether too is an all-embracing sea or atmosphere, a medium like air, and to it are related "vapours and exhalations," as to time are related exhalations and apparitions. "Thus, perhaps, may all things be originated from aether," as on time, "we and all the universe swim, like exhalations, like apparitions." And now as there is a mystery of the aether so to there is a mystery of time. For the aether, though much like air, is "rarer, subtler and more strongly elastic," and whereas one can paddle in the water with one's feet, and one can hold out one's hand in a breeze, the aether goes right through one's foot and hand. One can catch neither touch nor sight of it. Besides it is silent. Also there are the mysteries of vapours and exhalations, of precipitation and condensation. And so the mystery of time is analogous. Is not time also "rarer, subtler" and perhaps "more strongly elastic" than air, and perhaps, even than aether? It is difficult, perhaps, to say whether the mystery of time in the sentence quoted is the same as the mystery of aether or whether it is the mystery of a medium even rarer and subtler than aether of which the aether itself is an exhalation, a gross form. On the latter assumption there is this order of media: water, air, aether, time. In any case, the following sentence is not an unreasonable parody: "The great mystery of Aether, were there no other; the illimitable, silent, never-resting thing called aether" (notwithstanding its phlegmatism), "rolling, rushing on, swift" (these words show the traces of the analogy with the sea, but wind also rushes), "silent, like an all-embracing ocean-tide, on which we and all the universe swim like exhalations, like apparitions which are and then are not; this is forever literally a miracle; a thing to strike us dumb, for we have no word to speak about it."

So we can understand this case of a man who does not know what time is, as like that of the man who does not know what aether is. He is like one who breathes deeply to take one big breath of time, hoping to get wind of it in this way. And he would like to know how out of so much time and a trowel to make a star.

There, now I think I know what it is that this man who does not know what time is, does not know. He also did not get the drift.

16

Maurice Merleau-Ponty, "Temporality," from *The Phenomenology of Perception*

Maurice Merleau-Ponty (1908–1961), French philosopher, was especially interested in "prereflective" consciousness, which he described in paradoxical ways. With Jean-Paul Sartre and Simone de Beauvoir, he edited a political journal, Les Temps Modernes. *In the following text from* The Phenomenology of Perception, *he describes time as phenomenon.*

We say that time passes or flows by. We speak of the course of time. The water that I see rolling by was made ready a few days ago in the mountains, with the melting of the glacier; it is now in front of me and makes its way towards the sea into which it will finally discharge itself. If time is similar to a river, it flows from the past towards the present and the future. The present is the consequence of the past, and the future of the present. But this often repeated metaphor is in reality extremely confused. For, *looking at the things themselves*, the melting of the snows and what results from this are not successive events, or rather the very notion of event has no place in the objective world. When I say that the day before yesterday the glacier produced the water which is passing at this moment, I am tacitly assuming the existence of a witness tied to a certain spot in the world, and I am comparing his successive views: he was there when the snows melted and followed the water down, or else, from the edge of the river and having waited two days, he sees the pieces of wood that he threw into the water at its source. The 'events' are shapes cut out by a finite observer from the spatio-temporal totality of the objective world. But on the other hand, if I consider the world itself, there is simply one indivisible and changeless being in it. Change presupposes a certain position which I take up and from which I see things in procession before me: there are no events without someone to whom they happen

From *Phenomenology of Perception*, by M. Merleau-Ponty, Routledge.

and whose finite perspective is the basis of their individuality. Time presupposes a view of time. It is, therefore, not like a river, not a flowing substance. The fact that the metaphor based on this comparison has persisted from the time of Heraclitus to our own day is explained by our surreptitiously putting into the river a witness of its course. We do this already when we say that the stream discharges *itself,* for this amounts to conceiving, where there is merely a thing entirely external to itself, an individuality or interior of the stream which manifests itself outside. Now, no sooner have I introduced an observer, whether he follows the river or whether he stands on the bank and observes its flow, than temporal relationships are reversed. In the latter case, the volume of water already carried by is not moving towards the future, but sinking into the past; what is to come is on the side of the source, for time does not come from the past. It is not the past that pushes the present, nor the present that pushes the future, into being; the future is not prepared behind the observer, it is a brooding presence moving to meet him, like a storm on the horizon. If the observer sits in a boat and is carried by the current, we may say that he is moving downstream towards his future, but the future lies in the new landscapes which await him at the estuary, and the course of time is no longer the stream itself: it is the landscape as it rolls by for the moving observer. Time is, therefore, not a real process, not an actual succession that I am content to record. It arises from *my* relation to things. Within things themselves, the future and the past are in a kind of eternal state of pre-existence and survival; the water which will flow by tomorrow *is* at this moment at its source, the water which has just passed *is* now a little further downstream in the valley. What is past or future for me is present in the world. It is often said that, within things themselves, the future is not yet, the past is no longer, while the present strictly speaking, is infinitesimal, so that time collapses. That is why Leibnitz was able to define the objective world as *mens momentanea,* and why Saint Augustine, in order to constitute time, required, besides the presence of the present, a presence of the past and of the future. But let us be clear about what they mean. If the objective world is incapable of sustaining time, it is not because it is in some way too narrow, and that we need to add to it a bit of past and a bit of future. Past and future exist only too unmistakably in the world, they exist in the present, and what being itself lacks in order to be of the temporal order, is the not-being of elsewhere, formerly and tomorrow. The objective world is too much of a plenum for there to be time. Past and future withdraw of their own accord from being and move over into subjectivity in search, not of some real support, but, on the contrary, of a possibility of not-being which accords with their nature. If we separate the objective world from the finite perspectives which open upon it, and posit it in itself, we find everywhere in it only so many instances of 'now'. These instances of 'now', moreover, not being present to anybody, have no temporal character and could not occur in sequence. The definition of time which is implicit in the comparisons undertaken by common sense, and which might be formulated as 'a succession of instances of *now*'[1] has not even the disadvantage of treating past and future as presents: it is inconsistent, since it destroys the very notion of 'now', and that of succession.

We should, then, gain nothing by transferring into ourselves the time that belongs to things, if we repeated 'in consciousness' the mistake of defining it as a succession of instances of now. Yet this is what psychologists do when they try to 'explain' consciousness of the past in terms of memories, and consciousness of the future in terms of the projection of these memories ahead of us. The refutation of 'physiological theories' of memory, in Bergson for example, is undertaken in the domain of causal explanation; it consists in showing that paths in the brain and other bodily expedients are not adequate causes of the phenomena of memory; that, for example, nothing can be found in the body to account for the order of disappearance of memories in cases of progressive aphasia. The discussion conducted on these lines certainly discredits the idea of a bodily storage of the past: the body is no longer a receptacle of engrams, but an organ of mimicry with the function of ensuring the intuitive realization of the 'inventions'[2] of consciousness. But these intentions cling on to memories preserved 'in the unconscious', and the presence of the past in consciousness remains a simple factual presence; it has passed unnoticed that our best reason for rejecting the physiological preservation of the past is equally a reason for rejecting its 'psychological preservation', and that reason is that no preservation, no physiological or psychic 'trace' of the past can make consciousness of the past understandable. This table bears traces of my past life, for I have carved my initials on it and spilt ink on it. But these traces in themselves do not refer to the past: they are present;

---

1. 'Nacheinander der Jetztpunkte,' Heidegger, *Sein und Zeit*, for example, p. 422.

2. Bergson, *Matière et Mémoire*, p. 137, note 1, p. 139.

and, in so far as I find in them signs of some 'previous' event, it is because I derive my sense of the past from elsewhere, because I carry this particular significance within myself. If my brain stores up traces of the bodily process which accompanied one of my perceptions, and if the appropriate nervous influx passes once more through these already fretted channels, my perception will reappear, but it will be a fresh perception, weakened and unreal perhaps, but in no case will this perception, which is present, be capable of pointing to a past event, unless I have some other view of my past which enables me to recognize it as memory, which runs counter to the hypothesis. If we now go on to substitute 'psychic traces' for physiological ones, and if our perceptions are preserved in an unconscious, the difficulty will be the same as before: a preserved perception is a perception, it continues to exist, it persists in the present, and it does not open behind us that dimension of escape and absence that we call the past. A preserved fragment of the lived-through past can be at the most no more than an occasion for thinking of the past, but it is not the past which is compelling recognition; recognition, when we try to derive it from any content whatever, always precedes itself. Reproduction presupposes re-cognition, and cannot be understood as such unless I have in the first place a sort of direct contact with the past in its own domain. Nor can one, *a fortiori*, construct the future out of contents of consciousness: no actual content can be taken, even equivocally, as evidence concerning the future, since the future has not even been in existence and cannot, like the past, set its mark upon us. The only conceivable way, therefore, of explaining the relation of future to present is by putting it on the same footing as that between present and past. When I consider the long procession of my past states, I see that my present is always passing, and I can anticipate this passage, treat my immediate past as a remote one, and my actual present as past: ahead of it is then a vacuum, and this is the future. Looking ahead would seem in reality to be retrospection, and the future a projection of the past. But even if, *per impossible*, I could construct consciousness of the past with transferred presents, they certainly could not open a future for me. Even if, in fact, we form an idea of the future with the help of what we have seen, the fact remains that, in order to pro-ject it ahead of us, we need in the first place a sense of the future. If prospection is retrospection, it is in any case an anticipatory retrospection, and how could one anticipate if one had no sense of the future? It is said that we guess 'by analogy' that this inimitable present will, like all the others, pass away. But for there to be an analogy between presents that have elapsed and the actual present, the latter must be given not only at present, it must already announce itself as what will soon be past, we must feel the pressure upon it of a future intent on dispossessing it; in short the course of time must be primarily not only the passing of present to past, but also that of the future to the present. If it can be said that all prospection is anticipatory retrospection, it can equally well be said that all retrospection is prospection in reverse: I know that I was in Corsica before the war, because I know that the war was on the horizon of my trip there. The past and the future cannot be mere concepts abstracted by us from our perceptions and recollections, mere denominations for the actual series of 'psychic facts'. Time is thought of by us before its parts, and temporal relations make possible the events in time. Correspondingly it is necessary for the subject not to be himself situated in it, in order to be able to be present in intention to the past as to the future. Let us no longer say that time is a 'datum of consciousness'; let us be more precise and say that consciousness unfolds or constitutes time. Through the ideal nature of time, it ceases to be imprisoned in the present.

But does it enjoy an opening on to a past and a future? It is no longer beset by the present and by 'contents', it travels freely from a past and a future which are not far removed from it, since it constitutes them as past and future, and since they are its immanent objects, to a present which is not near to it, since it is present only in virtue of the relations which consciousness establishes between past, present and future. But then has not a consciousness thus freed lost all notion of what future, past and even present can possibly be? Is not the time that it constitutes similar in every detail to the real time the impossibility of which we have demonstrated; is it not a series of instances of 'now', which are presented to nobody, since nobody is involved in them? Are we not always just as far away from understanding what the future, the past and the present, and the passage between them, can possibly be? Time as the immanent object of a consciousness is time brought down to one uniform level, in other words it is no longer time at all. There can be time only if it is not completely deployed, only provided that past, present and future do not all three have their being in the same sense. It is of the essence of time to be in process of self-production, and not to be; never, that is, to be completely constituted. Constituted time, the series of possible relations in terms of before and after, is not time itself, but the ultimate recording of time, the result of its *passage*, which objective thinking always presupposes yet never manages to fasten on to. It is spatial, since its moments co-exist spread out before thought;[3] it is a present, because consciousness is contemporary with all times. It is a setting distinct from me and unchanging, in which nothing either elapses or happens. There must be another true time, in which I learn the nature of flux and transience itself. It is indeed true that I should be incapable of perceiving any point in time without a before and an after, and that, in order to be aware of the relationship between the three terms, I must not be absorbed into any one of them: that time, in short, needs a synthesis. But it is equally true that this synthesis must always be undertaken afresh, and that any supposition that it can be anywhere brought to completion involves the negation of time. It is indeed the dream of philosophers to be able to conceive an 'eternity of life', lying beyond permanence and change, in which time's productivity is pre-eminently contained, and yet a thetic consciousness *of* time which stands above it and embraces it merely destroys the phenomenon of time. If we are in fact destined to make contact with a sort of eternity, it will be at the core of our experience of time, and not in some non-temporal subject whose function it is to conceive and posit it. The problem is how to make time explicit as it comes into being and makes itself evident, having the *notion* of time at all times underlying it, and being, not an object of our knowledge, but a dimension of our being.

It is in my 'field of presence' in the widest sense—this moment that I am spending working along with, behind it, the horizon of the day that has elapsed, and, in front of it, the evening and night—that I make contact with time, and learn to know its course. The remote past has also its temporal order, and its position in time in relation to my present,

---

3. In order to arrive at authentic time, it is neither necessary nor sufficient to condemn the spatialization of time as does Bergson. It is not necessary, since time is exclusive of space only if we consider space as objectified in advance, and ignore that primordial spatiality which we have tried to describe, and which is the abstract form of our presence in the world. It is not sufficient since, even when the systematic translation of time into spatial terms has been duly stigmatized, we may still fall very far short of an authentic intuition of time. This is what happened to Bergson. When he says that duration 'snowballs upon itself', and when he postulates memories in themselves accumulating in the unconscious, he makes time out of a preserved present, and evolution out of what is evolved.

but it has these in so far as it has been present itself, that it has been 'in its time' traversed by my life, and carried forward to this moment. When I call up a remote past, I reopen time, and carry myself back to a moment in which it still had before it a future horizon now closed, and a horizon of the immediate past which is today remote. Everything, therefore, causes me to revert to the field of presence as the primary experience in which time and its dimensions make their appearance unalloyed, with no intervening distance and with absolute self-evidence. It is here that we see a future sliding into the present and on into the past. Nor are these three dimensions given to us through discrete acts: I do not form a mental picture of my day, it weighs upon me with all its weight, it is still there, and though I may not recall any detail of it, I have the impending power to do so, I still 'have it in hand'.[4] In the same way, I do not think of the evening to come and its consequences, and yet it 'is there', like the back of a house of which I can see only the façade, or like the background beneath a figure. Our future is not made up exclusively of guesswork and daydreams. Ahead of what I can see and perceive, there is, it is true, nothing more actually visible, but my world is carried forward by lines of intentionality which trace out in advance at least the style of what is to come (although we always wait, perhaps to the day of our death, for the appearance of *something else*). The present itself, in the narrow sense, is not posited. The paper, my fountain-pen, are indeed there for me, but I do not explicitly perceive them. I do not so much perceive objects as reckon with an environment; I seek support in my tools, and am at my task rather than confronting it. Husserl uses the terms protentions and retentions for the intentionalities which anchor me to an environment. They do not run from a central *I*, but from my perceptual field itself, so to speak, which draws along in its wake its own horizon of retentions, and bites into the future with its protentions. I do not pass through a series of instances of now, the images of which I preserve and which, placed end to end, make a line. With the arrival of every moment, its predecessor undergoes a change: I still have it in hand and it is still there, but already it is sinking away below the level of presents; in order to retain it, I need to reach through a thin layer of time. It is still the preceding moment, and I have the power to recapture it as it was just now; I am not cut off from it, but it would not belong to the

4. 'Noch im Griff behalte', Husserl, *Vorlesungen zur Phänomenologie des inneren Zeitbewusstseins*, pp. 390 and ff.

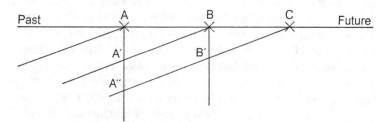

From Husserl (*Zeitbewusstsein*, p. 22). Horizontal line: series of 'present mo-ments'. Oblique lines: *Abschattungen* of the same 'present moments' seen from an ulterior 'present moment'. Vertical lines: Successive *Abschattungen* of one and the same 'present moment'.

past unless something had altered. It is beginning to be outlined against, or projected upon, my present, whereas it *was* my present a moment ago. When a third moment arrives, the second undergoes a new modi-fication; from being a retention it becomes the retention of a retention, and the layer of time between it and me thickens. One can, as Husserl does, represent this phenomenon diagrammatically. In order to make it complete, the symmetrical perspective of protentions would have to be added. Time is not a line, but a network of intentionalities.

It will doubtless be maintained that this description and this diagram do not bring us one step nearer to a solution. When we pass from A to B, and then on to C, A is projected or outlined as A′ and then as A″. For A′ to be recognized as a retention or *Abschattung* of A, and A″ of A′, and even for the transformation of A into A′ to be experienced as such, is there not needed an identifying synthesis linking A, A′, A″ and all other possible *Abschattungen*, and does this not amount to making A into an ideal unity as Kant requires? And yet we know that with this intellectual synthesis there will cease to be any time at all. A and all previous moments of time will indeed be identifiable by me, and I shall be in a way rescued from time which runs them into one another and blurs their identity. But at the same time I shall have lost all sense of before and after which is provided by this flux, and nothing will any longer serve to distinguish the temporal sequence from spatial multi-plicity. Husserl introduced the notion of retention, and held that I still have the immediate past in hand, precisely for the purpose of conveying that I do not posit the past, or construct it from an *Abschattung* really distinct from it and by means of an express act; but that I reach it in its recent, yet already elapsed, thisness. What is given to me is not in the first place A', A'', or A''', nor do I go back from these 'outlines' to their original A, as one goes back from the sign to its significance. What is given to me is A transparently visible through A', then the two through A'', and so on, as I see a pebble through the mass of water which moves over it. There are certainly identifying syntheses, but only in the express memory and voluntary recollection of the remote past, that is, in those modes derived from consciousness of the past. For example, I may be uncertain about the date of a memory: I have before me a certain scene, let us suppose, and I do not know to what point of time to assign it, the memory has lost its anchorage, and I may then arrive at an intellectual identification based on the causal order of events, for example, I had this suit made before the armistice, since no more English cloth has been available since then. But in this case it is not the past itself that I reach. On the contrary, for when I rediscover the concrete origin of the memory, it is because it falls naturally into a certain current of fear and hope running from Munich to the outbreak of war; it is, therefore, because I recapture time that is lost; because, from the moment in question to my present, the chain of retentions and the overlapping horizons coming one after the other ensure an unbroken continuity. The objective landmarks in relation to which I assign a place to my recollection in the mediatory identification, and the intellectual synthesis generally, have themselves a temporal significance only because gradually, step by step, the synthesis of apprehension links me to my whole actual past. There can, therefore, be no question of assimilating the latter to the former. The fact that the *Abschattungen* A' and A'' appear to me as *Abschattungen* of A, is not to be explained by the fact that they all participate in an ideal unity A, which is their common ground. It is because through them I obtain the point A itself, in its unchallengeable individuality, which is for ever established by its passage into the present, and because I see springing from it the *Abschattungen* A', A''... In Husserl's language, beneath the 'intentionality of the act', which is the thetic consciousness of an object, and which, in intellectual memory for example, converts 'this' into an idea, we must recognize an 'operative' intentionality (*fungierende Intentionalität*)[5] which makes the former possible, and which is what Heidegger terms transcendence. My present outruns itself in the direction of an immediate future and an immediate past and impinges upon them where they actually are,

5. Husserl, *Zeitbewusstsein*, p. 430. *Formale und transzendentale Logik*, p. 208. See Fink, *Das Problem der Phänomenologie Edmund Husserls*, p. 286.

namely in the past and in the future themselves. If the past were available to us only in the form of express recollections, we should be continually tempted to recall it in order to verify its existence, and thus resemble the patient mentioned by Scheler, who was constantly turning round in order to reassure himself that things were really there—whereas in fact we feel it behind us as an incontestable acquisition. In order to have a past or a future we do not have to bring together, by means of an intellectual act, a series of *Abschattungen*, for they possess a natural and primordial unity, and what is announced through them is the past or the future itself. Such is the paradox of what might be termed, with Husserl, the 'passive synthesis' of time[6]—and of a term which is clearly not a solution, but merely a pointer to the problem.

Light begins to be shed on the problem if we remember that our diagram represents an instantaneous cross-section of time. What there really is, is not a past, present and future, not discrete instants A, B and C, nor really distinct *Abschattungen* A′, A″, B′, nor finally a host of retentions on the one hand and protentions on the other. The upsurge of a fresh present does not *cause* a heaping up of the past and a tremor of the future; the fresh present *is* the passage of future to present, and of former present to past, and when time begins to move, it moves throughout its whole length. The 'instants' A, B and C are not successively *in being*, but *differentiate* themselves from each other, and corresponding A passes into A′ and thence into A″. In short, the system of retentions collects into itself at each instant what was, an instant earlier, the system of protentions. There is, then, not a multiplicity of linked phenomena, but one single phenomenon of lapse. Time is the one single movement appropriate to itself in all its parts, as a gesture includes all the muscular contractions necessary for its execution. When we pass from B to C, there is, as it were, a bursting, or a disintegration of B into B′, of A′ into A″, and C itself which, while it was on the way, announced its coming by a continuous emission of *Abschattungen*, has no sooner come into existence than it already begins to lose its substance. 'Time is the means offered to all that is destined to be, to come into existence in order that it may no longer be.'[7] It is nothing but a general flight out of itself, the one law governing its centrifugal movements, or again, as Heidegger says, an *ek-stase*. While B becomes C, it becomes also B′; and simultaneously A which, while

6. See, for example, *Formale und Transzendentale Logik*, pp. 256–7.
7. Claudel, *Art poétique*, p. 57.

becoming B, had also become A', lapses into A''. A, A' and A'' on the one hand, and B and B' on the other, are bound together, not by any identifying synthesis, which would fix them at a point in time, but by a transitional synthesis (*Übergangssynthesis*), in so far as they issue one from the other, and each of these projections is merely one aspect of the total bursting forth or dehiscence. Hence time, in our primordial experience of it, is not for us a system of objective positions, through which we pass, but a mobile setting which moves away from us, like the landscape seen through a railway carriage window. Yet we do not really believe that the landscape is moving; the gate-keeper at the level crossing is whisked by, but the hill over there scarcely moves at all, and in the same way, though the opening of my day is already receding, the beginning of my week is a fixed point; an objective time is taking shape on the horizon, and should therefore show up in my immediate past. How is this possible? How is it that the temporal *ek-stase* is not an absolute disintegration in which the individuality of the moments disappears? It is because the disintegration undoes what the passage from future to present had achieved: C is the culmination of a long concentration which has brought it to maturity; as it was being built up, it made its approach known by progressively fewer *Abschattungen*, for it was approaching *bodily*. When it came into the present it brought with it its genesis, of which it was merely the ultimate expression, and the impending presence of what was to come after it. So that, when the latter comes into being and pushes C into the past, C is not suddenly bereft of its being; its disintegration is for ever the inverse or the consequence of its coming to maturity. In short, since in time being and passing are synonymous, by becoming past, the event does not cease to be. The origin of objective time, with its fixed positions lying beneath our gaze, is not to be sought in any eternal synthesis, but in the mutual harmonizing and overlapping of past and future through the present, and in the very passing of time. Time maintains what it has caused to be, at the very time it expels it from being, because the new being was announced by its predecessor as destined to be, and because, for the latter, to become present was the same thing as being destined to pass away. 'Temporalization is not a succession (*Nachei-nander*) of ecstases. The future is not posterior to the past, or the past anterior to the present. Temporality temporalizes itself as future-which-lapses-into-the-past-by-coming-into-the-present.'[8]   Bergson

8. Heidegger, *Sein und Zeit*, p. 350.

was wrong in *explaining* the unity of time in terms of its continuity, since that amounts to confusing past, present and future on the excuse that we pass from one to the other by imperceptible transitions; in short, it amounts to denying time altogether. But he was right to stick to the continuity of time as an essential phenomenon. It is simply a matter of elucidating this. Instant C and instant D, however near they are together, are not indistinguishable, for if they were there would be no time; what happens is that they run into each other and C becomes D because C has never been anything but the anticipation of D as present, and of its own lapse into the past. This amounts to saying that each present reasserts the presence of the whole past which it supplants, and anticipates that of all that is to come, and that by definition the present is not shut up within itself, but transcends itself towards a future and a past. What there is, is not a present, then another present which takes its place in being, and not even a present with its vistas of past and future followed by another present in which those vistas are disrupted, so that one and the same spectator is needed to effect the synthesis of successive perspectives: there is one single time which is self-confirmatory, which can bring nothing into existence unless it has already laid that thing's foundations as present and eventual past, and which establishes itself at a stroke.

The past, therefore, *is* not past, nor the future future. It exists only when a subjectivity is there to disrupt the plenitude of being in itself, to adumbrate a perspective, and introduce non-being into it. A past and a future spring forth when I reach out towards them. I am not, for myself, at this very moment, I am also at this morning or at the night which will soon be here, and though my present is, if we wish so to consider it, this instant, it is equally this day, this year or my whole life. There is no need for a synthesis externally binding together the *tempora* into one single time, because each one of the *tempora* was already inclusive, beyond itself, of the whole open series of other *tempora*, being in internal communication with them, and because the 'cohesion of a life'[9] is given with its *ek-stase*. The passage of one present to the next is not a thing which I conceive, nor do I see it as an onlooker, I perform it; I am already at the impending present as my gesture is already at its goal, I am myself time, a time which 'abides' and does not 'flow' or 'change', which is what Kant says in various

9. Heidegger, *Sein und Zeit*, p. 373.

places.[10] This idea of a time which anticipates itself is perceived by common sense in its way. Everyone talks about Time, not as the zoologist talks about the dog or the horse, using these as collective nouns, but using it as a proper noun. Sometimes it is even personified. Everyone thinks that there is here a single, concrete being, wholly present in each of its manifestations, as in a man in each of his spoken words. We say that there is time as we say that there is a fountain: the water changes while the fountain remains because its form is preserved; the form is preserved because each successive wave takes over the functions of its predecessor: from being the thrusting wave in relation to the one in front of it, it becomes, in its turn and in relation to another, the wave that is pushed; and this is attributable to the fact that, from the source to the fountain jet, the waves are not separate; there is only one thrust, and a single air-lock in the flow would be enough to break up the jet. Hence the justification for the metaphor of the river, not in so far as the river flows, but in so far as it is one with itself. This intuition of time's permanence, however, is jeopardized by the action of common sense, which thematizes or objectifies it, which is the surest way of losing sight of it. There is more truth in mythical personifications of time than in the notion of time considered, in the scientific manner, as a variable of nature in itself, or, in the Kantian manner, as a form ideally separable from its matter. There is a temporal style of the world, and time remains the same because the past is a former future and a recent present, the present an impending past and a recent future, the future a present and even a past to come; because, that is, each dimension of time is treated or aimed at *as* something other than itself and because, finally, there is at the core of time a gaze, or, as Heidegger puts it, an *Augen-blick, someone* through whom the word *as* can have a meaning. We are not saying that time is *for* someone, which would once more be a case of arraying it out, and immobilizing it. We are saying that time *is* someone, or that temporal dimensions, in so far as they perpetually overlap, bear each other out and ever confine themselves to making explicit what was implied in each, being collectively expressive of that one single explosion or thrust which is subjectivity itself. We must understand time as the subject and the subject as time. What is perfectly clear, is that this primordial temporality is not a juxtaposition of external events, since it is the power which holds them together while keeping them apart. Ultimate

10. Quoted by Heidegger, *Kant und das Problem der Metaphysik*, pp. 183–4.

subjectivity is not temporal in the empirical sense of the term: if consciousness of time were made up of successive states of consciousness, there would be needed a new consciousness to be conscious of that succession and so on to infinity. We are forced to recognize the existence of 'a consciousness having behind it no consciousness to be conscious of it'[11] which, consequently, is not arrayed out in time, and in which its 'being coincides with its being for itself'.[12] We may say that ultimate consciousness is 'timeless' (*zeitlose*) in the sense that it is not intratemporal.[13] 'In' my present, if I grasp it while it is still living and with all that it implies, there is an *ek-stase* towards the future and towards the past which reveals the dimensions of time not as conflicting, but as inseparable: to be at present is to be always and for ever. Subjectivity is not in time because it takes up or lives through time, and merges with the cohesion of a life.

11. Husserl, *Zeitbewusstsein*, p. 442; 'primäres Bewusstsein . . . das hinter sich kein Bewusstsein mehr hat in dem es bewusst wäre . . .'
12. Ibid., p. 471: 'fällt ja Sein und Innerlich-bewusstsein zusammen.'
13. Ibid., p. 464.

17

James F. Sheridan,
"First Experience of Time,"
from *Mystery Delight*

James F. Sheridan, Professor of Philosophy at Allegheny College, integrates phenomenology with psychology and natural science in his work. His most important works are Once More from the Middle *and* Mystery Delight. *He is currently experimenting with computer poetry. His theme in the following text is the "discovery" of time by paleolithic humanity.*

Let's begin by considering the plight of some of our ancestors, the poor guys in the caves who were harassed by creatures which could see better than they could in the dark. They would have had a tremendous stake in knowing how long they had until daylight relieved those particular fears, eliminating some of the night stalkers and enabling the humans to use one of their best weapons, their eyes. The eyes are a great way to apprehend danger at a distance. But think of the poor guy in the middle of the night, sitting in a cave, just *waiting.* I'd be out of my skull! Visual clues would give no hope at all for a very long time. Because he was himself a being composed of various *rhythms,* he would be aware that something was going on, namely, him and probably the beasties. I suppose he could have used his heart beat or breathing rhythms as indicators of the time although I'm sure I wouldn't have had that much sense. That technique would have provided a very rough measure indeed but it had to have been better than nothing. But if he was as scared as I would have been, he'd certainly have a good idea of "taking" time. It took an almost unendurable amount of time for the daylight to come. He would have had a clear awareness of helplessness against the beasties and an even deeper sense of dependence just because of the necessity of *waiting* for time to *pass.* The independence of time from human manipulation would certainly have been a forceful deliverance of this situation. . . .

By permission of the author.

Due to this guy's efforts, his descendants managed to alter the situation to a more favorable balance. The guy is aware of the rough alternation of night and day. He's also aware that they fade into one another rather than abruptly changing. He is also aware that this process *takes time*. I don't know whether he can tell whether time is an *aspect* of the process or a *setting* within which the process occurs. I'd think it was a setting myself but I'm quite willing to suppose that's an idiosyncrasy. . . .

Anyway, I've got this guy waiting, aware that he can't control the process, especially to speed it up so daylight will come, that is, he's aware that there is some resistance to time change. In the dark, he probably wouldn't associate that change with motion and I'm with him. *This "passage" of time wouldn't be a motion.* It wouldn't have a spatial element to it because there is nothing to *see* in the dark. Thus he could have a kind of Bergsonian intuition of the passage of time which wasn't a locomotion. (I wonder whether different philosophies of time are written by night and day people?) He would be aware of himself as *persisting* while time *passed* and the change *went on*. Practicality and memory would join together to tell him that the process was *repetitive*. It came in more or less halves which lopped over into one another and succeeded one another. That's worth another look. First, by process I mean something with some internal "negation" or negations. On the face of it, it looks like time as apprehended in the dark wouldn't be thought of as a *process*. Maybe that's why Whitehead used terms like "passage" and "creative advance" when he wanted to mention that which was measured. These negativities were not clear and distinct, not sharp. There were "times" after daylight faded when it was dark and *not* light in as definite a sense of "not" as you want, even the logical "not." The same thing can be said of daylight after it arrived. But the division was itself gradual, both ways. The alternation, however was perfectly regular. The night always came after the day and the day after the night. Of course, which came "first" is as unanswerable as it always is from a mundane point of view.

Except for a few times that I stood on a dark platform on the El in Chicago, I cannot pretend that I have ever been exactly in this caveman's situation but I can say that I'm very much akin to him in being uncertain about my temporal location. I know that's partly because my habitual mode of wandering around in the world is as the sargent says, eyes front. I seldom look to the side. Until recently, I never looked behind. Like Sartre, I thought I was a man who had no past or at least no past which was worth anything more than a reservoir for the construction of fantasies. Most importantly, I never seldom looked up or down. My feed from the world is primarily horizontal. Recently, however, I've begun to look above me. I've long been interested in astronomical topics but always from books. I never bothered to go outside and look at the sky! After a bit, I decided I might be missing something so I tried it. I discovered something very interesting. As I looked at the sky, I was overwhelmed by the number of lights. I did the usual cookbook responses as to which of the lights were planets and which stars and bits and pieces of what I had learned from reading books flitted in and out of my head but all I accomplished by that meditation was to highlight some aspects of the display. I immediately moved to picking out two or three of the lights to serve as reference points, even calling one of them my "anchor star." Then I realized what I had done and stopped. *I realized I was lost.* When I raised my eyes to the stars, I no longer had any of the familiar feed from the horizontal, the feed in terms of which I usually guide myself, my built-in points of reference. Nothing about the night sky gave me any clue to what should be a reference point. I had to decide and to decide arbitrarily. . . .

As existentialists have taught us, being free, we are homeless. We *make* homes for ourselves but we do not *have* homes in totality. No, I won't start into the familiar existentialist sermon about anguish, boredom and death. I want to show that even in its most "sensible" aspect, the physical aspect has a contorted texture consistent with the other aspects of totality as they are lived by humans. To do that, I shall again return to the "beginning," the Big Bang. I have already said that we have to remember that expansion is not motion. I have also said that we have to remember that what is expanding is timespace. I'm not confident that the practitioners from whom I've learned what I know about that are clear about time being involved. They talk about it temporally which seems a little hard to do if time is changing, expanding. I'm going to take them more seriously perhaps than they take themselves. I want to ask again *where* the original concentration was which suddenly began expanding. I presume that my question is still unanswerable aside from fun things like "everywhere" or "nowhere." If "wheres" are about spatial location or about temporal location or both, then if temporality and spatiality are changing *as a whole*, we can't very well ask about the location of that whole.

To say that another way, unless we can specify some system, some framework, we cannot answer the question "Where is (or was?) the original egg." Because the framework itself is changing, expanding, the question is unanswerable. *Like myself, physical totality is lost.* No, I'm not saying "physical totality" in order to make room for suddenly importing a non-physical framework in which it might get located. I'd do that if I had to but I don't want to and certainly won't right now. There is more to totality than its physicality but I have no inclination to say that it's a "more" which is such that the physical could be "in" it. I simply mean again to signal my intention to display cosmic insanity in its physical aspects. I also intend to try desperately to force a coming together of observation and perception or the empirical and the experiential. The physical aspect of totality or totality as physical is as homeless as I am. The existentialists knew about the homelessness of the human but not about the homelessness of the physical aspect of totality. Of course, by extension, totality as a whole could hardly be anywhere, either! I've never had a lot of patience with talk about finitude and its dark companion, infinity, but if there's anything that is *inexhaustible* I suppose it's totality and infinity presumably has something to do with the last. I suppose that "capable of an unending number of formings" is about as good a definition of infinity as I could concoct. The inexhaustible would presumably differ very little at all from the infinitely exhaustible. I'm not sure just how all of this doesn't go together but I am sure that what I know of science won't quite tell me although it will help by adding that little touch of reality which is required for good fantasy. . . .

I'll come back to that at a later point but now I want to collect what I've said thus far about the temporal aspect of this issue. Let's go back to the guy in the cave. You remember that he is really anxious to have time *pass.* One of the ways for him to do that would be to engage in activities. As I indicated, I've seldom been in circumstances as extreme as his but I am a person who gets bored easily and I've learned how dolefully slowly the passage of time can be. What I usually do in those circumstances is to "kill" time by engaging in some activity, preferably one that is pleasant but if that's not available, any activity will do better than none. I *use up* time by engaging in activities which *take* time. That kind of talk suggests to me again that there is a reservoir of time there to be used. I know that I'm only doing a little business on some of the meanings of quite mundane terms but that's one of the less elaborate ways to try to achieve naivete. Nothing need be said to be true *because* it occurs in common sense but there must be some point to that repository of human experience. If there were a reservoir, would it be lodged in the indeterminate aspect of totality? I'm not sure. What does seem true, however, is that the guy in the cave is as lost with respect to time as I am to the vast reaches of space when I look at the night sky. We are equally lacking in frames of reference. The materials from which to make a home just aren't ready to hand. Beyond the cloud cover there are realms beyond encompassing. The poor guy in the cave doesn't even have a cloud cover to interrupt this expanse of time with which he's contending. But there's a striking difference in our situations, too. He has some reason to think of time as an activity. It passes. I have no reason to think of space as an activity. If I were traveling, I might well think of it as something to be used up but since I travel only under protest, I'll just note that and then press on.

How is it that engaging in activities helps time to pass? The most obvious answer is that I don't *notice* that passage. I don't object to that answer unless it gives me undue temptation to translate "passage" in terms of motion. I have no sense of a particulate aspect of time unless I have already spatialized it. But I think I have misspoken even now. I'm not sure that making-particulate or focusing upon the particulate is spatializing. Looking out into the space in the night sky is hardly particularizing (or particulatizing—if that's a word). I suspect that spatializing time is making it particulate only if we have already unitized it by treating it arithmetically, that is, in terms of equal differences or equal parts. I don't think that the first move in assessing time is spatializing in the sense of unitizing. When the guy in the cave made some moves to quell his anxiety, he would use some spin-off from assessing time in terms of the motion of the sun. That could be unitized but at first the divisions could be relatively rough, more like those on an ordinal scale than on an interval scale, matters of more and less rather than matters of equality and inequality. I suppose one might think of this situation as one which is merely a "qualitative" precursor of a quantitiatve scale and, no doubt, that's the way things have most often gone. My point is that this historical fact is neither a logical nor a cognitive necessity.

Neither is it cognitively necessary to say that the temporal passage of which the guy in the cave is aware is "really" composed of equal parts and he is simply too dumb to know that. The mode of apprehension which he uses gives him no reason to believe that temporal passage is in itself unitized. No. I'm not saying that he has an "intuition " of time. I suspect that one would only talk that way in a situation in which the idea that time was unitized had already become a part of the general intellectual set, so pervasive that the notion of temporal "instants" had become the official doctrine. The guy in the cave isn't intuiting at all. He's simply involved in a global apprehension combined with great fear. Do I want to say that he's right and the advocates of the unit are wrong? Not unless I can't help it. I would much prefer to stay with the phenomenological conviction that perspectives in and of themselves are equally fundamental. I do want to say that with effort, a modern person can approximate to this kind of naive apprehension as I suggested I had some intimation of it during my tours of the streets of Chicago. I want to say that this aspect of the mush is available even though the determinate aspect has come to the fore among eggheads, or at least among eggheads of a familiar persuasion. But I confess that I'm again tempted by the same inclination which I steadily refuse in others and contest in myself, the notion that what is earlier is somehow more fundamental. . . . I don't know whether in my own historic route I apprehended time as the guy in the cave did but even if I could say that I did, that still wouldn't make that apprehension any more fundamental than those which result in the sophistications I've discussed in the course of my argument thus far.

18

Mircea Eliade,
"Sacred Time and Myth,"
from *Sacred Time*

Mircea Eliade (1907–1986), Roumanian historian of religion, described the diverse religions of the world and their roots in the neolithic. His scholarly achievement is summed up in his three-volume work, A History of Religious Ideas; *his most important novels are* The Forbidden Forest *and* The Old Man *and the Bureaucrats.* A central topic for Eliade is the emergence of time from eternity as expressed in the rites of archaic religious communities. He discusses this topic in the following text.

The Heterogeneousness of Time

The problem we come to in this chapter is among the most difficult in all religious phenomenology. The difficulty is not simply that magico-religious time and profane time are different in nature; it is rather more the fact that the actual *experience of time as such* is not always the same for primitive peoples as for modern Western man. Sacred time does differ from profane; but, further, this latter reckoning itself differs in nature according to whether we are speaking of primitive or of modern society. It is not easy, at first, to determine whether this difference arises from the fact that the primitive's experience of profane time has not yet become completely detached from his ideas of mythico-religious time. But certainly this experience of time gives the primitive a kind of permanent "opening" on to religious time. To simplify the explanation and to some extent to anticipate the results of our study of it, we might say that the very nature of the primitive's experience of time makes it easy for him to change the profane into the sacred. But as this problem is primarily of interest to philosophic anthropology

Excerpts from Eliade, *Patterns in Comparative Religion*, 1958, Sheed and Ward. Reprinted with permission of the publisher.

and sociology, we shall only consider it in so far as it brings us to a discussion of hierophanic time.

The problem we are dealing with is, in fact, this: in what is sacred time distinguishable from the "profane" duration that comes before and after it? The phrase "hierophanic time", we see at once, covers a collection of widely varying things. It may mean the time during which a ritual takes place and therefore a *sacred time,* a time essentially different from the profane succession which preceded it. It might also mean mythical time, reattained by means of a ritual, or by the mere repetition of some action with a mythical archetype. And, finally, it might also indicate the rhythms of the cosmos (like the hierophanies of the moon) in that those rhythms are seen as revelations—that is, manifestations—of a fundamental sacred power behind the cosmos. Thus, an instant or a fragment of time might *at any moment* become hierophanic: it need only witness the occurrence of a kratophany, hierophany or theophany to become transfigured, consecrated, remembered because repeated, and therefore repeatable forever. All time of whatever kind "opens" on to sacred time—in other words, is capable of revealing what we may for convenience call the *absolute,* the supernatural, the superhuman, the superhistoric.

To the primitive mind, time is not homogeneous. Even apart from the possibility of its being "hierophanized", time as such appears under different forms, varying in intensity and purpose. Lévy-Bruhl, following Hardeland, counted five distinct sorts of time believed by the Dyaks to vary, each by its special quality, the pattern of a single day—in this case a Sunday: (1) Sunrise, favourable for the beginning of any work. Children born at this moment are lucky; but one must never choose this time to set off for hunting, fishing or travelling. One would meet with no success; (2) About nine in the morning: an unlucky moment; nothing begun then will succeed, but if one sets out on the road one need not fear bandits; (3) Middday: a very lucky time; (4) Three in the afternoon: a time of battle, lucky for enemies, bandits, huntsmen and fishermen, unlucky for travellers; (5) About sunset: a shorter "lucky time".[1]

Examples are not hard to find. Every religion has its lucky and unlucky days, its best moments even on the lucky ones, "concentrated" and "diluted" periods of time, "strong" and "weak" times, and so on. One point we must bear in mind from now on is the realization that time was seen as not being homogeneous even apart from all the valuations it came to

1. *Le Surnaturel et la nature dáns la mentalité primitive,* Paris, 1931, pp. 18–19.

receive in the framework of any given ritual system: certain periods are lucky and certain the reverse. In other words, time can be seen to have a new dimension that we may call hierophanic, as a result of which succession, by its very nature, takes on not only a particular cadence, but also varying "vocations", contradictory "dynamisms". Obviously this hierophanic dimension of time can be displayed, can be "caused", by the rhythms of nature, as with the Dyaks' five sorts of time, or the crises of the solstice, the phases of the moon and the rest; it may equally well be "caused" by the actual religious life of human societies, under such forms as those winter festivals which centre around the dead season of agricultural life, and so on.

Various authors have lately pointed out the social origins of the rhythms of sacred time (for instance Mauss and Granet); but it cannot be denied that the rhythms of the cosmos also played a leading role in the "revelation" and ordering of these systems of reckoning. We have only to recall how very important were the religious values placed upon the course of the moon or the stages of plant life in the spiritual fate of primitive man. The ideas of rhythm and of repetition to which we shall have occasion to return during the course of this chapter, may be considered as having been "revealed" by the hierophanies of the moon quite independent of later exemplifications of rhythm and repetition in the framework of social life as such. It has been said[2] that the social "origin" of the reckoning of sacred time is borne out by the discrepancies between religious calendars and the rhythms of nature. In point of fact this divergence in no way disproves the link between man's systems of reckoning and the rhythms of nature; it simply proves on the one hand the inconsistency of primitive reckoning and chronometry, and on the other the non- "naturalist" character of primitive piety, whose feats were not directed to any natural phenomenon in itself but to the religious aspect of that phenomenon.

Plant hierophanies brought home to us how very movable in the calendar the spring festival was. I have also shown that what characterized this spring festival was the metaphysical and religious significance of the *rebirth* of Nature and the *renewal* of life, rather than the "natural" phenomenon of spring as such. It was not because a calendar did not accord with astronomical time that sacred time was always arranged independently of the rhythms of nature. It was simply that those rhythms

2. Hubert and Mauss, "La Représentation du temps dans la religion et la magie", *Mélanges d'histoire des religions*, 1909, pp. 213 ff.

were only thought to be of value in so far as they were hierophanies, and this "hierophanization" of them set them free from astronomical time which served them rather as a sort of womb. A "sign" of spring might reveal *spring* before "nature's spring" made itself felt; the sign marked the *beginning* of a new era and nature's spring would soon come to confirm it—not as a mere phenomenon of nature but as a complete renewal and recommencement of all cosmic life. Of course the notion of renewal included a renewal of individuals and of society as well as of the cosmos. This is not the first time in this book that I have pointed out how, in the view of primitive spirituality, all things return to a unity, all levels correspond.

The Unity and Contiguity of Hierophanic Time

The heterogeneousness of time, its division into "sacred" and "profane", does not merely mean periodic "incisions" made in the profane duration to allow of the insertion of sacred time; it implies, further, that these insertions of sacred time are linked together so that one might almost see them as constituting another duration with its own continuity. The Christian liturgy for a given Sunday is one with the liturgy for the previous Sunday and the Sunday following. The sacred time in which the mystery occurs of the transubstantiation of bread and wine into the Body and Blood of Christ is different not only in quality from the profane succession from which it is detached like a space enclosed between the present and the future; not only is this sacred time linked with that of the Masses preceding and following it, but it can also be looked on as a continuation of all the Masses which have taken place from the moment when the mystery of transubstantiation was first established until the present moment. The profane succession, on the other hand, which flows between two Masses, not being transformed into sacred time, cannot have any connection with the hierophanic time of the rite: it runs parallel, so to speak, to sacred time which is thus revealed to us as a *continuum* which is interrupted by profane intervals in appearance only.

What is true of time in Christian worship is equally true of time in all religions, in magic, in myth and in legend. A ritual does not merely repeat the ritual that came before it (itself the repetition of an archetype), but is linked to it and continues it, whether at fixed periods or otherwise. Magic herbs are picked in those critical moments which mark a breaking-through from profane to magico-religious time—as,

for instance, midnight on the feast of St. John. For a few seconds—
as with the "herb of iron" (the Rumanian *iarba fiarelor*), and with
ferns—popular belief has it that the heavens open and magic herbs
receive extraordinary powers so that anyone picking them at that moment will become invulnerable, invisible and so on.

These instants of hierophany are repeated every year. In the sense
that they form a "succession"—sacred in nature, but a succession none
the less—it may be said that they *are continuous*, and go to make up a
single, unique "time" over the years and centuries. This does not
prevent these instants of hierophany from recurring periodically; we
might think of them as momentary openings onto the Great Time,
openings which allow this same paradoxical second of magico-religious
time to enter the profane succession of things. The notions of recurrence and repetition occupy an important place in both mythology
and folklore. "In the legends of sunken churches, castles, towns and
monasteries, the curse is never a final one: it is renewed from time to
time; every year, every seven years or every nine years, on the date of
the catastrophe, the town rises again, the bells ring, the lady of the
castle comes out of hiding, the treasures are laid open, the guards
sleep: but at the time fixed, the spell closes in again and everything
disappears. These periodic recurrences are almost enough to prove
that the dates themselves bring back the same happenings."[3]

Periodic Recurrence—The Eternal Present

In religion as in magic, the periodic recurrence of anything signifies
primarily that a mythical time is *made present* and then used indefinitely.
Every ritual has the character of happening *now*, at this very moment.
The time of the event that the ritual commemorates or re-enacts is
made *present*, "re-presented" so to speak, however far back it may have
been in ordinary reckoning. Christ's passion, death and resurrection
are not simply *remembered* during the services of Holy Week; they really
happen *then* before the eyes of the faithful. And a convinced Christian
must feel that he is *contemporary* with these transhistoric events, for,
by being re-enacted, the time of the theophany becomes actual.

The same may be said of magic. We saw that people set off to hunt
for simples with the words: "We will gather herbs to lay on the wounds
of the Saviour." By her magic rite, the healer makes herself contempo-

---

3. Hubert and Mauss, p. 205.

rary with Christ's passion; the herbs she picks owe their power to the fact that they *are* placed (or at least *can be* placed) on Christ's wounds, or grow at the foot of the cross. Her incantation takes place in the present. We are told how a healer met the Blessed Virgin or some other saint; told her of someone's illness, and was told by her what remedy to use, and so on. I will limit myself to one example, taken from Rumanian folklore (which has abundant material to choose from). "Nine brothers with nine different fathers met, all dressed the same, with nine well-ground hoes, and nine sharpened axes; they went half-way across the bridge of bronze; there they met Saint Mary; she was coming down a ladder of wax and began to ask them questions: 'Where are you going, you nine brothers with nine different fathers, all dressed the same?' 'We are going to the hill of Galilee to cut down the tree of Paradise.' 'Leave the tree of Paradise there. Go to Ion for his warts. Cut them off, chop them up and throw them to the bottom of the sea'."[4]

The scene is laid in that mythical time before the tree of Paradise had been cut down, and yet it takes place *now*, at this very moment while Ion suffers from pimples. The invocation does not simply invoke the Blessed Virgin's power, for all powers, even the divine, become weakened and lost if exercised in profane time; it establishes a different time, magico-religious time, a time when men *can* go and cut down the tree of Paradise, and Our Lady *comes down* in person on a heavenly ladder. And it is no merely allegorical establishment of it but a real one. Ion and his affliction are contemporary with the Virgin's meeting with the nine brothers. This contemporaneity with the great moments of myth is an indispensable condition for any form of magico-religious efficaciousness. Seen in this light, Søren Kierkegaard's effort to express the Christian status as "being contemporary with Jesus" is less revolutionary than it at first sounds; all Kierkegaard has done is to formulate in new words an attitude common and normal to primitive man.

Periodic recurrence, repetition, the eternal present: these three marks of magico-religious time taken together explain what I mean by saying that this time of kratophany and hierophany is not homogeneous with profane time. Like all the other essential activities of human life (hunting, fishing, gathering fruit, agriculture and the rest) which later became "profane" activities—though never totally so—rites too were revealed by the gods or by "ancestors". Every time the rite, or any

4. Pavelescu, *Cercetari asupra magiei la Romanii din Muntii Apuseni*, Bucharest, 1945, p. 156.

significant action (hunting, for instance) is repeated, the archetypal action of the god or ancestor is being repeated, that action which took place at the beginning of time, or, in other words, in a mythical time.

But this repetition also has the effect of establishing the mythical time of the gods and ancestors. Thus, in New Guinea, when a master mariner went to sea he personified the mythical hero Aori: "He wears the costume which Aori is supposed to have worn, with a blackened face and (in a way prematurely) the same kind of *love* in his hair which Aori plucked from Iviri's head. He dances on the platform and extends his arms like Aori's wings. . . . A man told me that when he went fish shooting (with bow and arrow) he pretended to be Kivavia himself."[5] He did not implore Kivavia's favour and help; he identified himself with the mythical hero. In other words, the fisherman lived in the mythical time of Kivavia just as the sailor identifying himself with Aori lived in the transhistoric time of that hero. Whether he *became* the hero himself, or merely a *contemporary* of the hero's, the Melanesian was living in a *mythical present* that could not possibly be confused with any profane kind of time. By repeating an archetypal action, he entered a sacred, an historical time, and this entry could only take place if profane time were done away with. We shall see further on how important it was for primitive man thus to do away with profane time.

The Restoration of Mythical Time

By every sort of ritual, and therefore by every sort of significant action (hunting, fishing, etc.) the primitive is placing himself in "mythical time". For "the mythical period, *dzugur*, must not be thought of simply as past time, but as present and future, and as a state as well as a period".[6] That period is "creative"[7] in the sense that it was then, *in illo tempore*, that the creation and arranging of the Cosmos took place, as well as the revelation of all the archetypal activities by gods, ancestors or culture heroes. *In illo tempore*, in the mythical period, anything was possible. The species were not yet fixed and all forms were "fluid". (There are memories of that fluidity even in the most highly developed mythological traditions; in Greek mythology, for instance, the time of

5. F. E. Williams, quoted by Lévy-Bruhl, *La Mythologie primitive*, Paris, 1935, pp. 163–4.

6. A. P. Elkin, quoted by Lévy-Bruhl, *Mythologie primitive*, p. 7.

7. Lévy-Bruhl, p. 8.

Ouranos, or of Cronos.) On the other hand, this same fluidity of "forms" will be, at the other end of time, one of the signs of the end of the world, of the moment when "history" comes to an end and the whole world begins to live in sacred time, in eternity. "The wolf shall dwell with the lamb: and the leopard shall lie down with the kid."[8] Then *nec magnos metuent armenta leones*, "herds of cattle shall not fear great lions".[9]

It would be impossible to overstress the tendency—observable in every society, however highly developed—to bring back that time, mythical time, the Great Time. For this bringing-back is effected without exception by every rite and every significant act. "A rite is the repetition of a fragment of the original time." And "the original time is the model for all times. What took place once upon a day is forever repeated. One need only know the myth to understand what life is about".[10] As for the expression and significance of the myth, we will consider exactly how far this formula of Van der Leeuw's is true: "One need only know the myth to understand what life is about." Let us note, for the moment, these two marks of mythical time (or, it may be, sacred, magico-religious or hierophanic time); (1) its repeatability (in the sense that every significant action reproduces it); and (2) the fact that, though it is looked upon as transhistoric, beyond all succession, and in a sense in eternity, this sacred time has, *in history*, a "beginning"—namely, that moment when the divinity created the world or set it in order, or that moment when the ancestor or civilizing hero made the revelation of any given activity, etc.

From the point of view of primitive spirituality, every beginning is *illud tempus*, and therefore an opening into the Great Time, into eternity. Marcel Mauss was right in saying that "the religious things that take place in time are legitimately and logically looked upon as taking place in eternity".[11] Indeed, every one of these "religious things" indefinitely repeats the archetype; in other words, repeats what took place at the "beginning", at the moment when a rite or religious gesture was, being revealed, at the same time expressed in history.

As I shall show at greater length later on, history, in the view of the

8. Isa. xi. 6.

9. Virgil, Fourth Eclogue, 22.

10. Van der Leeuw, *L'homme primitif et la religion*, Paris, 1940, pp. 120, 101.

11. "Représentation du Temps", p. 227.

primitive mind, coincides with myth: every *event* (every occurrence with any meaning), simply by being *effected in time*, represents a break in profane time and an irruption of the Great Time. As such, every event, simply by happening, by taking place in time, is a hierophany, a "revelation". The paradox of this event-being-also-hierophany, this historic-time-being-also-mythical-time is a paradox in appearance only; we have merely to try and place ourselves in the conditions of mind which produced it. For the primitive, at bottom, finds meaning and interest in human actions (in farm labour, for instance, or social customs, sexual life, or culture) in so far as they repeat actions revealed by his gods, culture heroes, or ancestors. Anything outside the framework of these meaningful actions, having no superhuman model, has neither name nor value. But all these archetypal actions were revealed then, *in illo tempore*, during a time outside recorded history, mythical time. By being revealed, they broke through profane time and brought mythical time into it. But, in the same act, they also created a "beginning", an "event" which entered the dreary and monotonous perspective of profane time (the time in which meaningless actions come and go) and thus produced "history", the series of "events with meanings" so different from the succession of automatic and meaningless acts. Thus, though it may seem paradoxical, what we may call the "history" of primitive societies consists solely of the mythical events which took place *in illo tempore* and have been unceasingly repeated from that day to this. All that the modern thinks of as truly "historic", that is, as unique and done once and for all, is held by the primitive to be quite devoid of importance as having no mythico-historic precedent.

Nonperiodic Recurrence

These observations contribute equally to our understanding of myth and to the explanation of that mythical, hierophanic, magico-religious time which is the subject of this chapter. We are now in a position to understand why sacred, religious time, is not always reproduced periodically; while a given feast (taking place of course in hierophanic time) will be repeated periodically, there are other actions which appear to be profane—but *only* appear to be—which, while they too were established in an *illud tempus*, can take place *at any time*. Man may set off at any time to hunt or to fish, and thus imitate a mythical hero, embodying him, re-establishing mythical time, leaving profane time, repeating the myth-history. To return to what I said a moment ago, *any* time may become a sacred time; at any moment succession may be changed to eternity. Naturally, as we shall see, the periodic recurrence of sacred time has an important place in the religious notions of all mankind; but it is extremely significant that the same contrivance of imitating an archetype and repeating an archetypal action can do away with profane time and transform it into sacred, quite apart from any periodic rites; it proves, on the one hand, that the tendency to "hierophanize" time is something essential, independent of any systems based on the framework of social life, independent of the normal means of abolishing profane time (like the "old year") and establishing sacred (the "new year") to which we shall be returning in a moment; and on the other hand, it reminds us of the "easy substitutes" we saw for establishing sacred space. Just as a "centre of the world", which is, by definition, in some inaccessible place, can nevertheless be constructed anywhere without any of the difficulties described by the myths and heroic legends, so too sacred time, generally established by communal feasts set by the calendar, may be attained at any time and by anyone, simply by repeating an archetypal, mythical gesture. It is important that we remember henceforth this tendency to go outside the frameworks of society in establishing sacred time: it is important in a way we shall very soon see.

The Regeneration of Time

Festivals take place in sacred time, or, in other words, as Marcel Mauss points out, in eternity. But there are some seasonal feasts—certainly the most important ones—which give us a glimpse of something more: the wish to destroy the profane time that is past and establish a "new time". In other words, the seasonal feasts which close one cycle of time and open another set out to achieve a *complete regeneration of time*. As I have elsewhere[12] studied in some detail the ritual scenarios marking the end of the old year and beginning of the new, I will give here only a summary at this important question.

The morphology of seasonal ritual drama is a very rich one. The researches of Frazer, Wensinck, Dumézil and other authors cited in the bibliography, make it possible to formulate the substance of it in the following way. The end of the year and beginning of the new year are marked by a series of rites: (1) purgations, purifications, the confessing of sins, driving off of demons, expulsion of evil out of the

12. *In The Myth of the Eternal Return.*

village and so on; (2) the extinguishing and rekindling of all fires; (3) masked processions (with the masks representing the souls of the dead), the ceremonial reception of the dead, who are entertained (with banquets, etc.) and led back at the end of the feast to the borders of the territory, to the sea, or the river, or wherever it may be; (4) fights between two opposing teams; (5) an interlude of Carnival, Saturnalia, reversal of the normal order, "orgy".

Needless to say, nowhere does the scenario for the end of the old year and beginning of the new include all these rites—and in any case this list does not exhaust them, for it omits the initiations and marriages by abduction which take place in some areas. All of them are none the less part of the same ceremonial framework. Each—at its own level, with its own particular outlook—aims at abolishing the time that composed the cycle now being brought to a close. Thus the purgation, the purifications, the burning of effigies of the "old year", the driving out of demons and witches, and generally of everything that represents the past year—all this is done to destroy the whole of the past, to *suppress* it. By extinguishing all fires, "darkness" is established, the "cosmic night" in which all "forms" lose their outlines and become confused. At this cosmological level, this "darkness" is identified with chaos, as the rekindling of the fires symbolizes creation, the reestablishing of forms and of limits. The masks which embody the ancestors, the souls of the dead paying ceremonial visit to the living (in Japan, Germany, and elsewhere) are also a sign that all barriers have been destroyed and all forms of life merged together. In this paradoxical interval between two "times" (between two Cosmoses) communication between the living and the dead becomes possible, between determinate forms and what is preformal, "larval". In a sense it may be said that in the "darkness" and "chaos" established by the liquidation of the old year, all forms merge together and the coalescence of all things ("night"—"deluge"—"dissolution") makes possible an effortless, automatic *coincidentia oppositorum* at every level of existence.

This wish to abolish time can be seen even more clearly in the "orgy" which takes place, with varying degrees of violence, during the New Year ceremonies. An orgy is also a regression into the "dark", a restoration of the primeval chaos, and as such precedes all creation, every manifestation of ordered form. The fusion of all forms into one single, vast, undifferentiated unity is an exact reproduction of the "total" mode of reality. I pointed out earlier the function and meaning of the orgy, at once sexual and agricultural; at the cosmological level, the "orgy" represents chaos or the ultimate disappearance of limits and, as time goes, the inauguration of the Great Time, of the "eternal moment", of non-duration. The presence of the orgy among the ceremonials marking the periodic divisions of time shows the *will to abolish the past totally by abolishing all creation.* The "merging together of forms" is illustrated by overthrowing social conditions (during the Saturnalia, the slave was master, the master obeyed his slaves; in Mesopotamia the king was dethroned and humiliated); by combining opposites (matrons were treated as courtesans, and so on); and by the suspension of all norms. License is let loose, all commands are violated, all contraries are brought together, and all this is simply to effect the dissolution of the world—of which the community is a copy—and restore the primeval *illud tempus* which is obviously the mythical moment of the *beginning* (chaos) and the end (flood or *ekpyrosis,* apocalypse).

Yearly Repetition of the Creation

That this is the meaning of the carnivalesque orgy at the end of the year is confirmed by the fact that the chaos is always followed by a new creation of the cosmos. All these seasonal celebrations go on to a more or less clear symbolic repetition of the creation. I will give only a few examples. During the new year ceremonial of the Babylonians, *akitu* (lasting for twelve days), they used to recite the creation poem, *Enuma Elish,* several times in the temple of Marduk; thus by oral magic and the rites that went with it, they brought into the present the struggle between Marduk and the sea-monster Tiamat, a struggle which took place *in illo tempore,* and which, through the god's final victory, put an end to the chaos. The Hittites had a similar custom: as part of the feast of the New Year, they recounted and re-enacted the archetypal duel between Teshub the god of the weather and the serpent Iluyankash.[13] The single combat between Marduk and Tiamat was acted out by a conflict between two groups of men,[14] and this ritual also occurs among the Hittites (at the time of the New Year),[15] and the Egyptians.[16] The turning of chaos into cosmos was

13. Cf. Gotze, *Kleinasien,* Leipzig, 1933, p. 130.

14. Labat, *Le Caractère religieux de la royauté assyro-babylonienne,* Paris, 1939, p. 99.

15. Gotze, p. 130.

16. Ivan Engnell, *Studies on Divine Kingship in the Ancient Near East,* Uppsala, 1943, p. 11.

reproduced: "May he continue to conquer Tiamat", they cried, "and cut short his days!" The struggle, Marduk's victory and the creation of the world thus became actually present.

At the time of the *akitu*, they also celebrated the *zakmuk*, the "feast of lots", so called because lots were then drawn for every month of the year; in other words, they were *creating* the next twelve months according to a notion shared by a great many other traditions. A whole series of rituals was connected with these: Marduk's descent into hell, the humiliation of the king, the driving out of ills in the guise of a scapegoat, and finally the marriage of the god with Sarpanitum—a marriage which the king re-enacted with a temple handmaid in the goddess' sanctuary[17] and which must have been the signal for a short time of communal license. We thus see a reversion to chaos (in which Tiamat is supreme, and all forms become confused) followed by a new creation (the victory of Marduk, all fates determined, and a sacred marriage or "new birth"). At the moment when the old world was dissolving into primeval chaos, they thus also effected the abolition of the old time, of what a modern would call the "history" of the cycle coming to an end.

In the primitive mind, the old time consisted of the profane succession of all the events without meaning, events, that is, with no archetypal models; "history" is the remembrance of those events, of what can only really be called "unmeanings" or even sins (in as much as they are divergences from the archetypal norms). As we saw, to primitives, true history is not that, but myth; all that true history records are the archetypal actions displayed by the gods, the ancestors or the culture heroes, during the mythical time, *in illo tempore*. To the primitive, all repetitions of archetypes take place outside profane time; it follows then, that, on the one hand, such actions cannot be "sins", divergences from the norm, and on the other, they have no connection with ordinary succession, the "old time" that is periodically abolished. The driving out of demons and spirits, the confessing of sins, the purifications and, specially, the symbolic return of the primeval chaos–all this indicates the abolition of profane time, of the old time during which occurred all the meaningless events and all the deviations.

Once a year, then, the old time, the past, the remembrance of all events not archetypal in character (in short, "history" in our sense of the word), are abolished. The symbolic repetition of the creation which follows this symbolic annihilation of the old world regenerates *time in*

17. Labat, p. 247.

its entirety. For it is no mere matter of a feast, bringing "the eternal moment" of sacred time into profane succession; it is further, as I have said, the total annihilation of all the profane time that made up the cycle now coming to an end. In the wish to *start a new life in the midst of a new creation*—an aspiration clearly present in all the ceremonies for beginning one year and ending another—there also enters the paradoxical desire to attain to an historic existence, to be able to live only in sacred time. What is meant is a regeneration of time in its totality, a transforming of succession into "eternity".

This need for a complete regeneration of time (which can be effected by repeating the creation every year) has been preserved even in traditions which are anything but primitive. I mentioned the things done in the Babylonian new year festival. The creation elements are equally obvious in the corresponding Jewish ceremonial. "When the time of the year returneth",[18] "in the end of the year",[19] there took place the struggle of Yahweh with Rahab, the defeat of the sea monster (the counter-part of Tiamat) by Yahweh and the victory over the waters which was equivalent to a repetition of the creation of the worlds, and at the same time, the salvation of men (victory over death, a guarantee of food for the coming year and so on).[20]

Wensinck points out still more traces of the primitive idea of the annual re-creation of the Cosmos, which were preserved in Jewish and Christian traditions.[21] The world was created during the months of Tishri or Nisan, that is, during the rainy season, the ideal cosmogonic period. To Eastern Christians, the blessing of water at the Epiphany also has a cosmogonic significance. "He [God] has created the heavens anew, because sinners have worshipped all the heavenly bodies; has created the world anew which had been withered by Adam, a new creation arose from his spittle."[22] "Allah is he who effects the creation,

18. Exod. xxxiv. 22.

19. Exod. xxiii. 16.

20. Cf. Johnson, "The Role of the King in the Jerusalem Cultus", in *The Labyrinth*, ed. S. H. Hooke, London, 1938, pp. 97 ff.

21. "The Semitic New Year and the Origin of Eschatology", *AOA*, 1923, vol. i, p. 168.

22. St. Ephraim the Syrian, *Seventh Hymn on the Epiphany*, 16; Wensinck, "The Semitic New Year and the Origin of Eschatology", *AOA*, 1923, vol. i, p. 169.

hence he repeats it."[23] This eternal repeating of the creative act, which makes every New Year the inauguration of an era, enables the dead to return to life and upholds the faithful in their hope of a resurrection of the flesh. This tradition also remains among Semitic peoples[24] as well as Christians.[25] "The Almighty awakens the bodies [at Epiphany] together with the spirits."[26]

A Pahlavi text, translated by Darmesteter,[27] says that "It is in the month of Fravartin, on the day of Xurdhath, that the Lord Orhmazd will cause the resurrection and the second body, and the world will be saved from powerlessness with demons, *drugs* ... And there will be plenty in all things; no one will have any more desire for food; the world will be pure and man will be free from the opposition [of the evil spirit], and immortal forever." Kazwini says that on the day of Nawroz, God will raise the dead, "give them back their souls and give his orders to the sky to rain upon them, and that is why people have the custom of pouring water on that day".[28] The close connection among the ideas of "creation by water" (aquatic cosmogony; periodic flood regenerating "historic" life; rain), of birth and of resurrection, are borne out by this phrase from the Talmud: "God hath three keys, of rain, of birth, of raising the dead."[29]

Nawroz, the Persian New Year, is at the same time the feast of Ahura Mazda (celebrated on "Orhmazd day" of the first month) and the day when the creation of the world and of man took place.[30] It is on the day of the Nawroz that "renovating the creation" takes place.[31]

23. *Qur'an*, xxix, 20 ff.

24. Lehman and Pedersen, "Der Beweis für die Auferstehung im Koran", *Der Islam*, v, pp. 54–61.

25. Wensinck, p. 171.

26. St. Ephraim the Syrian, *First Hymn on the Epiphany*, 1.

27. *Zend-Avesta*, Paris, 1892–3, vol. ii, p. 640, n. 138.

28. *Cosmography*, quoted by A. Christensen, *La Premier homme et le premier roi*, Uppsala, 1918–34, vol. ii, p. 147.

29. *Ta'anith*, ch. 1; Wensinck, p. 173.

30. Cf. the texts assembled by J. Marquart, "The Nawroz, its History and Significance", *Journal of the Cama Oriental Institute*, Bombay, 1937, no. xxxi, particularly 16 ff.

31. Albiruni, *The Chronology of Ancient Nations*, trans. Sachau, London, 1879, p. 199.

According to the tradition handed on by Dimashki,[32] the king proclaimed: "This is a new day of a new month of a new year; all that time has worn out must be renewed!" It is on that day, too, that the fate of men is determined for the whole year.[33] On the night of the Nawroz, innumerable fires and lights are to be seen,[34] and libations and purifications by water are performed to ensure plenty of rain in the coming year.[35]

At the time of the "Great Nawroz", too, everyone sowed seven sorts of grain in a jar, and "drew from their growth conclusions as to the year's harvest".[36] This is a custom similar to that of "fixing lots" in the Babylonian new year, and exists even to-day in the new year celebrations of the Mandeans and the Yezidis. Again, it is because the New Year repeats the creation that the twelve days between Christmas and Epiphany are still looked on as foreshadowing the twelve months of the year; peasants all over Europe judge the temperature and rainfall to be expected during each of the months to come by the "meteorological signs" of those twelve days.[37] The rainfall for each month was also decided in this way during the Feast of Tabernacles.[38] The Indians of Vedic times thought of the Twelve Days of the middle of the winter as an image and replica of the whole year,[39] and this same concentration of the year into twelve days also appears in Chinese traditions.[40]

Repetitions of the Creation Attached to Particular Occasions

All these things we have been looking at have one trait in common: they presuppose the notion that time is periodically regenerated by symbolic repetition of the creation. But the repetition of the creation

---

32. Christensen, vol. ii, p. 149.

33. Albiruni, p. 201; Kazwini, in Christensen, vol. ii, p. 148.

34. Albiruni, p. 200.

35. Albiruni, pp. 202–3.

36. Albiruni, p. 202.

37. Cf. Frazer, *The Scapegoat*, London, 1936, pp. 315 ff.; Dumézil, *Le Problème des Centaures*, Paris, 1929, pp. 36 ff.

38. Wensinck, p. 163.

39. *RV*, iv, 33.

40. Granet, *La Pensée chinoise*, p. 107.

is not narrowly bound up with communal ceremonies for the New Year. In other words, "old", "profane", "historic" time can be abolished and mythical, "new" regenerated time established *by repeating the creation* even during the course of the year and quite apart from the communal rites mentioned just now. Thus, for the Icelanders, the taking possession of land (*landnama*) was equivalent to the transformation of chaos into cosmos[41] and, in Vedic India, taking possession of an area was confirmed by the erection of a fire altar, regarded in fact as a repetition of the creation. The fire altar, in effect, reproduced the universe, and setting it up corresponded to creating the world; and whenever anyone built an altar of this sort, he was repeating the archetypal act of creation and "building" time.[42]

The Fijians called the ceremony of inaugurating a new chieftain the "creation of the world".[43] The same idea can be found, though not necessarily so explicitly, in more developed civilizations, where every enthronement is equivalent to a re-creation or regeneration of the world. The first decree the Chinese emperor promulgated on his accession to the throne was to determine a new calendar, and before establishing a new order of time, he abolished the old.[44] Assurbanipal saw himself as a regenerator of the cosmos, for, he said, "since the time the gods, in their friendliness, did set me on the throne of my fathers, Ramman has sent forth his rain ... the harvest was plentiful, the corn was abundant ... the cattle multiplied exceedingly."[45]

The prophecy of the Fourth Eclogue, *magnes ab integro saeclorum nascitur ordo* ... can in a sense be applied to every sovereign. For with every new sovereign, however insignificant he may be, a "new era" is begun. A new reign was looked upon as a regeneration of the nation's history, if not of the history of the world. We should be wrong to reduce these high-sounding formulae to what they came to be only as monarchies declined: mere boasting by the sovereign and flattery by his courtiers. The hope of a "new era" inaugurated by the new ruler

41. Van der Leeuw, *L'Homme primitif et la religion*, p. 110.

42. Cf. *Śatapatha-Brahmana*, vi, 5, i, ff.; "The fire-altar is the year" ... ibid., x, 5, 4, 10; "Of five layers consists the fire-altar [each layer is a season], five seasons are a year, and the year is Agni [the altar]", ibid., vi, 8, 1, 15.

43. Hocart, *Kingship*, Oxford, 1927, pp. 189–90.

44. Granet, *La Pensée chinoise*, p. 97.

45. Quoted by Jeremias in Hastings, *Encyclopedia of Religion and Ethics*, vol. i, p. 187 b.

was not only genuine and sincere, but also quite natural, if one looks at it with the vision of primitive man. In any case, there is not even any need of a new reign to open a new era; it is enough to have a wedding, the birth of a child, the building of a house or anything else of the sort. Man and the universe go on being regenerated, the past is destroyed, mistakes and sins are done away with, by any and every means, and nothing can stop it happening. However differently they may be expressed, all these means of regeneration are equally effective: they annihilate the time that is past, and abolish history by constantly going back to *illud tempus*.[46]

Thus, to go back to the Fijians, they repeat the creation of the world, not only when a new chieftain is crowned, but again every time the harvest is endangered.[47] Whenever the rhythms of nature are upset and life as a whole is threatened, the Fijians save themselves by returning *in principiuo*—they await, in other words, the re-establishing of the cosmos, not by a process of *repair*, but by *regeneration*. Similar ideas are behind the meaning of the "beginning", the "new", the "virginal", and so on, in popular medicine and in magic ("new water", the "new pitcher", the symbolism of the child, of the virgin, of the "immaculate", and so on). We saw (Periodic Recurrence—the Eternal Present) how magic can make actual a mythical event which guarantees the power of the medicine and the cure of the patient. The symbolism of "the new", and "not yet begun", also guarantees the concurrence in time of the thing done now with the mythical, archetypal event. As with a threatened harvest, a cure is got not by any sort of patching up but by a *new beginning*, which involves the return to *illud tempus*. (It is not essential that a sorcerer carrying out these rites should realize the theory underlying them; it is enough for the rites in question to flow from the theory implicit in them.)

Similar ideas, although of course disfigured by irrelevant additions and inevitable corruptions, can be seen in the techniques of mining and metallurgy.[48] On the other hand, initiation ceremonies (such as the "death" of the old man and "birth" of the new) are based on the hope that the past—"history"—may be abolished and a new time established. If the symbolism of water and the moon played so important

46. See *Myth of the Eternal Return*, chs. ii–iii.
47. Hocart, p. 190.
48. Cf. Eliade, "Metallurgy, Magic and Alchemy", *CZ*, Paris, 1938, vol. i, *passim*.

a part in the spiritual life of primitive men, it was precisely because it made the continued abolition and reestablishing of "forms", periodic disappearance and reappearance, the eternal return (which was in fact a return to the *beginnings*), clear and obvious. At every level—from cosmology to soteriology—the notion of regeneration is bound up with the conception of a new time, that is, with belief in man's sometimes being able to attain to *an absolute beginning.*

Total Regeneration

This obsession with regeneration is also expressed in all the myths and doctrines of cyclic time, which I studied in *The Myth of the Eternal Return.* Belief in a time that is cyclic, in an eternal returning, in the periodic destruction of the world and mankind to be followed by a new world and a new, regenerated, mankind—all these beliefs bear witness primarily to the desire and hope for a periodic regeneration of the time gone by, of history. Basically, the cycle in question is a Great Year, to use a term very common in Graeco-Oriental terminology: the Great Year opens with a creation and concludes with a Chaos, that is, by a complete fusion of the elements. A cosmic cycle includes a "creation", an "existence" (or "history", wearing-out, degeneration), and a "return to chaos" (*ekpyrosis, ragnarok, pralaya,* submergence of Atlantis, apocalypse). Structurally, a Great Year is to the year what a year is to the month and the day. But what is interesting to us at the moment is chiefly the hope of *a total regeneration of time* that is evident in all the myths and doctrines involving cosmic cycles; every cycle is an *absolute* beginning because all the past, all "history", has been completely abolished by reverting in a single instant to "chaos".

We thus find in man at every level, the same longing to destroy profane time and live in sacred time. Further, we see the desire and hope of regenerating time as a whole, of being able to live—"humanly", "historically"—in eternity, by transforming successive time into a single eternal moment. This longing for eternity is a sort of parallel to the longing for paradise which we looked at in the last chapter. To the wish to be always and naturally in a sacred place there corresponds the wish to live always in eternity by means of repeating archetypal actions. The repetition of archetypes shows the paradoxical wish to achieve an ideal form (the archetype) in the very framework of human existence, to be in time without reaping its disadvantages, without the inability to "put back the clock". Let me point out that this desire is no "spiritual" attitude, which depreciates life on earth and all that goes with it in favour of a "spirituality" of detachment from the world. On the contrary, what may be called the "nostalgia for eternity" proves that man longs for a concrete paradise, and believes that such a paradise can be won *here*, on each, and *now*, in the present moment. In this sense, it would seem that the ancient myths and rites connected with sacred time and space may be traceable back to so many nostalgic memories of an "earthly paradise", and some sort of "realizable" eternity to which man still thinks he may have access.

19

Thomas Mann,
"Excursus on the Sense of Time,"
from *The Magic Mountain*

Thomas Mann (1875–1955), German novelist and essayist, lived in Munich until 1933, when he was forced by the Nazis to emigrate. Philosophy, myth, and intellectual history figure prominently in his writing. His most important novel is The Magic Mountain, *in which young Hans Castorp, a student of engineering, visits his cousin Joachim at a sanatorium high in the Alps. Time (and much else) is subtly altered during his visit, as we see in the following text.*

When they came upstairs after the meal, the parcel containing the blankets lay on a chair in Hans Castorp's room; and that afternoon he made use of them for the first time. The experienced Joachim instructed him in the art of wrapping himself up, as practised in the sanatorium; they all did it, and each new-comer had to learn. First the covers were spread, one after the other, over the chair, so that a sizable piece hung down at the foot. Then you sat down and began to put the inner one about you: first lengthwise, on both sides, up to the shoulders, and then from the feet up, stooping over as you sat and grasping the folded-over end, first from one side and then from the other, taking care to fit it neatly into the length, in order to ensure the greatest possible smoothness and evenness. Then you did precisely the same thing with the outer blanket—it was somewhat more difficult to handle, and our neophyte groaned not a little as he stooped and stretched out his arms to practise his grips his cousin showed him. Only a few old hands, Joachim said, could wield both blankets at once, flinging them into psition with three self-assured motions. This was a rare and enviable facility, to which belonged not only long years of practice, but a certain knack as well. Hans Castorp had to laugh at this, lying back in his chair with aching muscles; Joachim did not at once see anything funny in what he had said, and looked at him dubiously, but finally laughed too.

"There," he said, when Hans Castorp lay at last limbless and cylindrical in his chair, with the yielding roll at the back of his neck, quite worn out with all these gymnastic exercises; "there, nothing can touch you now, not even if we were to have ten below zero." He withdrew behind the partition, to do himself up in his turn.

That about the ten below zero Hans Castorp doubted; he was even now distinctly cold. He shivered repeatedly as he lay looking out through the wooden arch at the reeking, dripping damp outside, which seemed on the point of passing over into snow. It was strange that with all that humidity his cheeks still burned with a dry heat, as though he were sitting in an over-heated room. He felt absurdly tired from the practice of putting on his rugs; actually, as he held up *Ocean Steamships* to read it, the book shook in his hands. So very fit he certainly was not—and totally anaemic, as Hofrat Behrens had said; this, no doubt, was why he was so susceptible to cold. But such unpleasing sensations were outweighed by the great comfort of his position, the unanalysable, the almost mysterious properties of his reclining-chair, which he had applauded even on his first experience of it, and which reasserted themselves in the happiest way whenever he resorted to it anew. Whether due to the character of the upholstering, the inclination of the chair-back, the exactly proper width and height of the arms, or only to the appropriate consistency of the neck roll, the result was that no more comfortable provision for relaxed limbs could be conceived than that purveyed by this excellent chair. The heart of Hans Castorp rejoiced in the blessed fact that two vacant and securely tranquil hours lay before him, dedicated by the rules of the house to the principal cure of the day; he felt it—though himself but a guest up here—to be a most suitable arrangement. For he was by nature and temperament passive, could sit without occupation hours on end, and loved, as we know, to see time spacious before him, and not to have the sense of its passing banished, wiped out or eaten up by prosaic activity. At four o'clock he partook of afternoon tea, with cake and jam. Followed a little movement in the open air, then rest again, then supper—which, like all the other meal-times, afforded a certain stimulus for eye and brain, and a certain sense of strain; after that a peep into one or other of the optical toys, the stereoscope, the kaleidoscope, the cinematograph. It might be still too much to say that Hans Castorp had grown used to the life up here; but at least he did have the daily routine at his fingers' ends.

There is, after all, something peculiar about the process of habituating oneself in a new place, the often laborious fitting in and getting used, which one undertakes for its own sake, and of set purpose to break it all off as soon as it is complete, or not long thereafter, and to return to one's former state. It is an interval, an interlude, inserted, with the object of recreation, into the tenor of life's main concerns; its purpose the relief of the organism, which is perpetually busy at its task of self-renewal, and which was in danger, almost in process, of being vitiated, slowed down, relaxed, by the bald, unjointed monotony of its daily course. But what then is the cause of this relaxation, this slowing-down that takes place when one does the same thing for too long at a time? It is not so much physical or mental fatigue or exhaustion, for if that were the case, then complete rest would be the best restorative. It is rather something psychical; it means that the perception of time tends, through periods of unbroken uniformity, to fall away; the perception of time, so closely bound up with the consciousness of life that the one may not be weakened without the other suffering a sensible impairment. Many false conceptions are held concerning the nature of tedium. In general it is thought that the interestingness and novelty of the time-content are what "make the time pass"; that is to say, shorten it; whereas monotony and emptiness check and restrain its flow. This is only true with reservations. Vacuity, monotony, have, indeed, the property of lingering out the moment and the hour and of making them tiresome. But they are capable of contracting and dissipating the larger, the very large time-units, to the point of reducing them to nothing at all. And conversely, a full and interesting content can put wings to the hour and the day; yet it will lend to the general passage of time a weightiness, a breadth and solidity which cause the eventful years to flow far more slowly than those poor, bare, empty ones over which the wind passes and they are gone. Thus what we call tedium is rather an abnormal shortening of the time consequent upon monotony. Great spaces of time passed in unbroken uniformity tend to shrink together in a way to make the heart stop beating for fear; when one day is like all the others, then they are all like one; complete uniformity would make the longest life seem short, and as though it had stolen away from us unawares. Habituation is a falling asleep or fatiguing of the sense of time; which explains why young years pass slowly, while

later life flings itself faster and faster upon its course. We are aware
that the intercalation of periods of change and novelty is the only means
by which we can refresh our sense of time, strengthen, retard, and
rejuvenate it, and therewith renew our perception of life itself. Such
is the purpose of our changes of air and scene, of all our sojourns at
cures and bathing resorts; it is the secret of the healing power of change
and incident. Our first days in a new place, time has a youthful, that
is to say, a broad and sweeping, flow, persisting for some six or eight
days. Then, as one "gets used to the place," a gradual shrinkage makes
itself felt. He who clings or, better expressed, wishes to cling to life,
will shudder to see how the days grow light and lighter, how they
scurry by like dead leaves, until the last week, of some four, perhaps,
is uncannily fugitive and fleet. On the other hand, the quickening of
the sense of time will flow out beyond the interval and reassert itself
after the return to ordinary existence: the first days at home after the
holiday will be lived with a broader flow, freshly and youthfully—but
only the first few, for one adjusts oneself more quickly to the rule than
to the exception; and if the sense of time be already weakened by age,
or—and this is a sign of low vitality—it was never very well developed,
one drowses quickly back into the old life, and after four-and-twenty
hours it is as though one had never been away, and the journey had
been but a watch in the night.

We have introduced these remarks here only because our young
Hans Castorp had something like them in mind when, a few days later,
he said to his cousin, and fixed him with his bloodshot eyes: "I shall
never cease to find it strange that the time seems to go so slowly in a
new place. I mean—of course it isn't a question of my being bored;
on the contrary, I might say that I am royally entertained. But when I
look back—in retrospect, that is, you understand—it seems to me I've
been up here goodness only knows how long; it seems an eternity back
to the time when I arrived, and did not quite understand that I was
there, and you said: 'Just get out here'—don't you remember?—That
has nothing whatever to do with reason, or with the ordinary ways of
measuring time; it is purely a matter of feeling. Certainly it would be
nonsense for me to say: 'I feel I have been up here two months'—it
would be silly. All I can say is 'very long.' "

"Yes," Joachim answered, thermometer in mouth, "I profit by it too;
while you are here, I can sort of hang on by you, as it were." Hans
Castorp laughed, to hear his cousin speak thus, quite simply, without
explanation.

20

Simone Weil,
"The Renunciation of Time,"
from *Gravity and Grace*

The French philosopher Simone Weil (1909–1943) is an authentic modern mystic. Gravity and Grace, *her most important work, contains a brief chapter on time, which is presented here in its entirety. The intense and luminous style is typical of Weil's writing.*

Time is an image of eternity, but it is also a substitute for eternity.

The miser whose treasure has been taken from him. It is some of the frozen past which he has lost. Past and future, man's only riches.

The future is a filler of void places. Sometimes the past also plays this part ('I used to be,' 'I once did this or that . . .'). But there are other cases when affliction makes the thought of happiness intolerable; then it robs the sufferer of his past (*nessun maggior dolore . . .*).

The past and the future hinder the wholesome effect of affliction by providing an unlimited field for imaginary elevation. That is why the renunciation of past and future is the first of all renunciations.

The present does not attain finality. Nor does the future, for it is only what will be present. We do not know this, however. If we apply to the present the point of that desire within us which corresponds to finality, it pierces right through to the eternal.

That is the use of despair which turns the attention away from the future.

When we are disappointed by a pleasure which we have been expecting and which comes, the disappointment is because we were
expecting the future, and as soon as it is there it is present. We want
the future to be there without ceasing to be future. This is an absurdity
of which eternity alone is the cure.

Time and the cave. To come out of the cave, to be detached, means
to cease to make the future our objective.

A method of purification: to pray to God, not only in secret as far
as men are concerned, but with the thought that God does not exist.

Piety with regard to the dead: to do everything for what does not
exist.

The suffering caused by the death of others is due to this pain of
a void and of lost equilibrium. Efforts henceforward follow without an
object and therefore without a reward. If the imagination makes good
this void—debasement. 'Let the dead bury their dead.' And as to our
own death, is it not the same? The object and the reward are in the
future. Deprivation of the future—void, loss of equilibrium. That is
why 'to philosophise is to learn to die'. That is why 'to pray is like a
death'.

When pain and weariness reach the point of causing a sense of
perpetuity to be born in the soul, through contemplating this perpetuity
with acceptance and love, we are snatched away into eternity.

Further Readings

Altizer, Thomas J. J., *Mircea Eliade and the Dialectic of the Sacred*, Philadelphia, Westminster Press, 1963.

Armstrong, *Cambridge History of Later Greek and Early Medieval Philosophy*, Cambridge, Cambridge University Press, 1967, "Plotinus".

Bell, Richard H., *Simone Weil's Philosophy of Culture: Readings Toward a Divine Humanity*, Cambridge, Cambridge University Press, 1993.

Braithwaite, R. B., Broad, C. D., and Macmurray, J., "Time and Change", Symposium, Aristotelian Society Supplementary Volume VIII (1928).

Findlay, J. N., "Time and Eternity", *Review of Metaphysics* 32 (1978).

———, *Plato: the Written and the Unwritten Dialogues*, New York, Humanities Press, 1974.

Heath, Louise Robinson, *The Concept of Time*, Chicago, University of Chicago Press, 1936.

Gale, R. M., *The Philosophy of Time*, London, Macmillan, 1962.

Gilson, Etienne, *The Christian Philosophy of St. Augustine*, New York, Random House, 1960.

Heidegger, Martin, *Being and Time* trans. J. Macquarrie and Edward Robinson, New York, Harper and Row, 1962. Division II, Ch. IV, "Temporality and Everydayness".

King-Farlow, John, "The Positive McTaggart on Time", *Philosophy* 49 (1974).

Lucas, J. R., *A Treatise on Space and Time*, London, Methuen, 1973.

Mellor, D. H., *Real Time*, Cambridge, Cambridge University Press, 1981.

Owen, G.E.L., "Aristotle on Time", in *Logic, Science and Dialectic: Collected Papers*, ed. Martha Nussbaum, Cornell, Cornell University Press, 1986.

Poulet, George, *Studies in Human Time* trans. Elliot Coleman, Baltimore, Johns Hopkins University Press, 1966.

Ricoeur, Paul, *Time and Narrative* trans. Kathleen McLaughlin and David Pellauer, Chicago, University of Chicago Press, 1984–88.

Sartre, Jean-Paul, *Being and Nothingness* trans. Hazel Barnes, New York, Philosophical Library, 1956, Part Two, Chapter Two.

Schlesinger, G., *Aspects of Time,* Cambridge and Indianapolis, Hackett, 1980.

Smart, J.J.C., "The River of Time", in Antony Flew, ed., *Essays in Conceptual Analysis,* London, Macmillan, 1956.

———, *Problems of Space and Time,* New York, Macmillan, 1964.

———, "Time", *Encyclopedia of Philosophy,* Vol. 8, New York, Macmillan, 1967.

Sorabji, Richard, *Time, Creation and the Continuum: Theories in Antiquity and the Early Middle Ages,* Cornell, Cornell University Press, 1983.

Suter, Ronald, *Interpreting Wittgenstein: A Cloud of Philosophy, a Drop of Grammar,* Ch. 9, "Augustine on Time", Philadelphia, Temple University Press, 1989.

Teselle, Eugene, *Augustine the Theologian,* London, Burns and Oates, 1976.

Index